6203

PRINCESS MARGARET ROSE

THE FIRST PRODUCTION STANIER PACIFIC

BRIAN RADFORD & BRELL EWART

PLATFORM
5

Published by Platform 5 Publishing Ltd., Wyvern House, Old Forge Business Park, Sark Road, Sheffield S2 4HG, England.

Printed by Echo Press, Echo House, Jubilee Drive, Belton Park, Loughborough, Leicestershire, LE11 0XS.

ISBN 1 872524 40 0

DEDICATION

This book is dedicated to the memory of

RICHARD SPENCER LEVICK

a member of the Midland Railway Trust
who tragically lost his life whilst working
on the restoration of locomotive parts.
His skill and knowledge in the art
of engineering were for many years generously
and unstintingly given to further the restoration
of steam locomotives that he loved both at the
Midland Railway Centre and elsewhere.

He will long be remembered by those who knew him.

Front end paper: A magnificent study of 46203 in blue livery by that doyen of railway photographers Eric Treacy, who captured her on film as she pulled away from London Euston in the summer of 1951 with an express bound for Liverpool.   *Courtesy Millbrook House Ltd.*

Back end paper: A fine study of 'Princess Margaret Rose' passing Carlisle Kingmoor motive power depot on 28th August 1962 with a down Scottish express — a sight of sheer majestic power captured by Rev. Eric Treacy as 46203 reached the last two weeks of her active career with BR.

Princess Margaret Rose

The Homestead
Yeldersley Lane
Bradley
Ashbourne
Derbyshire
DE6 1PJ

Michael Fry
184 Albyn Road
St Johns
Deptford
London

26th April 1993

Dear Mr Fry,

Please find a copy, signed by the authors of our book about
Princess Margaret Rose.

Regards,

Brell Ewart

CONTENTS

PREFACE

Many boys during the age of steam railways in Britain, when the network was of far greater size than that of 1990, had the cherished ambition to be an engine driver and for the overwhelming majority an ambition that would never be realised. When steam traction finished on British Railways in 1968, a watershed was reached and a vacuum left to the many enthusiasts and followers out of which, from very small beginnings, grew the railway preservation movement of today, with private railways and centres having multi-million pound business dealings and the capacity to own, maintain and run the largest steam locomotives to a standard well equal to that of the nationally-owned system of over two decades ago.

As a young schoolboy in the mid-fifties, my introduction to steam locomotives was through passing the locomotive shed at Barrow Hill and the yards of Staveley Works on my daily trek to and from school and seeing the many 8Fs, 9Fs and Austerities on their daily duties in the area. To return through the very same yards some thirty years later on the footplate of a 'Princess Royal' Class 8P No. 46203 named 'Princess Margaret Rose' owned by myself is truly a dream come true.

This book relates the life story of one of the most famous steam locomotives built together with the many quirks of fate that befell her over the years. Brian Radford, my co-author, has un earthed a number of previously unpublished items appertaining to the locomotive and the Stanier Pacifics which will undoubtedly be of interest and value to the connoisseurs. To return the locomotive to working order was the culmination of over two years planning and work by a totally dedicated and professional team of which I am very proud to be part and to whom the credit for the restoration goes. In all major restoration projects there are times of deep despair, problems to be overcome, deadlines to be met etc. and at all such moments in our project, Eric Riley our Locomotive Superintendent was always there to advise myself and the team with the cool, professional leadership, which had been a hallmark of the Midland Railway Trust's locomotive fleet for a good number of years.

The tragic death of our friend and colleague Richard Levick during the restoration of the locomotive, was a savage blow to us all and a sad loss to railway preservation. It was therefore one of the proudest moments we will ever witness to see 'Princess Margaret Rose' standing in Derby station on 2nd June 1990, awaiting departure with his memorial train. A finer and more appropriate tribute would have been impossible.

As to the future, I hope that 46203 will give as much pleasure to those who see and travel behind her as my interest in the hobby has given to me and who knows, in years to come, perhaps further chapters in her story will have to be written.

Brell Ewart

INTRODUCTION

When Mr (later Sir) William Arthur Stanier came to the L.M.S. on 1st January 1932, he quickly set about creating a modern locomotive fleet representing completely new L.M.S. designs rather than developments of pre-grouping locomotive types. His greatest priority was to be the design of a more powerful class of main line express locomotive, for hauling the heaviest 500 ton expresses on the West Coast main line from Euston to Manchester and Liverpool and on into Scotland and Glasgow some 400 miles away, which resulted only eighteen months later in the appearance of the 'Princess Royal' class Pacifics.

The two prototypes, Nos 6200, later named 'The Princess Royal', and 6201, later named 'Princess Elizabeth', emerged from Crewe works in July and November 1933 respectively. The subject of this book, No. 6203 'Princess Margaret Rose' named like her sisters of the class after lady members of royalty (one a Norwegian Queen), was the first of the production batch consisting of ten locomotives, ordered and built in 1935 and she has survived like her sister No. 6201 'Princess Elizabeth', to be preserved in working order.

6203, now restored to British Railways maroon livery as 46203 and owned by Derbyshire businessman and railway enthusiast Brell Ewart, has been given her first general repair for thirty years in the Midland Railway Trust's new restoration shop at Butterley Park, Midland Railway Centre, and was returned to steam for the first time since her 1962 withdrawal from service by British Railways on 11th May 1990.

This is her story.

CHAPTER ONE

THE DESIGN AND DEVELOPMENT OF THE NEW L.M.S. 'PACIFICS'

THE PROTOTYPES

Following the formation of the London Midland and Scottish Railway Company on 1st January 1923 the locomotive designs built in the early years followed on from those of the pre-grouping companies and the Midland 'small engine' policy was pursued by the building of more compound 4-4-0s. Although these were a successful type in good hands, they were not capable of meeting the demands of the heavier trains which were becoming an urgent requirement to meet the economic growth in traffic needs, particularly on the former L.N.W.R. main line out of Euston to the north, combined with the need to respond strongly to competition from the rival L.N.E.R. on the East Coast route to Scotland.

The 'Midland' answer in the shape of a large compound Pacific, drawings for which had been completed under the direction of Sir Henry Fowler and the frames cut, was circumvented by another section of the L.M.S. management who arranged for the trial of the Great Western four cylinder 4-6-0 No 5000 'Launceston Castle', which was exercised on the West Coast route and worked well. The outcome was the rejection of the 'Pacific' design and the introduction of Sir Henry Fowler's 'Royal Scot' 4-6-0s, built by the North British Locomotive Company in Glasgow and by the Derby Locomotive Works of the L.M.S.

However, Sir Josiah Stamp resolved to bring in a new Chief Mechanical Engineer, and by making first Henry Fowler and then his successor Ernest Lemon Vice-Presidents, the field was left open to bring in a new non-partisan C.M.E., William Arthur Stanier.

Stanier, born in Swindon in 1876, had until then been Collett's assistant, but since he would have had to wait until Collett had either retired or died, Stamp, with the agreement of the G.W.R. hierarchy, appointed Stanier to be the new Chief Mechanical Engineer of the L.M.S. as from 1st January 1932.

Stanier first attended the L.M.S. Locomotive Committee meeting held on 27th January 1932 and from then on his strong and purposeful influence began to be felt.

At the top of the list for new locomotive design required for express passenger work as we have said, was one capable of hauling the 500 ton-plus trains the 400 or so miles from Euston to Glasgow. This was to be based on some schemes evolved in Stanier's 'think tank' at Euston which involved both three and four cylinder 4-6-2 'Pacific' type locomotives. The three cylinder type had 19 inch diameter x 28 inch stroke cylinders placed just behind the leading bogie pivot centre and had 6 ft. 9 in. diameter driving wheels, whilst the four cylinder type had two inside cylinders of 16¼" diameter x 28" stroke set forward of the outside pair above the bogie pivot with the two outside cylinders placed over the trailing axle of the leading bogie. 6 ft. 6 in.

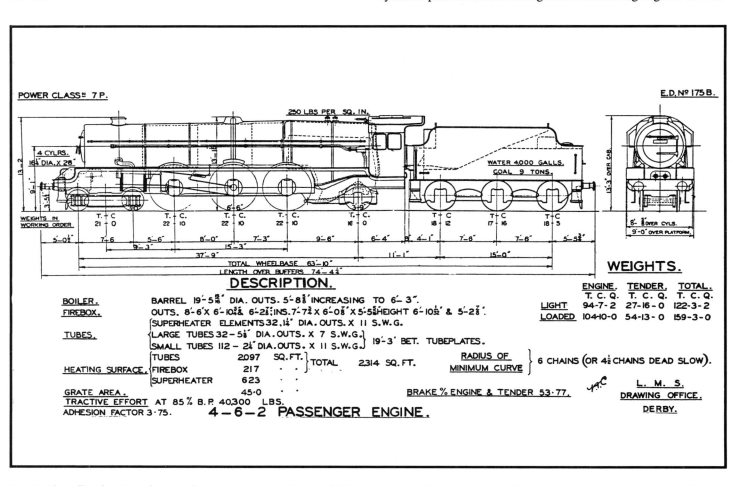

Fig. 1. The official L.M.S. diagram for the production batch of 'Princess Royal' Class Stanier pacifics.

J.B. Radford Collection

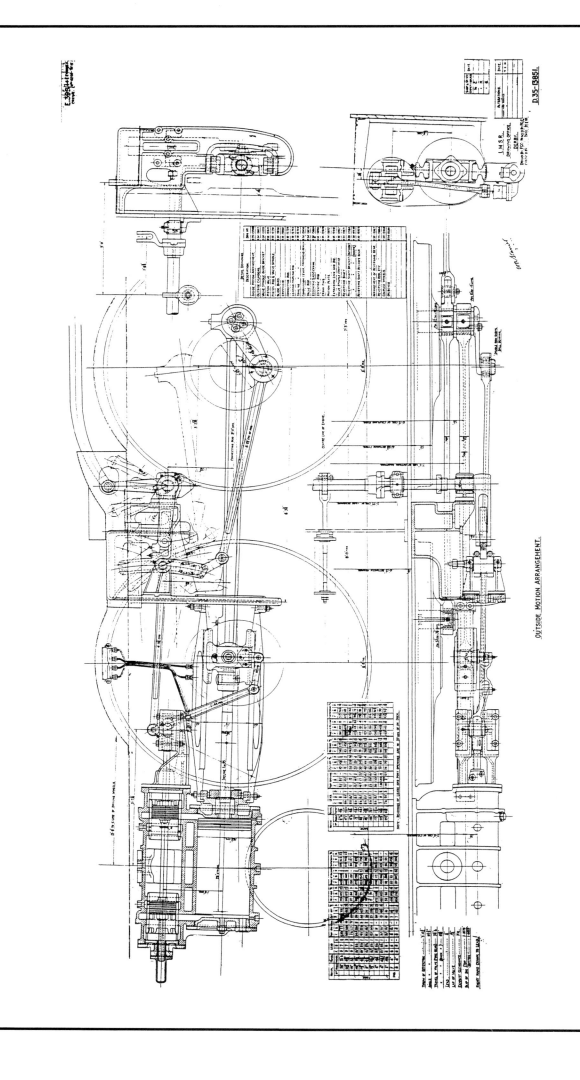

OUTSIDE MOTION ARRANGEMENT.

Fig. 2. The official L.M.S. drawing No. D35–13851 of the outside motion arrangement for 6203 and her sisters. *J.B. Radford Collection*

diameter driving wheels were used in this scheme and in both cases flat sided tenders holding 9 tons of coal and 4000 gallons on water were provided.

Stanier opted for the four cylinder type which was in many ways similar to the G.W.R. 'King' class but had a fundamental difference in having four sets of motion, thereby eliminating the G.W.R. 'rocking drive'.

The official descriptive booklet issued to mark the introduction of this type of locomotive onto the L.M.S. system explained the requirement thus:

LONDON MIDLAND AND SCOTTISH RAILWAY COMPANY

Chief Mechanical Engineer's Office,
EUSTON,
21st June 1933

NEW 4-6-2 "PACIFIC" TYPE SUPERHEATED 4-CYLINDER SIMPLE LOCOMOTIVE

As a result of about six years' experience with the "Royal Scot" locomotives, which have given very satisfactory service for the loads for which they were designed, it has been considered desirable to experiment with a still more powerful type of locomotive capable of hauling heavier trains of 500-tons loading between Euston and Glasgow. Previous experience has shown it desirable to provide an improved boiler with grate area of 45 sq.ft. to ensure satisfactory combustion during such long through runs. This large grate calls for a wide firebox to permit efficient firing and also a trailing truck of the Bissel type to carry the heavier weight at the trailing end of the engine. The wheel base thus develops into a 4-6-2 arrangement which is generally known as the "Pacific" type.

The tenders for these engines have been increased in both coal and water capacity to meet heavy requirements, 4000 gallons of water and 9-tons of coal being provided.

The standard type of water pick-up has, of course, been arranged on the tender, and in addition "Timken" roller bearings are being fitted to the six tender wheels.

The leading dimensions are as follows:-

4 simple cylinders	16¼" dia x 28" stroke.
Valve gear	"Walschaerts" long travel 7¼"
Coupled Wheel	6' 6" diameter

BOILER

Boiler pressure	250 lbs. per sq. inch.
Firebox heating surface	190 sq. ft.
Tubes	2523 sq. ft.
	2713 sq. ft.
Superheater	370 sq. ft.
Grate area	45 sq. ft.
Tractive effort	40,300 lbs. at 85% boiler pressure.

Additional official data provided was as follows:-

WHEELS

Bogie	3' 0" diameter
Coupled	6' 6" diameter
Trailing Truck	·3' 9" diameter

WHEELBASE

Coupled	15' 3"
Engine (total)	37' 9"
Engine and Tender	63' 10"

WEIGHT OF ENGINE (in working order)

	T. cwt. qrs.
Bogie	21. 0. 0.
Leading Coupled Wheels	22. 10. 0.
Intermediate Coupled Wheels	22. 10. 0.
Trailing Coupled Wheels	22. 10. 0.
Trailing Truck	16. 0. 0.
TOTAL	104. 10. 0.

TOTAL WEIGHT OF ENGINE AND TENDER (in working order):
158. 12. 0.

Three of the new 'Pacifics' were included in the 1933 Locomotive Building Programme and costs were 'charged to renewals' according to the L.M.S. Locomotive Committee minute 142 of July 1932. The official minutes record:

"Whilst the Royal Scot locomotive has proved satisfactory in service and has met what was anticipated when this type was designed, it is considered desirable that we should have information as to the efficiency and costs of the 'Pacific' type on Royal Scot workings. It is further proposed to build three 'Pacific' type locomotives of greater power and grate area than the "Royal Scots". It is important to realise that at that time the main reason for changing locomotives at Carlisle when a train was hauled by a 'Royal Scot' class 4-6-0 was because, after 300 miles of running, the firegrate needed thoroughly cleaning out. As the minute records, 'greater power and grate area' thus indicating the need to go to a 4-6-2 design.

Order No. 371 was placed on Crewe Works for the first two locomotives, to be numbered 6200 and 6201, and L.M.S. Lot No. 99 was issued to cover the build. Derby order number 8254 was issued on 20th November 1932 to cover work on these two locomotives done at Derby Locomotive Works and also work for the third locomotive No. 6202, an experimental steam turbine driven locomotive to be built to Crewe Order No. 371 and Lot No. 100. This third locomotive was originally intended to be like the first two, but Stanier had been impressed by seeing a 2-8-0 steam turbine driven locomotive at work on the Grangesberg—Oxelösund Railway in Sweden. He decided that the experience merited the construction of a prototype locomotive of this type for the L.M.S. to enable the idea to be fully evaluated under strict testing and performance conditions on a British Railway. A further Derby order, No. 8827 of 14th August 1934 covered work relating to the modifications carried out in 1934 to all three engines.

DESIGN FEATURES

Detailed design work began on the locomotives in the Locomotive Drawing Office at Derby and work on the 370 plus drawings went ahead with great despatch. The material specification ran to 361 pages and covered 25,000 different items. In the design scheme eventually adopted the horizontal inside cylinders drove a built up leading crank axle by means of 8 ft. 6½ in. centre connecting rods with a split big end, whilst the outside pair, inclined at an angle of 1 in 35, drove outside connecting rods of 108 inch centres. The twin exhaust steam passage arrangement was designed so that the steam from the inside cylinders emerged via the front orifice and from the rear cylinders via the rear orifice combining in a single blastpipe chamber before exhausting. A jumper blastpipe cap was fitted to prevent back pressure when working hard. Locomotive No. 6201 was later fitted experimentally with a double blastpipe and stovepipe chimney but the experiment proved unsuccesful and it was removed. The cylinder drain cocks were originally of the L.M.S. standard poppet type operated from the cab by a rather crude and complex lever system which was subject to wear in the linkage joints. Later, in the mid 1950s, the new British Railways design of steam operated drain cocks were fitted and proved to be much more successful. The inside admission eight inch diameter piston valves, with six valve rings per head, were actuated by Walschaerts valve gear with an eccentric drive for the inside set, and the reversing mechanism was the standard screw and rod type situated on the left hand side of the footplate. The valve gear arrangements for No. 6203 and her sisters are shown in Figs. 2 & 3.

The overall length of the engine (front buffer face to rear dragbox face) was 49 ft. 1½ in. with coupled wheelbase of 8 ft. plus 7 ft. 3 in. and a total wheelbase of 37 ft. 9 in. The leading four wheeled bogie was supplied with side bolsters and a carefully designed side check spring arrangement and, in view of its long 7 ft. 6 in. wheelbase, bar frames were used to reduce weight. The trailing truck, of the Bissel type, was anchored to a stretcher carried between the main frames and the load on the truck was transmitted from the main frames by side bolsters. A side check spring arrangement was also provided. These side check spring arrangements on both bogie and Bissel truck were a development of the French De Glehn design from the earlier part of the century. Stanier introduced the G.W.R. type cast-steel axlebox with a pressed-in brass insert and a white metal crown. The coupled axle journals were ten inches in diameter and ten inches long. Driving wheel axleboxes running hot on the 'Princess Royal' class were to prove a rarity in service as the lubricating oil, mechanically fed from the lubricators, entered the axlebox at the top with the oil being delivered right on the top centre line of each journal. The main frames of the locomotives were 1¼" thick steel on Nos. 6200-1 and 1⅛" thick high tensile steel on 6203-12. They had a spliced trailing end, the outside portion being splayed out to give room for the firebox which was rivetted to the main frame through an expansion plate just

7

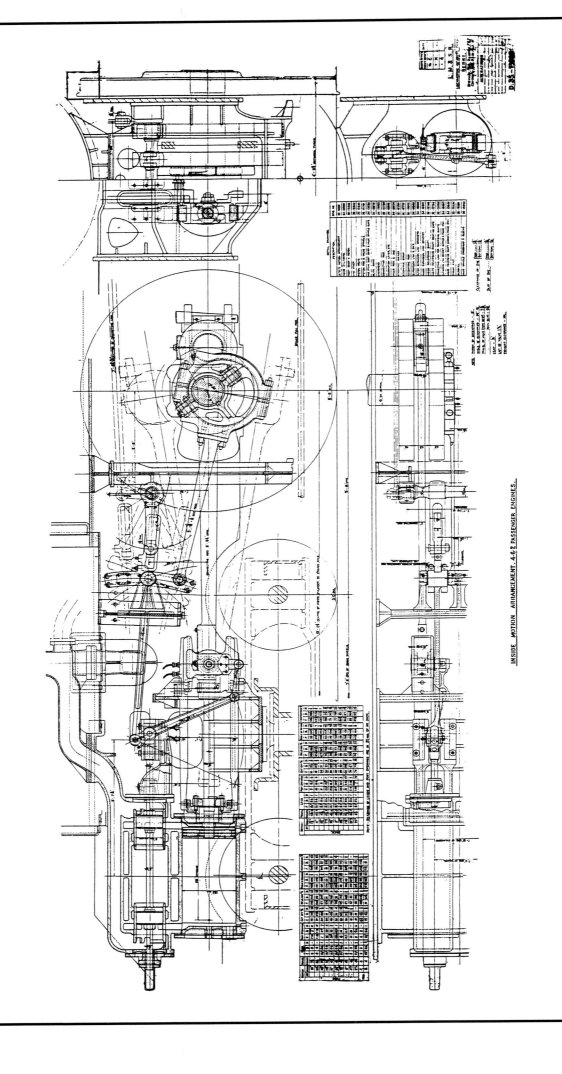

Fig. 3. The official L.M.S. drawing No. D35–13968 of the inside motion arrangement for 6203 and her sisters.   *J.B. Radford Collection*

behind the centre line of the trailing driving axleboxes, the inner frame narrowing over the trailing truck. Both the inner and outer joined up at the rear buffer beam, the inner frame housing the drag box. The boiler barrel was tapered from the throatplate to the smokebox tubeplate and the Belpaire firebox had carefully proportioned waterlegs to ensure efficient circulation of water. The firebox of the first three boilers had a short combustion chamber and tubes 20 ft. 9 in. long, but subsequent boilers had a longer chamber and tubes shortened to 19 ft. 3 in. Beginning with 16 flue low temperature superheat on the first two engines, Stanier soon found an urgent necessity to increase these to 24, 32 and even some 40 flues on the special boiler for No. 6202, for he had discovered that there was a restriction in steam flow at the superheaters where the inadequate cross sectional area provided formed a bottle neck, thus throttling steam supply to the cylinders. Consequently the practice of using low degree superheat, which had hitherto been used by the G.W.R. and which Stanier had brought with him and adopted for 6200 and 6201, turned out to be unsuitable for L.M.S. conditions where indifferent qualities of coal could seriously affect performance by influencing steaming efficiency and furthermore the slightly larger diameter of superheater elements with a single return loop probably meant a core of wet saturated steam in each path, as Stanier observed at a Locomotive Engineers meeting in 1940. The next step was a double pass element and more of them. Stanier wrote to F.A.Lemon (Works Manager) at Crewe on the subject on 4th July 1935:

> "I should be glad if you would arrange to have two sets of tubeplates of both copper and steel prepared for the conversion of 4-6-2 boilers from 2 row to 4 row elements. These can be prepared to a stores stock order and also the header and any other material ordered in anticipation of authority being obtained for the conversion. This matter is urgent as I wish to convert the boiler taken of Engine No. 6200 as quickly as possible in order that it may be ready for Engine No. 6201 when next in shops"

The driver's position was on the left hand side of the cab which had sliding side windows and small side windscreens to act as a draught protector for the crew when looking out beyond the cab sides. All steam supplies to the various controls in the cab were supplied from a manifold at the top of the boiler backplate. The whistle which had to be fitted in the horizontal position because of gauge considerations, was of the old Caledonian design . . .'which gives a melodious note', to quote the official booklet.

CLASS NAME

The new class of 4-6-2 express locomotives was called 'THE PRINCESS ROYAL' class and the reason for the choice is given in a letter from Hewitt Beames, who was at that time Deputy Chief Mechanical Engineer of the L.M.S., to the Editor of the 'Railway Gazette' dated September 22nd 1933 — which explained:

> ". . . .the reason which led to the naming of the first of our 4-6-2 locomotive 'The Princess Royal'. This engine was designed to take over the working of trains heavier than the 'Royal Scot' engine was designed for, and as such one might almost call her 'a super Royal Scot'. As Her Royal Highness, The Princess Royal, is Colonel-in-Chief of the Royal Scots it therefore seems a most appropriate name for the new engine, and she graciously gave permission for this.'

6200 was completed at Crewe Works on 27th June 1933 and was shortly afterwards at first incorrectly named 'PRINCESS ROYAL' and not 'THE PRINCESS ROYAL', this being quickly corrected. She was handed over for traffic on 1st July 1933, made a run from London (Euston) to Crewe on 1st August 1933 for the benefit of a special party of invited guests and members of the press, and made her first revenue earning trip to Glasgow with the 'Royal Scot' train on 22nd September 1933 after extensive running in trials. Sister engine No. 6201 'Princess Elizabeth' was completed at Crewe on 3rd November 1933.

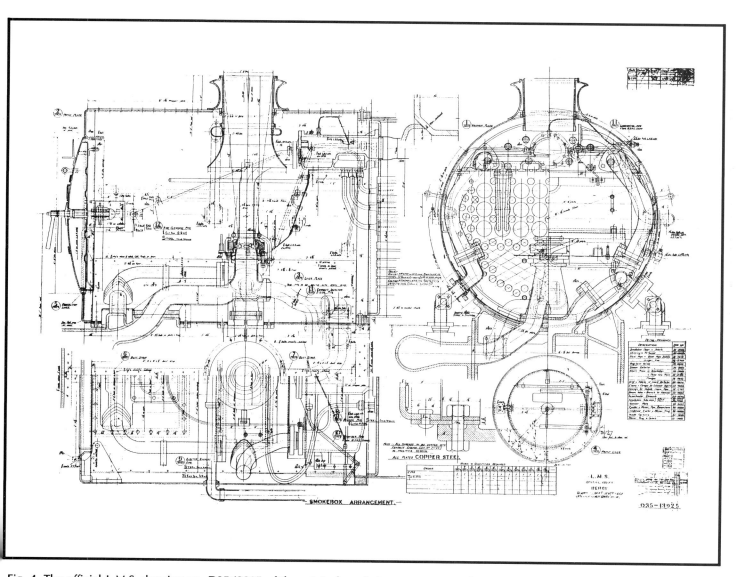

Fig. 4. The official L.M.S. drawing no. D35-13925 of the original smokebox arrangement for 6203−6212.

J.B. Radford Collection

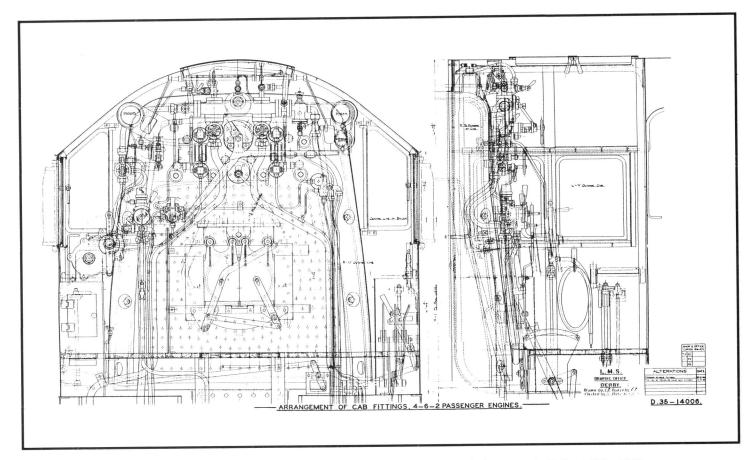

Fig. 5. The official L.M.S. drawing no. D35-14006 showing the arrangement of the cab fittings as built for 6203 – 6212.

J.B. Radford Collection

THE PRODUCTION BATCH

The production batch of ten 'Pacifics' following on behind, Nos. 6203–12, had boilers modified to take account of some of the findings recorded above as new, although as we shall see there were to be some further changes later. 6203 was built as part of Crewe order No. 395 and L.M.S. Lot No. 120, as Crewe new number 253, at an authorised (June 1934) cost of £10,700, being the first to be completed on 1st July 1935, the last being completed in the October.

BOILER DESIGN

6203 herself was originally built with domeless boiler No. 9101, having three rows of superheater elements providing 24 flues each of 5⅛'' diameter and 141 small tubes of 2¼'' diameter giving 2218 sq. ft. of heating surface. Subsequent boiler changes on 6203 were as in the table below:-

Date Outshopped	Boiler No.	Tubes Small	Large	Notes
6/1935	9101	141	24	Boiler with 3 rows elements
15/12/1936	9100	112	32	Ex 6202 'Turbomotive'
18/12/1938	9101	141	24	Ex 6209
20/12/1941	9106	112	32	Ex 6209
26/ 7/1944	9102	141	24	Ex 6211
8/12/1947	9106	123	32	Ex 6210
24/ 5/1951	9108	123	32	Ex 46204
9/10/1955	9101	123	32	Ex 46206
14/ 8/1958	9100	112	32	Ex 46202 – still fitted

However there is an unexplained reference in a letter dated 15th January 1936 to No 6203 having been fitted with the boiler off 6200 and another letter dated 14th October 1935 from G.R. Nicholson at Crewe recording that Mr (R.C.) Bond had asked to be told as soon as possible what would be involved in changing the latest type of 4-6-2 boiler from an engine originally fitted with it and replacing it with one of the first three boilers with the smaller fireboxes. The letter from G.R.Nicholson continued:

"...I believe the two ash pans are different and shall be glad if you will confirm this. Is there is any other alteration apart from the boiler clothing?".

D.W. Sandford was asked to get Mr. Henderson to look at it, but there is no filed reply. However the change is not recorded on the engine's

official record cards and if it took place at all, cannot be confirmed. The suggestion though is very interesting. Boiler No. 9100, still fitted to the engine today, was one of ten boilers (9100–9) built to Crewe order B395 in 1935 and was originally fitted as new to locomotive No. 6202 — Stanier's turbine driven locomotive. No. 6202 later had new boiler No. 9236 fitted, having 40 flues of 5⅛'' and 81 small tubes of 2¼'' diameter respectively and giving a total heating surface of 1951 sq. ft. Boiler No. 9100 had a dome and domed regulator fitted to it at Crewe in December 1952 as part of Job No. 5542 NWO (new work order) No. E780. The original boiler for 6203 showed a number of changes from the design used for 6200 and 6201 as E.A. Langridge, who was a design engineer in the Derby design office, fascinatingly recalled in a letter to D.F. Tee dated 11th November 1964 :

"The tale of the Duchess boilers goes back to that for the 'Turbo'. You know that was the long barrel chap as on 6200 with a few more superheater elements in the first place. Dr. H.L. Guy and Struthers of Metro Vickers urged W. A.S. (Stanier) to get a higher superheat and I was given the job to improve the boiler. So I cut out the vertical firebox tubeplate and put a drumhead one in front of a combustion chamber and arranged the firebox plates to lap over each other — no scarfing required. Our suppliers always pressed the copper tube plates but we did the steel ones and the size of press settled the amount of combustion chamber we could get in . . . I also noticed on ordinary combustion chamber boilers you get two humps where the barrel portion fades into the firebox front plate. It was difficult to explain on a drawing as the vertical and horizontal radii are constantly changing, and I had to go to Crewe and stand by while the pattern maker shaved the blocks to the correct shape. Having got over that, the problem was to stay the copper to the steel throat plate as there was no flat surface: so I had to go and do that on the actual plates. I hadn't the faintest idea how to dimension the thing and was thankful when I had actually marked off the first tubeplate from which a template was made. It seems to have been alright as the scheme was perpetuated for the replacement boilers on the 6200's and used on Coronations. I put the tubes up in diameter and, of course, increased the number of large tubes. Originally 6200 had two rows of large tubes with two elements in each — the steam making one pass — in order to keep up the cross section area thro' superheater and reduce pressure drop. We (later) put on a dome housing (the) regulator

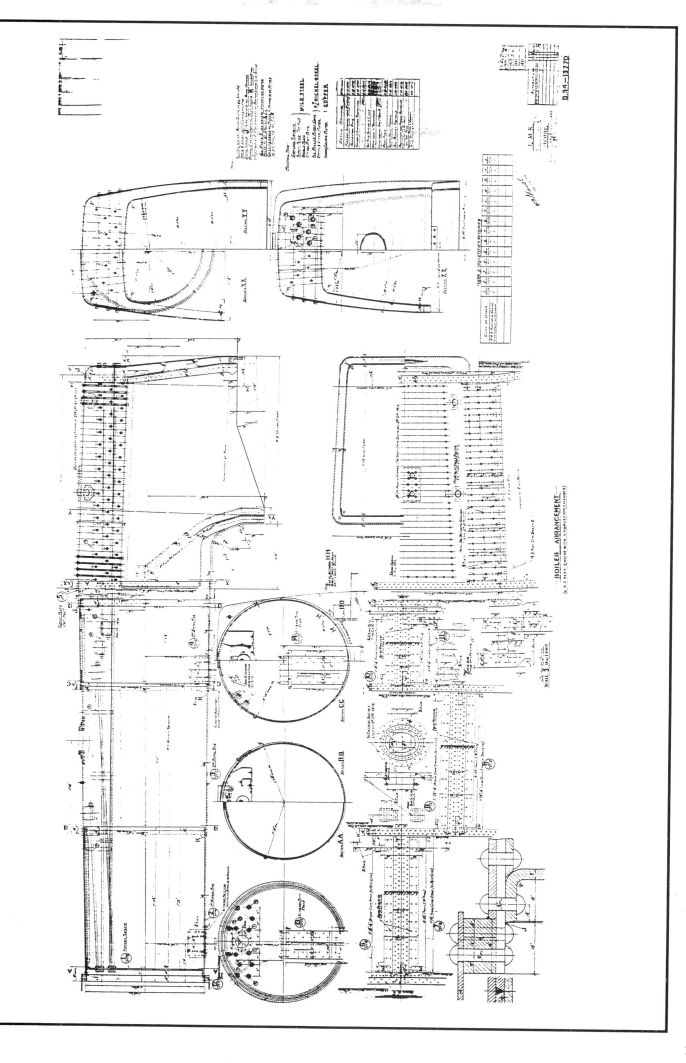

Fig. 6. The official L.M.S. drawing No. D34–13770 showing the boiler arrangement for the 6203–6212 with the combustion chamber.

J.B. Radford Collection.

and abolished the G.W. organ mouth collectors in the firebox corners. The regulator in the smokebox suffered from distortion — hot gases, hot and cold steam all in one casting - and the regulator rod -2¼" diameter G.W. style rod — an appalling affair — was replaced by the usual short rotating rod. By the time the 'Coronation' came along, the barrel was concentric not lying on one side of its cone as in G.W. — a most expensive boiler shop assembly job and plate development. Also in the 'Coronation' the famous 2 ft. 0 in. figure between the copper and firebox roof plates was abandoned in favour of 1 ft.10 in. which allowed the biggest barrel diameter on 6 ft. 9 in. wheels. We had pads on the boiler underside just in case the wheels when new at 6 ft. 9 in. took up the full rise in the axlebox gap."

An interesting development of the decision to place pads under the boilers of the boiler seatings on 'Coronations' came when the heavy overhaul was carried out on 'Duchess of Hamilton' in 1985—1990 the overall height of the locomotive had to be lowered in order to be able to pass under overhead wires. The new height was achieved by removing the pads under the boiler, this being a possible option since the tyres were worn down to the last turning size and thus the boiler when lowered remained clear of the wheels.

An earlier proposal to fit the regulators in the domes of all the 'Princess Royal' boilers, rather than where they had been positioned in the superheater headers, had been considered as early as October 1935 and implemented on boilers Nos. 6048 and 6049 fitted to engines 6200 and 6201 and also on boiler 9236 built new for 6202 to replace boiler 9100. However the change was surprisingly not carried out on the rest of the class until 1952—56, the superheater header itself not being replaced in the process, but being merely blanked off as required. Records also show that there was a further proposal issued on 30th June 1941 to have a regulator in the dome fitted up to a later boiler in order to create a spare for the earlier 'Princess Royal' type.

Boilers Nos. 9100, 9105 and 9235 (originally fitted to Locomotives Nos. 6202, 6207, and 6212) had 32 superheater flues and 112 small tubes the latter being increased in size from 2¼" dia. to 2⅜" dia. at a subsequent retube, this increasing the heating surface from 2097 sq. ft. to 2167 sq. ft. respectively. Boilers 9101—9104 had 24 flues of 5⅛" diameter and 141 small tubes of 2¼" diametery giving a total of 2218 sq. ft. heating surface. This was later still changed to 32 flues and 123 small tubes of 2⅜" diameter increasing the heating surface up to 2299 sq. ft. Boilers Nos. 9106—9109 (originally fitted to engines 6208—6211) started out with 32 flues and 112 2¼" small tubes and were also later fitted with the increased size of small tubes this giving them an increase in heating surface from 2097 to 2299 sq. ft. Boiler No. 9236, the second spare boiler, was built with a dome as new and a 40 element superheater to get the high degree of superheat necessary for driving the turbines on engine No. 6202 to which it was fitted and with which it remained for most of the engine's life. Boiler No. 9100 then went into the pool for the rest of the class, its final move being onto 6203 in 1958 and to which it is still fitted. An interesting letter from T.F.Coleman to D.W.Stanford at Derby and dated 5th November 1935 survives and referring to Drawing No D/4173 of the tube arrangement for boilers with five rows of elements says:-

"I noted that the small tubes were 2¼" diameter. Why is this when it has been arranged that they should be 2⅜" for future?"

No letter of response has survived so far as is known, but interestingly, apart from boiler No. 9236, the small tube outside diameter of 2⅜" was used after that date with increased heating surface as a consequence. Engines 6202—12, unlike 6200 and 6201 had boilers made from mild steel plate, and the combustion chamber was lengthened from the short version fitted to 6200 and 6201. As to cab controls these were very similar to the two prototypes except that 6203—12 had combined vacuum and steam brake valves unlike 6200 and 6201 where they were separate.

The Derby Locomotive Drawing Office of the C.M.E. on London Road where the design work for the 'Princess Royal' Class locomotives was done, seen here on 1st May 1936. Most of the draughtsmen here would have been involved in the design of both the prototype and production 'Princess Royal' class engines.

L.M.S. Official, courtesy Brian Radford

The centre cylinder block being positioned between the frames of 6200 in the heavy machine shop prior to being bolted in place.

L.M.S. Official, courtesy Brian Radford

THE SANDING SYSTEM

It is worth noting that according to L.M.S. official records and correspondence, engines 6203−12 had gravity fed trickle sanding gear fitted from new to which some modifications had to be made very early in the life of the locomotives when blockages became regular occurrences in the delivery pipes, resulting in a lack of sand at the rail. Bearing in mind the routes on which these engines worked together with the weather conditions that could prevail at any time of the year in the hills, failure of this equipment could well lead to trains coming to a stand unable to move. Urgent action was clearly needed and T.F. Coleman, in charge of the Derby drawing office, wrote to G.R. Nicholson at Crewe Works on 4th November 1935 only five months after 6203 had entered traffic (even less for some other members of the class), recording that Stanier had drawn his attention to the fact that the sanding gear was not working properly. Nicholson carried out an examination of engines at Camden Shed on 6th November and suggested the addition of sloping plates in the sand boxes to prevent sand packing there. After trials with a butterfly type sand valve, which did not result in a satisfactory outcome, the decision was taken to convert all the engines 6203−12 from trickle to Midland type steam sanding. 6203 herself was modified on 6th April 1936 according to the official record card for the locomotive.

TENDER DESIGN

The flat sided design which had been built for the first two engines and the 'Turbomotive', held 9 tons of coal and 4000 gallons of water, but because of problems caused to the fireman in getting sufficient coal down to the front shoveling plate, a new design of tender tank/bunker was introduced for engines 6203−12 when new. These had flat sides, but were curved over at the top edge, and also had a better slope for self trimming of the coal. The numbers of this batch were 9124 to 9133 (of which 6203 had the first) and they weighed 27 tons 16 cwts light and 54 tons 13 cwts loaded. Further problems

however became a repeated occurrence on long runs, particularly in adverse conditions when the 9 tons of coal proved scarcely adequate, so in 1936 a further modified version holding 10 tons of coal was built. 6203 received No. 9374 at a heavy general overhaul at Crewe, returning to traffic with it on 19th January 1937, whilst the old tender passed to 'Royal Scot' Class 4-6-0 No. 6130. Others passed second-hand to other 'Royal Scot' and 'Jubilee' class 4-6-0 locomotives. These new tenders were originally intended for the 'Jubilee' Class 4-6-0s but were specially altered to provide for the 10 ton coal capacity by extending the curved side sheet upwards to the limit of the loading gauge. They weighed 27 tons 16 cwts light and 55 tons 13 cwts loaded, to which the coal pusher fitted to tender No. 9359 attached to engine No. 6206, added a further ton. 'Princess Margaret Rose' was the last engine of the class to get one of these tenders and Appendix 5 lists all the 'Princess Royal' locomotive tenders and the engines to which they were allocated.

BUILDING A 'PRINCESS ROYAL'

Material Ordering

Following on from the design stage and sometimes contemporary with it the ordering of all the materials to be used in the manufacturing process of the locomotive needed to be put in hand, the period of time from date of ordering to material actually being delivered to the locomotive works ranging from a few weeks to six or seven months.

Frames

The main frames for both engine and tender on the production batch were cut out ten at a time using a coal-gas flame cutter in the heavy machine shop at the Crewe works of the L.M.S., and it was here that they were also slotted and drilled, reducing the original 3 tons of plain steel plate to some 2¼ tons each, pairs of engine and tender frame plates then being set up to form both of the basic chassis. Here too in the shop the complex cylinder castings, which involved the use of

Building a Princess Royal – The boiler of 6200 being held vertically inside the boiler shop tower to enable the front tubeplate to be rivetted in position.   *L.M.S. Official, courtesy R.T. Ellis*

over sixty moulds and cores following their casting in the Crewe Works foundry, were machined, bored, and drilled before being mounted in their respective positions between or outside the frames together with other items including drag boxes (which were also cast items) and frame stretchers. The completed basic chassis was then mounted on temporary accommodation wheelsets and moved by rail through the works to the main erecting shop where it was lifted onto frame stands, positioned over a set of rails, to enable the erection of the engine to continue.

Boiler and Firebox

The boilers of the 'Princess Royal' class, like all new L.M.S. boilers at the time, were constructed in the old part of Crewe works nearest the station. This is the area now occupied by the Crewe Heritage Centre. The manufacture of the various component parts that went to make up the boiler involved considerable expertise. Oil fired furnaces heated up the various plates that required forming to a white hot heat, their movement to and from the furnaces on special forks supported by an

overhead crane involved the need to counter-balance the weight carried. This was achieved by up to seven men seated in a row on the opposite end who, at the given signal when the plate had reached its correct position in the furnace, all jumped off together, allowing the plate to be lowered quickly, under its own weight, onto supporting firebricks in the furnace. For removal, the same produce was repeated in reverse, with the plate heated to the required temperature. The plate was next swung into position on the giant 700 ton hydraulic press where it was formed whilst hot into its required shape by being pressed over a mould (called a flanging block). This process sometimes required several re-heats in the furnace to achieve the necessary shaping. The throat plate blank for instance was squeezed between flanging blocks weighing some 41 tons in order to form the intricate shape, joining as it does the boiler barrel to the firebox and as specifically referred to in a E.A.Langridge's letter detailed in the earlier part of this chapter.

The boiler barrel required the careful rolling of three flat plate sections into a circular shape before joining them end to end and then attaching the steel firebox wrapper plate, front and rear tubeplates, and the inner copper firebox. This was fixed to the outer wrapper plate at the base through the foundation ring from which the ashpan hung from locating lugs and being held tight by steel wedges. Some 2,500 stays were required to hold the inner and outer firebox sections together providing the water space to the required width, an essential part of the boiler to ensure its correct operation under steam. In the boiler shop a tower had been added on the top of the old roof at one end of the shop which had originally been constructed with a height to suit the much shorter boilers of the L.N.W.R. days. This extra height enabled a boiler to be stood on end in order to facilitate the use of multi spindle drilling and hydraulic rivetting machines on the barrel, firebox and smokebox end of the boilers. This procedure was made possible by the additional use of a deep pit into which the boiler could be lowered to enable the rivetting machine to work on the top and intermediate sections of the boiler. Following this the boilers were completed in the boiler mounting shop by the addition of the main steam pipes followed by fire tubes, superheater flues which were screwed into the firebox tubeplate, and following the expanding of all tubes, the superheater elements were fitted, over 2,700 feet of tubes being used, and then by the addition of boiler fittings including the extensive array of controls and valves at the firebox end. These had where required been cast in the Crewe works own brass foundry and machined and fitted up in the brass finishing shop. Inside the firebox the cast iron firegrate sections were fitted making up the 45 square feet of grate area. The boiler lagging for the insulation of the barrel and firebox, covered by an outer skin of thin steel boiler cladding sheets, was the last to be applied following the hydraulic testing of the boiler at 30% above working pressure followed by the steam testing, it being tested in steam twice, first at 10lb/sq. in. over the working pressure and then at normal working pressure. A 'Princess Royal' boiler weighed 18 tons 1 cwt unmounted and 24 tons 17 cwt 1 qr fully mounted. Later modified boilers with a combustion chamber weighed 25 tons 10 cwt 1 qr.

Final Erection

In the main erecting shop the now completed boiler was lowered into position on the frames and although the frames were not wheeled, the motion, pipework and cab were fitted. As a matter of interest there were 56 points on the motion where needle roller bearings were used all requiring grease gun lubrication for maintenance. When all the motion in the cylinder area had been fitted the whole locomotive would be lifted by overhead cranes and the driving wheels fitted followed by the rear truck and bogie. Due to the very condensed areas of motion around the cylinders and remembering that the inside cylinders were position over the front bogie, the fitting of the bogie was usually left until very late on in the construction and also in later overhauls. Photographs taken of 'Princess Royal' class locomotives under repair often show the bogie removed to allow easier access for the fitters. With the locomotive on its driving wheels the connecting rods could be fitted joining the crossheads on the inside pistons to the leading driving crank axle whilst after fitting of the coupling rods, the outside connecting rods were fitted to join the crossheads to the centre driving wheel crankpins.

Wheels and Axles

The process of casting the driving wheels in the steel foundry involved the use of a two part mould with cores for the crankpin and axle holes, and 35 cwts. of the finest moulten steel, heated to a temperature of 1,500 degrees Centigrade, was poured into the space formerly occupied by the wooden pattern in order to produce the casting. After a few hours to allow the casting to cool sufficiently, the black moulding sand would be broken away to reveal the casting which then had to be dressed (cleaned up) by pneumatic chisel before removal to the wheel shop. Here a machine was employed to simultaneously turn the rim, face the centre boss and bore the hole for the axle. The pairs of wheels were then assembled using a 150 ton hydraulic press to force

With the main frames now on stands in the main erecting shop, this fascinating view shows the boiler of 6200 being gently lowered into position on 20th June 1933.

L.M.S. Official, courtesy R.T. Ellis

At 4 p.m. on the same day the boiler is now in place and various groups of workmen busy themselves on various tasks.

L.M.S. Official, courtesy R.T. Ellis

them onto either end of a plain or cranked axle as appropriate, the operation taking five minutes to achieve at a carefully controlled rate, thus keeping stress in the metal to a minimum. The axles, both plain and crank, had all been previously machined from forgings of the highest quality steel. Next came the process of fitting the wheelsets with the steel tyres upon which they would run. The tyres, rolled from ingots of high quality steel, were produced to the unmachined state by an outside company — usually Steel Peach and Tozer of Sheffield. With wear taking place all the time during the life of the locomotive it would be necessary for the locomotive to be re-tyred several times during its life span. The finished bore of the tyre is between 1/16" and ⅛" less in internal diameter when cold than the outside diameter of the wheel itself and thus, when the tyre is heated with gas jets and expands in size, the wheel can be lowered into it. As the tyre cools down to normal ambient temperature it contracts and an interference fit is achieved with the tyre tightly gripping the wheel rim. The rolling into a groove of a specially shaped 'Gibson ring' on the inside face of the wheel prevents any movement of the tyre during the course of its life. The wheelset was next spun on a rig at 260 revolutions per minute (equivalent to 60 miles per hour on the track) and temporary weights attached in various places to remove any oscillation due to out of balance forces. These temporary weights were in turn later replaced by cast lead weights poured in a moulten state between side plates rivetted onto the wheel itself each side of the spokes just inside the outer rim. These are known as the counter balance weights and enable smooth running in service to be assured, in so far as it is possible to balance the reciprocating masses of an engine in motion.

Coupling and Connecting Rods

The Crewe drop-forge had, of course, also been hard at work fashioning the coupling and connecting rods from low alloy manganese molybdenum steel together with other motion parts from less high quality steel. For instance, from 12 cwt. steel billets of rectangular shape in the case of the connecting rods, heated no less than five times

to white hot heat, the billets were worked to a rough forged shape to match a side view template followed by the machining of the flats and sides (complete with their fluting) in the machine shop, a special circling machine milling the rod ends to their rounded shape. After boring, the phosphor-bronze bushes were pressed into the eye ends, thus completing the rods enabling them to be taken to the erecting shop for fitting to the engine. All other forged motion parts were similarly treated to a finished state.

As it was fitted to a particular locomotive, each item would be stamped with the number of the engine and also where necessary, the handing of the part. e.g.'R' for right hand, 'L' for left hand and 'I' for inside This was to enable identification on future works visits of parts from the particular engine together with the correct location of the item.

The Tender

In the tender shop within Crewe works construction of the tenders ran concurrently with that of the engines in the erecting shop, construction sequences being basic frame assembly with its fitting up completed before the tanks were fitted. The original tenders were fitted with 'Timken' roller bearing axleboxes for all six wheels but surprisingly this was not repeated on the subsequent replacement tenders. Following wheeling, the tender was moved out of the shop to be coupled to the engine on the outside storage tracks.

With many of the above operations being carried out concurrently, a locomotive of the 'Princess Royal' class could be assembled from already finished component parts in the erecting shop in only 5½ working days. Over 1,000 men throughout the works were involved in the whole process of manufacture and construction.

Painting

Next came the visit to the paint shop where the locomotive received its new livery, lining out, plus numbers and letters and power classification code in transfers. The original livery of all the class was L.M.S.

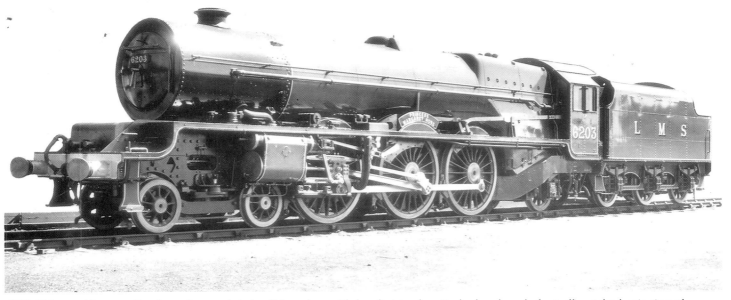

6203 'Princess Margaret Rose' stands complete in all her glory with her first tender attached and ready for traffic at the beginning of July 1935 before working her first train to London Euston on the 4th. *L.M.S. Official, Crown Copyright, courtesy National Railway Museum*

'crimson lake' with 12'' small numerals in gold shaded black. The Rolling Stock Committee meeting of 31st May 1923 — minute 53 records the L.M.S.Board's decision to recommend adoption of the old Midland 'crimson lake' for coaching stock and resolved that in future passenger engines be painted 'crimson lake' and freight engines black without lining.

Cost of Construction

The official records show that the cost of 6203 as built was :

    Engine £8,538-0s-0d
    Tender £1,154-0s-0d
    TOTAL £9,692-0s-0d

This total figure was a saving of over £1,000 per locomotive on the original authority figure of £10,700 each. The cost of locomotives 6203–12 was charged to Capital Renewals as per the Mechanical and Electrical Engineering Committee Minute No. 147 of July 1932. It is interesting to note that for this production batch of locomotives the unit cost had been reduced considerably from the first two locomotives built. No. 6200 'The Princess Royal' had cost £12,657 and 6201 'Princess Elizabeth' £11,675. Clearly with the production of a larger batch of locomotives some economies of scale were obtained, but another significant factor was the switch from steel castings to fabricated parts made by using welded construction. The Costs Office at Crewe Works produced a chart of comparative costs dated 26th September 1935 and also the weights of components, a few of which are tabulated below:

Item	Cost of Casting £ - s - d	Cost of Fabrication £ - s - d	Cost Saving £ - s - d	% Saving
Platform support	8- 7- 9	3-14- 4	10- 1- 3	67
Buffer beam gusset	17- 4- 8	6- 6- 5	10-18- 3	63
Pony truck stretcher	113-16- 4	53-18- 9	59-19- 7	53
Bogie pivot bracket	5- 5- 0	3-19-10	1- 4- 2	23
Ashpan *	54-13-10	33-13- 3	21- 0- 7	38

* This was a part rivetted and part pre-fabricated comparison against a wholly rivetted item.

Only complicated items such as the reversing link carrier and the frame stay and main frame stretcher for the bogie pivot showed significant savings of 34% and 61% respectively in favour of a cast item compared to a fabricated one.

The savings themselves were spread right across the board and included wages, workshops expenses and superintendence. However with many smaller items and even large items such as the inside and outside cylinders, wheels and axleboxes, castings made in the steel and brass foundry were still the only option.

INTO SERVICE

Firstly came the weighing on the weigh-bridge to ensure that the weight on each set of wheels on both engine and tender was accurately distributed in accordance with design calculations with any adjustments being made by increasing or decreasing the tension on the springs.

Following a stationary test in steam and a short trial trip, which enabled minor adjustments to be made, the brand new L.M.S. 4-6-2 'Princess Royal'class locomotive No. 6203 worked her first trip to Euston from Crewe on 4th July 1935 and on the 6th of that month was officially allocated to Camden Locomotive Depot, London to begin her life in the top link.

Sister locomotives 6204–12 were completed at Crewe between July and October 1935 and following their completion the L.M.S. intended to add a further five locomotives, to be numbered 6213–17, to the class. In fact order No. E402 was placed in July 1936 to add these to the 1937 building programme but there was a change of direction and the L.M.S. Shareholders meeting held on 26th February 1937 was advised of new plans for a high-speed service between London and Glasgow due to start on 5th July 1937 with streamlined locomotives in blue and silver livery and with coaches to match. E.A. Langridge, writing to D.F. Tee again, tells the 'behind the scenes'story thus:

"You may know what a fluke it was that the 'Coronation' came about. At various times in a D.O. (drawing office) a chief draughtsman will say 'see what you can do about this 5X or that business'. We were ordering up E402 quite in the usual way as another five 'Princesses' with latest boiler 6213–7, when he said 'see what you can do to get the biggest boiler and wheels on a 4-6-2'. Two schemes were got out within a week — as WAS (Stanier) was off to India on that engine riding enquiry with (E.S.) Cox — both had the big boilers — one with a 'Princess' cylinder layout and the other — which I did — based on the L.& Y. 4-6-0 four cylinder arrangement, which seemed to me far superior to the Western way. Mr Coleman, the C.D. (chief draughtsman) hadn't much hope of getting it passed by Stanier. . . . . . but the impossible came off and Coleman was told to go ahead 'tout de suite'. Stanier was away for six months and Crewe had done the boiler and above platform and Derby the rest by the time he saw the drawings. We had one of the finest drawing office staffs at that period at Crewe and Derby — the pick of Horwich, Crewe, Stoke, and Derby — and I think we made a fine job of it. Coleman took all the draughtsman at Derby engaged on the job to see 6220 (they abandoned the number '6213' as being unlucky) in all its glory in the paint shop. Later we went down to Tamworth one afternoon to see and hear it on the 'up Scot', running like a sewing machine. I did the motion arrangement and was interested in trying out the old bent rocking lever: there was nothing in it actually, so we made ours straight. The valve spindle guides were done by a Horwich man, so was the reversing shaft — made hollow to increase the diameter and resist twist. Later on I got across an idea — also from Horwich — to put a big lead on the valves — Horwich had it on Crabs (2-6-0s) — and its effect is to increase steam opening when notched up — helps power at high speed. If you make the

On Wednesday 17th July 1935, 6203 passes Brent signal box with the 10 a.m. Glasgow Central to Euston express *Ken Nunn collection*

6203 arriving at Glasgow Central station with the down 'Royal Scot' on 1st August 1935 after the 401 mile run from London Euston. *J.F.Clay*

steam port in the liner wider and the piston head on the exhaust side wider as well, you can also get a longer opening to exhaust at lower cut offs as well — the valve head always over runs the port on the exhaust side except when highly notched up (that makes the old G.W. habit of giving port sizes on engine diagrams quite useless — they mean nothing, anymore than heating surface figures do)."

So ends Eric Langridge's recollections of his view of the events which led to the building of the new 'Princess Coronation' class 4-6-2 engines or 'Duchesses' as they became colloquially, but not officially, known. It also completes our story of the design of 6203 'Princess Margaret Rose' and her sisters.

The class as a whole were built and eventually named as follows:

No.	Name	Date to Traffic
6200	The Princess Royal	27th June 1933
6201	Princess Elizabeth	3rd November 1933
6202	(The 'Turbomotive')	19th June 1935
6203	Princess Margaret Rose	1st July 1935
6204	Princess Louise	19th July 1935
6205	Princess Victoria	24th July 1935
6206	Princess Marie Louise	1st August 1935
6207	Princess Arthur of Connaught	9th August 1935
6208	Princess Helena Victoria	16th August 1935
6209	Princess Beatrice	23rd August 1935
6210	Lady Patricia	6th September 1935
6211	Queen Maud	18th September 1935
6212	Duchess of Kent	21st October 1935

The first of a series of three photographs of 6203, still less than one month old, and 'Royal Scot' class 4-6-0 6104 'Scottish Borderer' backing down into Glasgow Central station from Polmadie motive power depot prior to taking expresses to the south on 2nd August 1935. *J.F.Clay*

6203, now attached to her train, awaits the departure signal on the same day, Friday 2nd August 1935 at the head of the up 'Royal Scot' to London Euston.
J.F.Clay

'Princess Margaret Rose' starts away from Glasgow Central in fine style at the beginning of her long journey to London Euston. *J.F.Clay*

The final list of approved names was only confirmed after a long sequence of events which included the involvement of the general public through the national newspapers of the day. Suggestions apparently included characters from Longfellow's 'Hiawatha', the ancient kings of Mercia, great churchmen and even a suggestion by the Mayor of Crewe that they be called the 'Crewe' class. After official permission had been received to use the name 'Princess Royal', public response at one time caused the L.M.S. Vice-President to suggest that the next ten be named after dominions or colonies, but Stanier was keen to continue the Princess theme.

Of the list above 6202 was at one time to have been 'Princess Marina', 6206 'Princess Maud', 6207 'Princess Alice', 6208 'Princess Helena' only, 6210 'Princess Alexandra', 6211 'Princess Patricia', and 6212 'Princess Ingrid' and shortly afterwards 'Princess Ena'.

No. 6210 'Lady Patricia' was eventually named after Princess Patricia of Connaught who forfeited her royal status in 1919 upon marrying a commoner, Lieutenant Alexander Ramsay, R.N. although at one point the name was to have been 'Lady Patricia Ramsay', while 6211 'Queen Maud' was named after the wife of the King of Norway, the family having long links with the British Royal Family.

CHAPTER TWO

AT WORK FOR THE L.M.S.

As previously stated, 6203 'Princess Margaret Rose' left Crewe on her first trip south to Euston on 4th July 1935 and two days later was officially allocated for a brief period to the famous top link shed at Camden, London, with the shed code of 1B. She was soon in regular service along with her sisters on the Anglo–Scottish expresses, finding use on the 'Royal Scot', 'The Night Scot', and 'The Mid-Day Scot' trains to and from Glasgow Central station. On these London–Glasgow trips the new 'Princess Royals' no longer worked the down 'Royal Scot' one day and the up 'Royal Scot' the next, but returned after servicing on the very same day.

6203 also, on several occasions in the first few weeks of service, worked the so-called 'Liverpool Flyer', the 5.25 p.m. express from Liverpool (Lime Street) to London (Euston). The train was timed to cover the 152.7 miles from Crewe to Willesden in only 142 minutes. In this period she also on at least one occasion worked the 18.05 'Merseyside Express' from Euston to Liverpool, a train never lighter than 500 tons tare and timed at 200 minutes for the 189.6 miles from London Euston to Mossley Hill station on the outskirts of Liverpool. However all was not entirely well, for on November 27th 1935 Stanier had written to T.F. Coleman in the Derby design office as follows:

"NEW 4-6-2 ENGINES Nos. 6203–6212

My attention has been repeatedly drawn to the reports of enginemen that the latest 4-6-2 engines do not appear as powerful as the first three engines.

Mr Chambers has already had a conversation with you on the matter when it was pointed out that the steam port opening about 15% cut-off and also in other positions, is slightly less than that with the first three engines. (sic)

It is suggested that an increased lead should be provided which would have the effect of increasing the port opening and I shall be glad if you will look into the matter and let me know what alterations would be necessary in order to try this out on an engine.

Please give this matter special attention and let me have the information at the earliest possible moment.

W.A.Stanier"

The reference to 'three' engines must be a lapse of memory by Stanier since the remarks clearly do not apply to 6202 which was driven by steam turbines.

Three days later came the reply in the form of a letter to F.A.Lemon at Crewe stating that one engine was to be fitted up experimentally, having the lap decreased by 1/16" and the lead increased by 1/16", and asking for Experiment Form No. 1 to be sent.

Coleman replied to Stanier on 3rd December that at 15% cut-off the average port opening of the new engines was only 1/64" less on the outside cylinders, whilst the inside cylinders were practically identical with the original engines, and advised him of his instruction to have one set of valve heads made at Crewe to be fitted as early as possible to one engine for trial. Engine No. 6206, in Crewe Shops at the time, was the engine selected for the experiment and on 9th December Stanier asked to be advised of the number of the engine "in order that my representative can ride on the engine at an early date.".

Unfortunately the outcome of this trial is not recorded since the correspondence has not survived as far as we know.

Another small design issue here also deserves mention is that 6212 had an arrangement of clamping dogs around the periphery of the smokebox door fitted on the instructions of R.A. Riddles. But when the Crewe drawing showing this reached T.F. Coleman at Derby he wrote to G.R. Nicholson at Crewe on 14th November 1935:-

"I do not particularly favour this arrangement in conjunction with the type of door in question and am of the opinion that the new type of hinge and bar is a better job. The use of dogs will not be perpetuated."

An instruction was issued on 16th November that the smokebox cross bars should be changed to the hinged type and material was to be prepared for fitting to the engines when available at the shops.

One other problem which occurred was the overheating of crossheads and a modification was carried out on engine No. 6210 to stiffen the frame stretchers by having the flanges turned down instead of up except for the hind flange.

In addition engine No. 6210 was also modified (in November 1935) by having ⅝" thick plates fitted to each leg of the motion plate to stiffen it.

In 1936 'The Mid-Day Scot' was accelerated to include a stop at Penrith as well as Lancaster, only 59 minutes being allowed for the 51.2 miles between the two stations, entailing an ascent of Grayrigg Bank with the usual load of at least 14 vehicles at an average speed of over 40 miles per hour.

In the Railway Magazine for July 1936 timings of runs between Lancaster and Penrith during the first week of the accelerated 'Mid-Day Scot' services made by Cecil J Allen were published, and one of those runs featured 'Princess Margaret Rose', the only locomotive to keep to the new timings in the first week, the run being timed on Thursday May 7th 1936.

Locomotive : Class 7P 4-6-2 No. 6203
Loaded Coaches : 14
Load tons tare/gross : 445/470

Distance Miles	Location	Sched. mins.	Actual m.s.	Speed m.p.h.
00.0	LANCASTER	0	0.00	
03.1	Hest Bank		4.58	
06.3	CARNFORTH	8	8.01	67
09.5	m.p.9.5 (Yealand Summit)		11.05	55
13.6	Milnthorpe		14.53	67.5
15.5	Hincaster Jn		16.46	59
19.1	OXENHOLME	21	20.44	50
22.0	m.p.22		24.29	
24.0	m.p.24		27.19	42.5
26.1	Grayrigg		30.21	41
32.2	TEBAY	36	36.31	66.5
35.0	m.p.35		39.41	
37.7	Shap Summit	45	44.19	31.5
39.7	Shap		46.51	
47.0	Clifton & Lowther		53.06	78
50.0	m.p.50		55.30	
51.2	PENRITH	59	57.34	

Calculated equivalent drawbar horse power :

Carnforth–m.p. 9.5	1660
Oxenholme–m.p. 24	1560
m.p. 24–Grayrigg	1770
Tebay–Shap Summit	1790

No. 6203 made the best of the un-piloted times in the week under review by Cecil J.Allen, being over 4¼ minute quicker than the run behind No. 6208 with the same load as the previous day. Shap summit was passed ¾ minute inside booked time, with a net gain to Penrith of 1½ minutes.

As O.S. Nock has observed, the top link firemen of the L.M.S. had to adjust their firing techniques from those of the 4-6-0s which steamed well with an even fire all over the grate. With 'Princess Royals' good steaming was effected by keeping a thicker fire at the firehole door end and thinning it off towards the front end of the firebox.

The L.M.S. Engine History Card for 6203 quite interestingly actually records the amount of coal issued for trips and consumed per mile as follows:-

The down 'Royal Scot' with thirteen vehicles on, storms through Bushey behind 6203 with water spilling from the tender vent pipes after picking up water on the troughs. The date is August or September 1935.

H Gordon Tidey

Year	Mileage	Coal issued (tons)	Consumption (lb per mile)
1935	48,585	1125	52
1936	95,476	2353	55
1937	74,941	1741	52
1938*	74,017	1735	53

* 1938 being 53 weeks in operating records terms.

During the first week of the 1936 accelerated 7½ hour timings for the 'Mid-Day Scot', the performances of both 6203 (already referred to) and 6212 were recorded over the section of the line between Lancaster and Penrith, which included the stiff climb to Shap summit, a distance of 51.2 miles for which a scheduled 59 minutes was allowed as previously stated. Locomotive No. 6212 'Duchess of Kent' made the inaugural run on 4th May 1936.

As John Powell has observed in his book 'Stanier Pacifics at Work', this was a gruelling section of the line to be tackled after a train had already covered some 230 miles and beyond which a further section of line some 120 miles in length and also not without difficulties lay, and as Driver P.G.Johnson shrewdly commented at that time. "It's a long drag up Shap in either direction with a green fire or a green fireman!".

The grade from Carnforth, only a little above sea level, represents a continuous average gradient of 1 in 183. So for an average speed requirement of 50.9 mph the engine had to be worked very efficiently indeed in order to produce the requisite 1650 e.d.b.h.p..

The run with No. 6203 which represents the driver's first attempt at meeting the new requirements was a very creditable effort, the time taken being 57 minutes 34 seconds against the scheduled 59 minutes with a trailing load of 14 coaches (470 tons gross), the engine producing a maximum D.B.H.P. of 1790 over the section Tebay to Shap

L.M.S.R. MIDDAY SCOT : LANCASTER—PENRITH

Distance	Engine, 4-6-2 No. .. .. Load, vehicles .. .. ,, tons tare .. .. ,, ,, full	Schedule	6212 16 493 520		6205 14 443 470		6208 14 443 470		6203 14 445 470		6206 14 447 475		*6129 16 503 530		6210 16 503 530	
miles		min.	m.	s.	m.	s.	m.	s.	m.	s.	m.	s.	m.	s.	m.	s.
0·0	LANCASTER	0	0	00	0	00	0	00	0	00	0	00	0	00	0	00
3·1	Hest Bank	—	5	28	4	55	5	14	4	58	5	16	4	58	5	26
6·3	CARNFORTH	8	8	40	8	04	8	20	8	01	8	28	7	59	8	34
9·5	Milepost 9¼	—	12	00	11	24	11	45	11	05	11	52	11	10	12	01
13·6	Milnthorpe	—	16	05	15	29	15	56	14	53	16	02	15	00	16	22
15·5	*Hincaster Junction* ..	—	18	03	17	32	18	06	16	46	18	07	16	57	18	23
19·1	OXENHOLME	21	22	23	21	53	22	52	20	44	22	41	20	59	22	28
22·0	*Milepost 22*	—	26	18	25	41	26	59	24	29	26	57	24	38	26	14
24·0	*Milepost 24*	—	29	02	28	22	29	49	27	19	30	07	27	17	29	04
26·1	Grayrigg	—	32	06	31	21	33	00	30	21	33	33	30	05	32	06
32·2	TEBAY	36	38	09	37	45	39	23	36	31	39	53	35	56	38	20
35·0	*Milepost 35*	—	41	24	41	19	42	56	39	41	43	17	39	09	42	00
37·7	*Summit*	45	46	30	46	29	48	34	44	19	48	21	43	36	47	16
39·7	Shap	—	49	00	49	02	51	27	46	51	50	49	46	02	49	41
47·0	Clifton	—	55	00	55	13	57	52	53	06	56	24	52	29	55	53
50·0	*Milepost 50*	—	57	41	57	37	60	27	55	30	58	29	54	59	58	20
51·2	PENRITH	59	59	26	59	30	62	16	57	34	60	24	56	43	60	07

* " Royal Scot " 4-6-0, piloted by Midland compound 4-4-0 No. 1194

Fig. 7. Full table of runs between Lancaster and Penrith during the first week of the accelerated 'Mid-day Scot'.

From the Railway Magazine, July 1936

At rest on Camden motive power depot on Monday 26th August 1935 after almost two months in traffic. The leading driving wheels are chocked and fitters are on the footplate.
Harold N James

Summit.

From 4th May 1936 the down 'Royal Scot', the 10.00 a.m. from London Euston, was also accelerated by ten minutes to both Glasgow and Edinburgh, arriving at 5.45 p.m. and 5.50 p.m. respectively. The 'Mid-Day Scot' was then accelerated even further, leaving a full half hour later at 2.00 p.m. from Euston and arriving at 9.35 p.m. and 9.55 p.m. respectively, the whole of the 30 minutes being saved by faster running.

A non-stop run to Crewe, where, the footplate crews were changed and the through portion of the Plymouth—Glasgow service was added, was followed by fast running even with the increased load and including the demanding section of the line from Lancaster to Penrith with its testing gradients including the 1 in 75 covering the last four miles over Shap Wells to the north of Tebay. R.E.L.Charlwood, who was a prolific recorder of train performance, made a record of several runs by 'Princess Royals' in the 1936—37 period with the 'Mid-Day Scot' trains and 6203 figured among his observations.

With a trailing load of some 470 tons (gross) she covered the 31.4 miles (scheduled at 37 minutes at an average speed of 50.9 mph) in 36 minutes 18 seconds at an average speed of 51.9 mph with an initial speed of 67 mph and a final speed of 31.5 mph giving an equivalent drawbar pull of 1555 h.p..

That fine photographer Maurice Earley captured 6203 on film at work on this service at Tebay in July 1936.

On 6th July 1936 the 'Royal Scot' was also accelerated even further and was timed to run from London to Glasgow in 7½ hours without a stop. Although this run was shown as 'non-stop', the 'down' train actually stopped alongside Carlisle Kingmoor depot, a distance of 301 miles from Euston, to change enginemen and also at Symington, where the Edinburgh portion of the train was detached, but there were no stops for passenger purposes, and the same locomotive was used throughout the journey. From the September of 1936 the 'up Royal Scot' to London Euston was accelerated by an extra ten minutes, being timed to arrive at London Euston at 5.25 p.m.

These accelerations of the services had proved possible in part by the findings of a series of dynamometer test car runs carried out the previous November using Nos. 6203 'Princess Margaret Rose' and 6209 'Princess Beatrice' from Euston to Glasgow and back using the normal timings of the 'Royal Scot' trains.

No. 6203, with a boiler having three rows of superheater elements totalling 24 in all at that time, ran to Crewe with a 544 ton train on 25th November and thence to Symington with 480 tons following on to Glasgow with a trailing load of 343 tons. By comparison 6209 with a boiler having four rows of superheater elements, numbering 32 in all, ran from Glasgow to Euston hauling 314 tons to Symington and from there 481 tons to London on 27th November. Camden and Carlisle train crews were used on the Euston—Carlisle section and Polmadie men between Carlisle and Glasgow.

The tests were written up as dynamometer car test report No. 59, and used the ex Lancashire and Yorkshire dynamometer car No. 45050, now preserved at the Midland Railway Centre, Butterley.

The results of the test are shown in Appendix 8 Tables 1 to 5. The

main conclusion drawn was that No. 6209, with the 4 rows of elements, showed an average reduction of 4.9% in coal consumption and 5.7% water per drawbar horse power compared with No. 6203 with only 3 rows of elements.

These tests followed earlier tests with No. 6201 'Princess Elizabeth' in June 1934 and were to be followed later by further tests in April and May, 1936 comparing No. 6202 the 'Turbomotive' with ordinary reciprocating locomotive No. 6212 'Duchess of Kent' on the same route. No. 6202 was subjected to further coal and water consumption tests in June 1937, (L.M.S. Test Reports Nos. 48, 61 and 71 respectively).

It is worth remembering here that the theory that achieving high superheat temperature rose directly from the number of elements was later found not to be the whole truth and that it was very much compromised by the resistance to the flow of hot gases along the superheater flues together with the throttling of the steam supply to the cylinders at the superheater header as already noted in Chapter 1.

On 24th August 1935, No. 6203 had been officially transferred to Polmadie Motive Power Depot, Glasgow, on the Northern Division of the L.M.S. in exchange for No. 6201 'Princess Elizabeth' which was transferred to the Western Division, but by 29th February 1936 she was back at Camden M.P.D. where she remained allocated for three and a half years until 21st October 1939.

On 15th February 1936 instructions had been sent out that in future engine number transfers on the cab sidesheets were to be 10" deep, 14" 'L M S' letters and 2⅛" deep classification figures. All were to be plain black style in gilt with black shading for red passenger engines. The cast iron smokebox door number plates were also to be plain block style in future. Existing stocks of transfers were to be used up and the new style applied to new engines. This instruction was changed on 25th June 1936 the new one stating that the transfers were to be vermillion shaded whatever the type of locomotive.

Mention must now be made of the round trip non-stop tests carried out on November 16th and 17th 1936 from London Euston to Glasgow Central and back using No. 6201 'Princess Elizabeth' to evaluate the performance of the new class.

The test train was made up of seven coaches weighing 225 tons (230 tons gross) and included the ex-Lancashire and Yorkshire Dynamometer Car No. 1. A schedule of six hours was set and the special train left Euston at 9.50 a.m., ten minutes ahead of the regular 'Royal Scot' working, in the hands of Driver T.J. Clarke assisted by Fireman T. Fleet and Passed Fireman A. Shaw, all from Crewe North depot.

A standby locomotive was required to be available in case of locomotive failure and after choosing No. 6210, the final choice fell on No. 6203 'Princess Margaret Rose'. She might well have had to have been used on the return run because 6201 had suffered a white metal failure on the left hand outside crosshead slipper block. Robert A. Riddles, then Principal Assistant to the Chief Mechanical Engineer Ernest Lemon (for Stanier as previously noted was in India at the time), left the celebration dinner, and had the engine sent to St. Rollox Works

where he and some of the staff worked through the night to re-metal the block, machine it and re-fit it so that she was ready for the return trip the following day.

After leaving Glasgow at 1.10 p.m., most of the return journey was undertaken in torrential rain and with the added load of an extra coach bringing the tare weight up to 255 tons (260 tons gross). Euston was reached in 344 minutes 15 seconds compared with a schedule time of 360 minutes, giving an average speed of 70 mph for the whole route including the climbs up to the summits at Beattock and Shap.

Top speed going north was 95.5 mph at Sear's crossing near Cheddington (in later years this location was to gain fame as the spot where the Great Train Robbery took place), and coming south, 95 mph on the approaches to Crewe on level track.

These excellent results confirmed the L.M.S. decision to continue with non-stop runs apart from a crew change at either Crewe or Carlisle and led eventually to the introduction of the 'Coronation Scot' streamlined service planned for the following summer.

Going north the schedule of 360 minutes had been cut by rather less of a margin to 353 minutes 38 seconds, nevertheless a most creditable performance.

Almost immediately after the test runs between Euston and Glasgow 6203 entered the shops at Crewe for a Heavy General Overhaul between 30th November 1936 and 19th January 1937, and during this visit both engine and tender were repainted on the driver's side only, in shop grey and lined out for the purpose of recording each member of the class, 6203 being the model to receive names and numbers from 6203—12. This was done on 31st December 1936 and January 1st 1937 as recorded both officially and by the late W. Leslie Good, a railway enthusiast and excellent photographer of the time. Before leaving the shops in full livery, she received the changes outlined above in terms of lettering and transfers, and 6203 also received her larger 10 ton tender No. 9374, the old one being re-allocated to 'Royal Scot' Class 4-6-0 No. 6130.

The March 1937 issue of the 'L.M.S. Magazine', the official organ of the company carried a most interesting item on page 119 as follows:

"102.5 mph was reached at milepost 39, south of Leighton Buzzard, during a vacuum brake test with a special recording car running between Euston and Crewe on May 3rd 1936. The train consisted of seven coaches hauled by the engine 6203, the total weight, including the locomotive being 366 tons."

This official report confirmed by stop-watch timings by experienced recorder the late W. Rowing Coleby, credits No. 6203 'Princesss Margaret Rose' with the highest recorded speed attained by any locomotive of the 'Princess Royal' class so far as can be determined.

Although L.N.E.R. Class A3 Pacific No. 2570 'Papyrus' had achieved 108 mph on a run down Stoke bank, the gradient assistance was far more than on the descent between Tring and Cheddington where 6203 achieved her record speed. Only 'Flying Scotsman', 'Papyrus', and 'Silver Link' had at that time exceeded a recorded speed of 100 mph if we discount 'City of Truro's' un-authenticated feat with the 'Plymouth Mail'.

As a result of these tests one outcome was the adoption of direct admission brake valves on the new coaching stock being built for the 'Coronation Scot' trains which were due to be introduced the following year.

As to 'Princess Margaret Rose' herself she was to feature as one of the set of fifty cigarette cards issued by W.D. & H.O. Wills (Imperial Tobacco Company) in 1936 depicting 'Railway Engines' both British and Foreign.

The card depicted No. 6203 in full L.M.S. red livery, and the description on the reverse side read:

'2. "PACIFIC" EXPRESS LOCO. "PRINCESS MARGARET ROSE" *L.M.S.R.* For hauling the most important Anglo—Scottish Expresses on the West Coast route, including the "Royal Scot", "Mid-day Scot" and "Night Scot" the L.M.S.R. employ 4-6-2 locomotives of the "Princess Royal" Class, each named after a member of the Royal Family, and weighing with tender, in working order, 158 tons 12 cwt. Like the G.W.R. 'King' and 'Castle' class engines, these engines have four cylinders and a boiler pressure of 250 lb per sq. in. On such duties as the "Royal Scot" express, these engines may work right through between Euston and Glasgow (401½ miles) or Euston and Edinburgh (399¾ miles).'

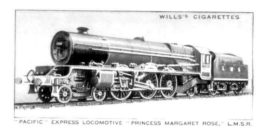

"PACIFIC" EXPRESS LOCOMOTIVE "PRINCESS MARGARET ROSE," L.M.S.R.

One cigarette card in the series was included in each pack of ten cigarettes and albums for mounting the set of 50 cards in, with the descriptions printed alongside, could be purchased for one old penny (1d).

Above: 'Princess Margaret Rose' at Symington probably in the autumn of 1935, but certainly before February 1936, at the head of the 'Royal Scot'. The stop at Symington was made to allow the Edinburgh portion to be attached to the rear of the train.

Locomotive and General Railway Photographs

Facing page upper: A fine action study of 6203 heading northwards through Oxenholme in late 1935. The train is likely to be the 'Royal Scot'.

Rail Archive Stephenson

Facing page lower: Standing on Crewe North motive power depot in 1936 whilst allocated to Camden motive power depot. *J.L. Stevenson*

6203 'Princess Margaret Rose' speeding over Dillicar troughs with a fourteen coach southbound 'Royal Scot' picking up water as she goes.
Maurice W Earley

Another action shot of 'Princess Margaret Rose' picking up water, this time from the troughs just to the south of Lichfield station, as she speeds towards London Euston with the up 'Royal Scot' in August 1935.
P.E. Hawes

Getting into her stride through Wavertree Junction about 1937–38, 6203 heads up an express to London Euston as the fireman leans from the cab probably to check that the exhaust steam injector is working.
Eric Treacy courtesy Millbrook House Ltd.

Underneath the signal gantry at Shrewsbury in the late 1930s, 6203 makes an imposing study of elegance as she stands with a local train, very likely a running-in turn after a works visit to Crewe.

W.H. Whitworth/Rail Archive Stephenson

'Princess Margaret Rose' is seen here again on a Camden motive power depot. Her smokebox door is open and there is a tube-cleaning brush leaning against the buffer beam. The smokebox doornumber plate has decorated corners, an embellishment applied by some depots.

P. Ransome-Wallis Collection

Nearly two decades later 'Princess Margaret Rose' was also featured in a series of 'Loco. 100' 50 cent postage stamps from Niu-Tuvalu. (Fiji). The stamps were in pairs, one stamp depicting side and end elevations and the other an action shot of 46203 hauling a B.R. train in the 1950s.

L.M.S. drivers of these days, as can readily be understood, gained a certain notoriety with the 'Princess Royals' in their charge. Among these was Driver T.J. Clarke who drove No. 6201 'Princess Elizabeth' on the non-stop run referred to above and who was featured in the advertisement for Hornby Trains placed by Meccano in the L.M.S. Magazine, the official journal of the company. As a matter of interest a 'Locomotive (sic) and tender in presentation box' cost the model railway enthusiast of the day the handsome price of 105/- (£5.25p) at Christmas 1937.

Another driver who gained considerable respect amongst his peers was Lawrence Alfred (Laurie) Earl of Camden Shed. He was a top link driver having joined the L.M.S. in 1901. In 1916 he began driving and moved to main line work in 1926. He always spoke well of the 'Princess Royals' and never considered them to be inferior to the later 'Princess Coronations'. He was featured as the writer in 'Speeding North with the Royal Scot', published by the Oxford University Press in 1939 (in collaboration with Horace Greenleaf) and written in 'Boys Own Paper' style. Here are three short extracts to give a flavour of Driver Earl's record of a journey with a 'Princess Royal' locomotive, in this case No. 6206 'Princess Marie Louise', as he prepares her and describes a run from Euston to Carlisle. As a footnote it was said that he had been disappointed that he had not been picked to drive 6201 on the non-stop run, but a Crewe rather than a Camden driver had been chosen because of route knowledge on the northern section.

From 'Speeding North With The Royal Scot'.

"CAMDEN DEPOT

It is exactly 8.40 a.m. as my fireman and I enter the foreman's office and sign on our duty cards. A cheery exchange of greetings with the other men -who, like ourselves, are starting the day's work, or who have just finished — and we peruse the official Notices to see if there is anything that requires our special attention.

When we are familiar with the contents of the Notices, we consult the Train Arrangement Board. This is a large board on which are chalked each day the times of various trains from Euston. By the side of these details are written, also in chalk, the numbers of the locomotives that will haul the trains, and of the 'pits' in which they are standing.

I glance down at the list until I see the times of my own train. Against it is written '6206'.

So we are to have 'Princess Marie Louise' to-day. Well it will give us a good run.

We cross the tracks to the pit where No. 6206 is waiting. Faint wisps of steam are floating away from its chimney, and the powerful body glistens in the morning sunshine. The cleaners have been busy, but other men besides them have been at work on it, for the fire is roaring away merrily and the engine is making that gentle sizzling sound which indicates a good head of steam. It takes up to six hours to get up steam on one of these big locomotives, so it was early in the morning that a man kindled the fire in 6206. He used some small pieces of wood wired together, and some small coal. The wood soon began to burn and ignited the coal; then more coal was thrown on until there was a nice steady blaze.

Without loss of time my fireman and I 'prepare' the engine for the day's run. First, I call at the Store and obtain oil. With this I lubricate all the exposed moving parts, such as the big ends of the connecting-rods, coupling-rods, and so on. While I am doing this the fireman obtains his shovel, the tools we may want on the journey, a case containing detonators and flags (for use in emergency), a hand lamp, a bucket, and some sponge cloths. He also gets oil and fills the lamps which form the headcode in front of the engine; see the smokebox door is screwed up tightly; and make sure there are proper quantities of coal and water in the tender, and sand in the sandboxes. After he gives his attention to building up the fire. Over a ton of coal will be ablaze when we pull out of Euston with our train so he has to get busy with his shovel.

All this preparation takes an hour. I use 20 pints of oil applying it judiciously through my long necked can to 67 different points. There are, however, many places on an engine that require oil but which are out of the driver's reach; so the locomotive is built with a system of mechanical lubrication which automatically oils the hidden parts. The lubricators hold sixteen pints of oil. After I have satisfied myself that they are full, I take a final look round to see if everything is in order, then climb up onto the footplate to await the 'signal' to set back into Euston.

Top link L.M.S. driver Laurie Earl, a section of whose epic description of a journey north with the 'Royal Scot' is reproduced in the text.
Courtesy The Railway Magazine

The sandwiches and tea that will be our refreshment on the journey are stowed away in the lockers on the tender; the tools are in the bucket; there is a nice head of steam in the boiler; all we want now is permission to join our train.

AT EUSTON

The hands of the big station timepiece point to exactly ten o'clock. The starting signal is 'off'. The guard is blowing his whistle and waving his green flag. I reply with a piercing note from my engine whistle, ease open the regulator, and take my stand by the lookout window.

Like a giant greyhound freed from the leash, our powerful No. 6206 glides forward with its 420-ton train, to the accompaniment of quickening bursts of exhaust from the chimney. Good-bye, London; we are off to Carlisle ! . . . . Over the points we go, on to the Down Through Road.

My fireman (his name is Tom) picks up his shovel and commences stoking. I adjust the reversing-wheel, so that the pistons receive a good pressure of steam, and take my stand in front of my look-out window. The beat of the pistons and the exhaust from the chimney are making a nice rhythmic sound as No. 6206 gets into its stride. 'Sh-sh-sh-sh', 'Sh-sh-sh-sh', 'Sh-sh-sh-sh','Sh-sh-sh-sh', it seems to say as it gathers speed.

The Distant, Home, and Starting signals are all 'off', so we can forge ahead. Tom admits water to the boiler by opening an injector steam valve and works the water regulator valve. The engine is moving along comfortably now, so I turn the reversing-wheel slightly and therefore reduce the amount of steam admitted to the cylinders. Steam, as you know, expands, and this expansion is utilised to the fullest extent. The pistons travel the whole length of the cylinders, but we do not admit steam for the entire length. The reversing-wheel governs the length of this admission, the expansion of the steam itself forcing the pistons along the remainder of their travel. Thus by 'notching up' the reversing wheel to, say

A superb study of a 'Princess Royal' class locomotive as 6203 is turned on the Camden turntable. The vacuum stand-pipe is connected to the locomotive to power the vacuum motor on the turntable. *Real Photographs Company*

Above: With Caledonian style semaphore headcode on the top lamp bracket, 6203 heads the fourteen coach up 'Royal Scot' past Hay Fell near Stonehaven in 1935. *F.R. Hebron, courtesy Rail Archive Stephenson*

The official L.M.S. photograph of 6203 'Princess Margaret Rose' in shop grey livery which gave a clearer picture. The location is Crewe works, the date is 31st December 1936 and the engine had just had her first heavy general overhaul and been attached to her second tender, No. 9374 with ten tons coal capacity.

L.M.S. Official, J.B. Radford Collection

25%, steam is cut off at 25% of the pistons' stroke, the expanding steam following the pistons for the full length of the stroke. And this is what is happening now.

We are no sooner out of Euston than we pass through a tunnel which we call Park Street Bridge. I pull the whistle lever. There is a loud shriek, and we plunge inside, clouds of smoke and steam enveloping us and some of it finding its way into the cab. The tunnel is only 166 yards long and we are soon out again into the open.

On our left now is the Camden Locomotive Depot, at which we arrived a short time ago, and on our right is the big L.M.S. Goods Depot of the same name. We have been climbing steeply since we started − a 1 in 70 gradient − but No. 6206, putting forth its utmost power, has breasted this slope without complaint.

GARSTANG TO CARLISLE

Tom is resting for a moment, filling his lungs with this revivifying air, and absorbing the view. The engine is working beautifully, its efforts quite in keeping with the scenery. The rhythm of the wheels and the beat of the pistons echo from the rocky vastness as we thread our way through the mountains of Westmorland. How small are the works of man when compared with those of nature! Our locomotive and train, which looked so imposing as we left London, are now dwarfed into insignificance by those ever increasing fells, which are gathering round us like giants watching a dwarf at play. Yes, earth and rock are more wonderful than steel!

I disturb the silence of the scene by sounding the whistle. Greyrigg Station. We are still on time; ay, the people in these lonely out-of-the-way places put their clocks and watches right when 'The Royal Scot' goes by! What is more, they come along to the rail side and eagerly await our approach. The climb has told upon No. 6206 for we are now down to 40 miles an hour, good going considering everything. We are on a falling gradient again and the engine forges ahead. We rejoin the River Lune, which we crossed at Lancaster, but what a difference! Here it is a tumbling, rushing mountain torrent, pouring tumultuously out of a great defile. The fells are now somewhat different to those of a few miles back. The latter were rather rough and crude, but those here are smooth and rounded, overgrown with grass of a very fine texture.

Low Gill Station and 60 miles an hour. Tom, who has been firing, is once more taking a breather. We are now in the Lune Gorge, one of the best pieces of scenery between London and Glasgow, and among the peaks. The line veers to the right and brings us almost head-on to towering Gibbet Hill, junction of Yorkshire and Westmorland; the tiny stream that forms the boundary between the two counties can be seen threading its way along the base. To the left is Bleasdale Fell 1,556 feet high, Illdale Head (1,553 feet)

and Fell Head (2,045 feet). Faster and faster we are going. Tom has closed the injector - for the boiler is full of water - has worked the coal pusher (Note: No. 6206 was the only Princess Royal to have a coal pusher) and is now looking ahead through his window. For what? For the water troughs that are flying towards us at the moment. Quickly he comes to the scoop handle, lowers the dip, and collects another thirteen hundred odd gallons for the locomotive's consumption. Yes, even in this wild land of constant rainfall, artificial aids to watering have to be adopted for the benefit of the railway engines.

I grasp the whistle lever and hold it down for several seconds as we tear through Tebay at 75 mph. I look at my watch. It says 2.21. The 262 mile-post has been passed and we are true to schedule. Tebay is another railway town, a junction for Darlington.

We are now on a rising gradient, which will soon increase to 1 in 75 for 4 miles. Bravely the locomotive breasts this, the ascent to Shap Summit. I have opened the regulator wide and worked the reversing-wheel to 30% We are now in the track of the winds; and it is raining! Not the sudden downpour that one experiences in city streets, but a fine penetrating rain that shrouds the peaks in mist. I operate the sand valves so that the rails are sanded and the engine's wheels will therefore grip well, thus maintaining our speed. But the rain is really nothing; it is snow that becomes the enemy to us railways. In winter this particular stretch of line has to be cleared of snow almost every day. I have even driven engine No. 6100 to Carlisle on Christmas Day, in the teeth of a blizzard, as far as the eye could see the desolate country-side was smothered in a deep blanket of frozen whiteness.

As we pass Scout Green the steepest part of the line commences. Tom has opened the injector and is hurling more shovelfuls of coal into the fire-box. How well the engine is taking the gradient! Short, staccato sounds are coming from the chimney as smoke and steam are forced up into the atmosphere. The beat of the pistons is as rhythmical as a roll of drums.

Up, up, we go. How lovely everything is! Kidsty Pike, 2,560 feet high, soars above us, backed by the long hill known as High Street Ridge. Great outcrops of granite are everywhere, and deeply pitted slabs of rock, adding an eerie note to the wild lonely fells. Shap is the lowest possible point at which it is possible to get over the Westmorland Range, that great barrier between England and Scotland. How it rains! And the sighing of the wind! Both are whisking round the cab like disgruntled sprites annoyed by this assault by man upon their stronghold. Pity the poor travellers in pre-railway times, who went over this very road on foot, on horse-back, or by coach!

The thing I am looking for comes into sight. It is a lonely little

'Princess Margaret Rose' makes a fine sight as she heads through the London suburb of Kilburn with the down 'Mid-day' Scot' just before the second world war.

Eric Treacy courtesy Millbrook House Ltd.

signal-box perched on what seems to be the roof of the world. On it is painted a single word of four letters, 'SHAP', and it signifies that we have reached the summit of our climb. The great barrier has been overcome; we have climbed 915 above sea-level in 31 miles, that is since leaving Carnforth, and No. 6206 has taken the 1 in 75 gradient at 32 miles an hour, a magnificent performance with a 420-ton train.

As we pass that little cabin the signalman leans from his window and greets us with a smile and a wave of the hand. Tom and I return his salute with equal pleasure. If ever there was an 'outpost of duty', it is the signal box on the summit of Shap!...."

"......... We are approaching Carlisle, and speed must be reduced. I close the regulator, move the reversing wheel, and gradually apply the brake. Back goes the needle 80, 75, 70, 65, 60, 55, 50, 45. Tom opens the blower, lays aside his shovel, and watches for signals. I see ahead the Distant signal for 'No. 13 Carlisle Signal Box'. It is 'On'. A long shriek escapes from our whistle as I pull down the lever, at the same time braking still further. Back goes the needle again; 40, 35, 30, 25, 20; we are restricted to 20 miles an hour here. The signalman in No. 13 Box has lowered both Home and Distant signals outside his cabin.

A maze of tracks is ahead, with many signals. On our right is Upperby Locomotive Depot, to which we will be going soon. The lines on the right connect with Newcastle, served by L.N.E.R. trains, and those on the left with Maryport. Our journey is over, and the train is proceeding towards the big, imposing station that we see looming ahead. Men at work on the many tracks stop their labours for a moment to watch the advance of the Down 'Royal Scot' that left Euston at ten o'clock this morning. The home signal is 'off' as steadily No. 6206 picks its way over the metals and heads for Platform No. 2, where a respite of two minutes will be granted after its five-hour dash throughout the whole length of England.

We are entering the station. The ring of our connecting-rods echoes under the great glass roof. Giant letters on the wall announce the station's name, and porters, with rich Cumberland accents are shouting 'Carlisle, Carlisle, next stop Glasgow'. There are many people on the platform, waiting to welcome friends. Leaning out of the side of the cab, I watch the platform edge and slowly press down the brake handle. Obediently the engine stops, and the 420-ton train comes to a halt. We have arrived. The station timepiece says exactly three o'clock. We have travelled 299 miles and have reached our destination 'on time', despite two permanent way slacks en route. I move the reversing-wheel forward to 75%, for the benefit of the relief driver, and open the release valves to the cylinders to prevent steam in the latter condensing. The engine will not move now. Tom tests the water-gauges and opens an injector to prevent an escape of steam while the train is in the station. Our foot-plate work for to-day is done; and with a feeling of satisfaction we wipe our hands on some sponge-cloths and await the relief driver and fireman who at this moment I can see walking along the platform towards us.'

CHANGE OVER AT CARLISLE

The new driver and fireman are Scotsmen from Glasgow. They are both old friends of mine, and I call the former Mac, and his mate Jock. As they climb into the cab we exchange friendly greetings. 'Good afternoon, Mac; and you, too Jock'. 'Good afternoon to ye', replies Mac, as he stows his food-basket in the locker on the tender from which I have just taken my own; 'ye're reet time ageen, I see. Had a bonny journey doon?' 'Sure we have, Mac. Had two p.w. slacks in Lancashire, but came over Shap true to schedule.' 'Ay, nasty place, Shap. Did it rain o'er much to-day?' 'Not more than usual'. I pick up my oil-can and prepare to climb down onto the track. 'I'll just give her the usual look-over, Mac, before you go to bonnie Scotland'.

I walk round the engine and examine the external parts to see if anything has become displaced on the journey, or if any of the bearings have been 'running hot'; but everything is in order, so I give a drop of oil to the big ends, slide-bars, and all the bearings that can be lubricated, then get back again onto the footplate.

"Everthing's O.K. Mac. We'd better be going now, or you'll be taking us onto Glasgow. Good-day Mac; good-day Jock; and a good journey." 'Ay, thank ye. We'll be seeing ye later. Good-day". We get down to the platform and make our way round the engine. They are gazing at it in admiration, as the people did at Euston. Mac is testing the water gauge glasses while Jock opens an injector and looks at the gauge on the tender. Travellers are getting out of the train, and making their way towards the station exit. An old gentleman, benign and bespectacled, comes to me half-apologetically. "I must say, driver, the train has made a remarkably

good run; or it has seemed to me. I believe we touched 80 miles an hour in places. Can you tell me where we attained this extraordinary speed?" "Why certainly", I answer. "We were doing 80 at Cheddington, at Shilton, and at Milford. Then again at Betley Road, Hartford, Calthwaite, Southwaite, and after we left Wreay. But I assure you that is nothing extraordinary." "Isn't it really? A very fine performance. I must be getting back now. Thank you very much indeed.".....No. 6206 emits a shrill whistle, and once more moves forward with its lovely train. we can see Jock firing away just as Tom did when we left Euston. The engine's chimney is sending forth short sharp beats of exhaust, and with quickening pace "The Royal Scot" goes on its way to Glasgow, 102 miles ahead.

Rapidly the carriages glide before us, the soft "dit-dit","dit-dit", over the rail joints, becoming quicker as each coach goes by. Passengers are leaning out of the windows, waving handkerchiefs to friends left behind, the restaurant-car conductor is again canvassing the train, this time for tea, and before we realize it is the last coach has gone and we are staring rather enviously at the rapidly departing tail-lamp on the train that is vanishing north. The merry 'chuff', 'chuff', 'chuff','chuff', of No. 6206 is getting fainter and faster, and in a moment 'The Royal Scot' is out of sight and hearing.'

This marvellous narrative encapsulates the very essence of the glorious days before the Second World War when steam reigned supreme on the railways of Britain and any journey of length was taken utilising rail travel.

O.S. Nock records that he observed 'Princess Margaret Rose' at Crewe on 6th August 1935 with the down 'Royal Scot' express running non-stop to Carlisle where there would be a crew change for the remaining leg to Glasgow, no doubt a similar exacting trip to Driver Earl's run on No. 6206.

On 28th October 1938 'Princess Margaret Rose' entered Crewe Works for her second Heavy General Repair, having run 94,377 miles since her last heavy repair carried out from 5th August 1937 to 10th September 1937 and with her tender having covered 148,958 miles without repair since its fitting when new during the December, 1936/January 1937 works visit. Prior to this second heavy general repair she had been shopped for a special repair from 5th August to 10th September 1937 and had a light overhaul between 29th November and 13th December 1937 during which she'd had her boiler changed to No. 9101, which had recently been taken off engine No. 6209 and repaired, this being fitted to No. 6203 on 5th December 1937. On completion of this second heavy general repair she emerged from the works on 12th January 1939.

No. 6203 and her sisters continued to be the mainstay of motive power on the fastest and heaviest trains until the introduction of the 'Princess Coronation' class of streamlined Pacifics in 1937 and the introduction of the crack 'Coronation Scot' trains. Princess Margaret Rose's sisters were gradually moved away from Camden as the new 'Princess Coronation' class entered service one by one, the 'Princess Royals' being found work on other express services.

In 1938 'Princess Royal' class locomotives began working regularly into and out of Aberdeen. From Carlisle they worked north on the 10.50 p.m. from Euston, returning on the 1.55 p.m. express fish train from Aberdeen to Crewe where the locomotive was changed for the final leg of the journey to Broad Street, London.

In the April 1939 issue of Railway Magazine, Cecil J. Allen included a table of more runs between Crewe and London (Euston) comparing 'Princess Royal' class locomotives including the 'Turbomotive' (6202) with the 'Royal Scot' class 4-6-0s. Details of the run behind No. 6203 'Princess Margaret Rose' are recorded in column 6.

Cecil J. Allen added that the run behind 6200 'The Princess Royal' in column 8 was the finest in the table and 'one of the most remarkable' at that time recorded behind an L.M.S. Pacific. See Fig. 8.

In the first six years of their existence up to 1939, the 'Princess Royal' class locomotives had therefore aquitted themselves well, and properly handled regularly gave superb performances on the most difficult L.M.S. routes. The crews were delighted with them, once they had gained the experience in handling them, for they required different techniques, particularly for the fireman having to master the art of firing a wide firebox in order to overcome the severe and testing London—Glasgow route.

With the outbreak of the second world war in September 1939 the 'Princess Royals' had become even more scattered and on 21st October 1939, with the 'Princess Coronation' Pacifics taking over much more of the work at Camden, 'Princess Margaret Rose' broke new ground with a transfer to Edge Hill Depot, Liverpool where she began working expresses to and from Euston in tandem with No. 6202, which herself remained on the London—Liverpool link for most of her work-

The down 'Royal Scot' headed by 6203 in immaculate condition, overtakes a London Underground train at Bushey station in 1939.

C.R.L. Coles

An Eric Treacy masterpiece. 6203 is captured heading through Wavertree Junction with an express about 1938, passing 'Jubilee' class 4-6-0 5705 'Seahorse' of Farnley Junction depot on the left.

Eric Treacy courtesy Millbrook House Ltd.

Distance		Run No. Engine No. " Type " Name Load (coaches) " (tons tare) " (tons full)	Schedule	1 6130 4-6-0 Liverpool 10 299 315	2 6113 4-6-0 Cameronian 11 347 365	3 6202 4-6-2 (Turbo) 11 335 355	4 6207 4-6-2 Princess Arthur of Connaught 12 374 400	5 6202 4-6-2 (Turbo) 14 429 455	6 6203 4-6-2 Princess Margaret Rose 14 431 460	7 6208 4-6-2 Princess Helena Victoria 14 438 470	8 6200 4-6-2 The Princess Royal 15 466 500	9 6207 4-6-2 Princess Arthur of Connaught 15 482 515
Miles			min.	m. s.	m. s.	m. s.	m. s.	m. s.	m. s.	m. s.	m. s.	m. s.
0.0	CREWE		0	0 00	—	0 00	0 00	0 00	0 00	0 00	0 00	0 00
4.8	Betley Road		—	6 49	—	7 10	7 09	8 05	7 46	7 28	8 00	7 52
8.0	Madeley		—	10 14	—	10 32	10 37	11 53	11 30	11 10	11 45	11 45
10.5	Whitmore		—	12 50	—	13 03	13 17	14 38	14 15	13 58	14 33	14 24
14.7	Standon Bridge		—	16 02	—	16 25	16 50	18 19	17 49	17 36	18 10	18 06
19.2	Norton Bridge		—	19 30	—	20 03	20 31	22 17	21 35	21 08	21 36	21 55
								p.w.s.				
24.5	STAFFORD*		26	24 08	0 00	24 55	26 09	27 10	26 17	25 37	25 38	26 18
				sigs.								
28.6	Milford		—	29 52	6 53	30 05	32 09	32 08	30 55	30 21	30 06	30 37
33.8	RUGELEY		—	36 13	11 49	34 47	36 50	36 50	35 31	35 01	34 41	35 13
37.1	Armitage		—	39 02	14 34	37 33	39 31	39 37	38 07	37 45	37 17	38 00
41.8	LICHFIELD		41	43 00	18 36	41 35	43 27	43 38	42 00	41 53	41 03	42 09
48.1	TAMWORTH		—	47 44	23 36	46 37	48 14	48 35	46 40	46 47	45 34	47 24
						p.w.s.		p.w.s.		p.w.s.		
51.6	Polesworth		—	50 48	26 38	50 50	51 06	53 15	49 25	50 00	*sig. stop	50 33
55.8	Atherstone		—	54 51	30 30	55 20	54 45	57 50	52 52	54 06	56 57	54 34
						sigs.						
61.0	NUNEATON		58	59 40	35 12	60 25	59 13	62 37	57 15	58 43	62 03	59 20
64.6	Bulkington		—	62 58	38 04	64 05	62 35	66 52	61 30	62 00	65 20	62 47
70.0	Brinklow		—	67 33	43 45	68 50	67 15	70 29	65 12	66 42	69 58	67 46
75.5	RUGBY†		72	72 23	49 04	73 55	72 17	75 30	70 10	71 20	74 44	72 50
77.8	Hillmorton		—	74 59	51 54	76 30	75 10	sigs.	73 10	73 47	77 18	75 27
82.3	Welton		—	80 11	57 56	81 20	80 22	85 50	78 48	78 39	82 30	80 46
88.4	Weedon		—	84 38	62 41	85 40	84 42	90 30	83 32	83 12	86 58	85 28
95.3	BLISWORTH		—	90 13	68 24	91 10	89 47	95 48	89 11	88 50	92 13	91 13
98.2	Roade		93	92 37	71 02	93 40	92 05	98 15	91 46	91 29	94 37	93 54
103.3	Castlethorpe		—	96 37	75 11	97 30	95 48	102 3	95 50	95 44	98 24	98 02
105.7	Wolverton		—	98 30	77 00	99 30	97 38	103 53	97 39	97 36	100 04	99 50
111.4	BLETCHLEY		104	103 03	81 53	104 00	102 22	108 23	102 30	102 31	104 20	104 36
117.9	Leighton		—	108 11	87 47	109 15	107 50	113 37	108 08	108 18	109 26	110 22
										sigs.		
122.0	Cheddington		—	111 37	91 39	112 32	111 27	116 59	111 51	113 47	112 42	113 58
126.4	TRING		118	115 23	96 05	116 20	115 48	120 48	116 11	120 11	116 39	118 12
130.2	Berkhamsted		—	118 28	99 57	119 35	119 21	123 51	119 41	123 52	119 53	121 36
137.2	King's Langley		—	123 29	105 15	125 02	125 00	128 48	125 14	129 28	125 09	127 22
											sig. stop	
140.7	WATFORD		—	125 58	107 50	127 48	127 51	131 17	128 01	132 10	136 18	130 09
146.7	Harrow		—	130 40	112 38	132 42	132 58	135 46	132 56	137 11	142 31	135 01
150.0	Wembley		—	133 05	115 08	135 20	136 05	138 08	135 29	139 47	145 10	137 28
						sigs.				sigs.	sigs.	
152.7	WILLESDEN JC.		140	136 13	117 02	139 55	139 46	141 23	138 04	143 35	147 16	139 25
										sigs.	sigs.	
158.1	EUSTON		148	—	123 47	—	—	—	146 59	—	155 40	146 52
152.7	Net times (min.)‡		142	133½	††123¾	135½	138½	136½	‡138¾	137	§132	§140½

* Service slack slight. † Service slack severe. ‡ Crewe-Willesden Jc. § Equivalent net time to a stop at Willesden Jc.
* Arrived at Polesworth in 48 min. 38 sec. from Crewe, and left 49 min. 12 sec. from Crewe. Arrived at 20½ milepost in 126 min. 2 sec. from Crewe and left 130 min. 18 sec. from Crewe. †† From Stafford to Euston

Fig. 8. Table of runs between Crewe and London Euston printed by Cecil J Allen in the April 1939 issue of the Railway Magazine as part of his 'British Locomotive Practice and Performance' series of articles.

courtesy 'The Railway Magazine'

ing life. Here No. 6203 took her share of working the 'Merseyside Express' trains where the 'Princesses' were required to take a train of some 500−550 tons gross the 189.6 miles from London(Euston) to Mossley Hill in the Liverpool suburbs in just 200 minutes.

From 6th April 1940 No. 6203 found herself transferred yet again, this time to Holyhead, along with sister locomotives Nos. 6204 and 6205, principally to work the 'Irish Mail' expresses.

The 'Irish Mail' was booked to leave Holyhead at 12.13 p.m. arriving at Euston at 5.30 p.m. with stops at Chester, Crewe, and Rugby. The morning run from London left Euston at 8.45 a.m. and arrived at Holyhead at 2.05 p.m. There was also an evening 'Irish Mail' publicly advertised to leave at 8.45 pm although the actual working departure time was 8.50 p.m.

At the end of September 1940 (28th), she moved to Crewe, returning to Holyhead for just one week, 2nd−9th November, before moving back to Edge Hill again, this time for a much longer spell, chiefly again to work the 'Merseyside Express'. This crack train left Liverpool at 10.10 each morning and ran non-stop to London Euston, arriving at 1.30 p.m. The return working from Euston left at 6.05 p.m. and arrived in Liverpool at 9.40 p.m., also conveying through car-

riages for Southport which were worked forward separately by another engine, arriving there at 10.30 p.m.

This service to and from Liverpool was in connection with steamer services to Belfast and Dublin (North Wall) which sailed 10.15 p.m. on weekdays. On summer Fridays and Saturdays a second train ran from Euston at 6.15 p.m. to meet the heavy demands of weekend passenger traffic to and from Ireland. The morning services from Liverpool connected with early morning steamer arrivals from Belfast and Dublin. 'Princess Royal' class locomotives based at Camden were used on this service during this period and her use on these trains enabled No. 6203 to record many fine high speed runs.

It is also worth noting that during the 1937 season for instance, an extra fifty special trains were also run between London (Euston) and Liverpool (Riverside) in connection with Cunard 'White Star' cruises and Canadian Pacific sailings at various times. 'Princess Margaret Rose' would undoubtedly have had a hand in some of this additional traffic. Liverpool was then of course a thriving major port for passenger liner sailings.

Just over two years after moving to Edge Hill Depot, 'Princess Margaret Rose' found herself transferred back to Camden on 26th

Naked power – another study by the late Eric Treacy as 6203 storms through Edge Hill on the outskirts of Liverpool with an express for London Euston just before the war.

Eric Treacy, courtesy Millbrook House Ltd.

December 1942 for a brief three month spell before moving back to Edge Hill, yet again, on 3rd April 1943. She moved to Crewe North Shed on loan on 9th October 1943 this being confirmed as a permanent transfer on 27th November. Here she worked forward those heavy expresses to Scotland requiring an engine change at Crewe.

Edge Hill again became her home depot on 20th May 1944 from where she saw out the end of the second world war. Transferred at this time with 6203 were Nos. 6200, 6201, 6204, and 6205 thus allowing the London to Liverpool express haulage to be almost monopolised by 'Pacifics'. Like her sisters No. 6203 retained her L.M.S. crimson lake livery, albeit often rather dirty, and giving a neglected appearance, due to wartime economies at depots.

As a matter of interest by 1st September 1945, some ten years after the production batch were first built, the 'Princess Royals' were allocated as follows:-

Camden	1B	6202		
Crewe North	5A	6201	6204	6206 – 12
Edge Hill	8A	6200	6203	6205

No. 6203 was taken out of traffic on 18th September 1947 and

entered the works at Crewe for her fifth heavy general overhaul having run 32,976 miles since her last heavy repair. At this repair she received exchange boiler No. 9106 (ex-No. 6210) with a 32 element superheater in replacement for the 24 element boiler 9102. This replacement boiler had 123 small tubes of 2⅜" diameter and 32 superheater flues of 5⅛" diameter giving a total heating surface of 2299 square feet.

She returned to traffic on 8th December 1947 after 71 days out of use, resplendent in new L.M.S. black livery, as introduced in 1946, lined out in maroon and straw and with shaded 'grotesque' sans serif lettering in straw yellow with a fine maroon line just inside the edges of the letters and numbers. The nameplate letters and border were painted in straw letters with a maroon background and bufferbeams in plain unlined vermillion. The valances were lined in maroon with straw yellow each side and boiler cladding bands were also similarly lined at the smokebox and, at the firebox front and in front of the cab. Six of her sister locomotives Nos. 6200–2, 6206, 6210, and 6211, also received this livery between February 1947 and February 1948.

Whilst still in Crewe Shops 6203 had been re-allocated 'on loan' to Crewe North depot on 18th October 1947 from where she was to see out her final days as an L.M.S. locomotive.

A surprisingly clean 'Princess Margaret Rose', despite the general neglect during the second world war, sweeps past Camden with a train of immaculate L.M.S. coaching stock in a view dated between December 1942 and April 1943.   *Eric Treacy courtesy Millbrook House Ltd.*

Above: 6203 bursts from Northchurch Tunnel, Berkhamsted, with a down express, most probably for Liverpool, on Tuesday 17th June 1947 in her last year as an L.M.S. engine. *E.R. Wethersett, courtesy Ian Allan Library*

Facing Page: Kenton station is seen in the background as 'Princess Margaret Rose' heads a down express through this Middlesex residential area north of Harrow on Saturday 26th April 1947. *E.R. Wethersett, courtesy Ian Allan Library*

Bushey station is again the location for this almost head-on study of 6203 as she sweeps through with a down express to Manchester about 1946.

R.F. Dearden, courtesy Ian Allan Library

'Princess Margaret Rose' heads through Tring station in Hertfordshire with an unidentified express on Saturday 28th September 1946.

R.F. Dearden, courtesy National Railway Museum

By the end of that year, when the London Midland and Scottish Railway Company ceased to exist as a separate entity, No. 6203 had run well over three quarters of a million miles in traffic, as recorded below :-

YEAR	MILES RUN
1935	48,585
1936	95,467
1937	74,941
1938	74,017
1939	83,612
1940	57,999
1941	40,375
1942	58,887
1943	57,016
1944	51,086
1945	54,674
1946	67,434
1947	45,690
Total	809,792

So far as her repair history is concerned she had been in Crewe Works for five Heavy General Repairs as follows :

TAKEN OUT OF TRAFFIC	*RETURNED TO TRAFFIC*
30th November 1936	19th January 1937
28th October 1938	12th January 1939
15th November 1941	20th December 1941
11th June 1944	26th July 1944
18th September 1947	8th December 1947

No. 6203 had also received four heavy overhauls, seven light overhauls, four heavy special repairs, and two light special repairs. At each heavy general repair a repaired boiler from another engine of the class was fitted.

As to modification; steam sanding gear had been fitted as mentioned earlier on 6th April 1936 and cab doors, stops and guide plates on 19th January 1937 at the same time as the new 10 ton tender No. 9374 had been allocated to the locomotive. It was also at this repair that the boiler with four rows of superheater elements, in place of the three row one, was fitted along with a hinged smokebox door bar to give easier access to the smokebox during servicing.

In August 1944 she had been fitted with a separate water scoop for the boiler top feed trays instead of a one combined with the trays themselves, and in July 1945, she had a steel (instead of copper) tube ejector exhaust pipe fitted.

The last day of the London Midland and Scottish Railway Company before it became 'Nationalised' and absorbed into the new 'British Railways', was Wednesday 31st December 1947 and it dawned to find 6203 'Princess Margaret Rose' hauling the down 11.05 p.m. (30th December) Birmingham—Glasgow sleeping car express northwards. Presumably she had been attached to the train at Crewe, being allocated to Crewe North Shed at the time, but the record we have of the working (courtesy of the Scottish Locomotive Owners Group Archives — T.L.Jehu Collection) records her arrival at Carlisle at 07.46 a.m. no less than 219 minutes behind time. The reason for this is not recorded but 6203 left 210 minutes late and lost a further 58 minutes between Carlisle and Glasgow, all due to signal checks. The run is recorded as follows:

Date: Wednesday 31st December 1947.
Locomotive: 6203 7P.
Train: 4.23 a.m. (ex-Carlisle) (11.05 p.m. Birmingham—Glasgow sleeping car express).
Load: 332 tons from Carlisle, 249 tons from Carstairs.

Distance (miles)	Location		Sched. time	Actual time	Late (mins.)
00.00	Carlisle	arr.	04.07	07.46	219
		dep.	04.23	07.53	210
08.50	Gretna	pass			
25.75*	Lockerbie	pass	04.49	08.47	233
39.75	Beattock	arr.	05.10	09.25	
		dep.	05.15	09.33	258
	Beattock Summit	pass		10.02	263
66.75	Symington	pass			
73.50§	Carstairs	arr.	06.04	10.30	
		dep.	06.10	10.35	265
89.50	Motherwell	arr.	06.32	10.58	
		dep.	06.36	11.01	265
102.25	Glasgow Central	arr.	06.55	11.23	268

* Calls to set down only if required
§ Train divides

Signal Checks:

15 mins.	Carlisle No. 3 to Kingmoor
10 mins.	Kirkpatrick to Castlemilk
22 mins.	Dinwoodie to Beattock South
3 mins.	Beattock North
5 mins.	Greskine
2 mins.	Strawfank Jnc. & Carstairs No. 3
3 mins.	Gushetfaulds Jnc.

What 'Princess Margaret Rose' was employed on for the remainder of that last day as an L.M.S. locomotive remains un-recorded, but with the birth of the new 'British Railways' on 1st January 1948, a new chapter in the life of No. 6203 was about to open up.

CHAPTER THREE

WORKING FOR BRITISH RAILWAYS

On 1st January 1948 'Princess Margaret Rose', along with all of the other members of her class, and as part of the L.M.S. locomotive and rolling stock fleet, was taken into the stock of the newly formed British Railways and by that date Crewe North had become the home shed of all the 'Princess Royal' class locomotives for a brief period with the exception of 46202 which remained at Camden.

In order to avoid the confusion of having locomotives with the same numbers entering the B.R. stock book by the amalgamation of the four railway companies upon the formation of British Railways, the locomotives of respective companies had numbers added to their respective existing series. In the case of the ex-L.M.S. locomotives they were generally renumbered by adding 40000 to the existing number, although the range extended into the 50000 series and there were some numbering complications.

6203 was duly renumbered 46203 during week ending 8th May 1948, receiving an L.M.S. style five figure number-plate on the smokebox door and a repainted number on the cabsides, although the tender remained lettered L.M.S. for some time afterwards. Later the large size 'lion and wheel' crest replaced the L.M.S. lettering but she was to remain in L.M.S. black livery until May 1951. However before that date, on 14th February 1948, she had been re-allocated back to Edge Hill to recommence working 'The Merseyside Express' and other expresses such as 'The Manxman' which ran in the summer only in connection with the steamship service to the Isle of Man from Liver-

pool. This was a morning express from Euston departing at 10.40 a.m. and with through coaches to Southport. The train called only at Stafford, running non-stop through Crewe, and was timed into Liverpool Lime Street station at 2.18 p.m.

The up 'Manxman' left Lime Street at 2.10 p.m. calling only at Mossley Hill and Crewe, then running a distance of 156 miles from Crewe to Euston in 152 minutes, reaching London at 5.30 p.m.

By the summer of 1950 'The Merseyside Express' was timed to leave Liverpool Lime Street at 10.00 a.m. and run non-stop to Euston arriving at 1.45 p.m. (1.52 p.m. on Saturdays) whilst the return from Euston gave arrival at Mossley Hill at 9.48 p.m. (9.52 p.m. on Saturdays) and Lime Street at 10.06 p.m.

When 46203 (6203) had been first built the L.M.S. had given the class the power classification 7P, and this was denoted on the locomotives above the cabside numerals. The method of classification was derived in part from the old Midland Railway gradings brought in by Paget for his 1906 Control System, augmented by a mean effective pressure–speed curve derived from tests on the Lancashire and Yorkshire Railway. Thus power classification was measured in terms of passenger or freight locomotive tractive effort in tons at 50 m.p.h. and 25 m.p.h. respectively. Passenger locomotives at that time ranged from the diminutive 1P up to 6P. The table below shows the classifications and Tractive Effort ranges at 50 m.p.h.

'Princess Margaret Rose', now a member of the British Railway locomotive fleet but with the L.M.S. lettering still on the tender, heads through Ashton, Northants with a northbound express (possibly for Liverpool) on Saturday 26th June 1948.   *L Hanson*

46203 still in black livery and with L.M.S. on the tender passes through Bushey on the relief line with a train of thirteen coaches heading towards London Euston and nearing the end of the journey from Liverpool Lime Street.

C.R.L. Coles

Classification	Tractive Effort (tons)
1P	1.5 — 2.0
2P	2.0 — 2.5
3P	2.5 — 3.0
4P	3.0 — 3.5
5P	3.5 — 4.0
6P	4.0 — 4.5

The 'Princess Royals' extended beyond that range and were therefore classified 7P with a value of 4.5 to 5.0 tons tractive effort at 50 m.p.h. All frictional resistances were ignored, the figures quoted being the theoretical force at the rim of the tyre when new.

At Nationalisation the LMS system, evolved from the Midland one to take account of the much more powerful locomotives which had arrived on the scene, was initially further developed in the first year of British Railways existence, but in 1949 all locomotives were generally re-classified, the effect of which was to further sub-divide the Class 7 locomotives into Classes 7 and 8.

The technical formula used as a basis for the evaluation for passenger and mixed traffic locomotives was :

Free gas area through tubes x grate area x tractive effort at 85% boiler pressure/10,000

The result of this gave a factor to be read against a chart graded from Class 1 to Class 8.

The cylinder tractive effort is given by the formula :-

$$\frac{Nd^2SP}{4480D}$$

where N = number of cylinders
d = cylinder diameter in inches
S = piston stroke in inches
P = mean effective pressure (lb/sq.in)
D = diameter of coupled wheels in inches

Calculating the drawbar pull as 0.00335 x D.B.H.P. (for superheated engines taken as 30.7 x grate area in sq. feet) the appropriate power classification could be derived which placed the 'Princess Royal' locomotives in Class 8, having a factor of over 901.

In May 1951 46203 was repainted in 'Caledonian' blue livery, lined out in black, blue and white, along with a number of other ex-L.M.S. Pacifics and B.R. express locomotives of the former G.W.R., L.N.E.R., and S.R.. The repainting of 'Princess Margaret Rose' was carried out during the heavy general repair at Crewe Works.

This new livery was part of an overall decision to paint approximately two hundred express passenger steam locomotives in this colour, a policy adopted at a Railway Executive meeting on 17th January 1949 (minute No. 1849) and in response to a letter from the British Transport Commission dated 11th January 1949. Three electric main line locomotives were also to be blue and some eight hundred more express passenger steam locomotives were to be painted in the former Great Western dark green colour, lined out in yellow and black.

This decision followed the appearance in May 1948 of fourteen selected trains in proposed new colours, the locomotives being turned out in ultramarine blue for express passenger and apple green for ordinary passenger, both lined out in red, yellow and grey, the goods locomotives being painted in unlined gloss black. Public reaction was not enthusiastic, the blue being considered too dark and the green rather bilious.

It was during this heavy general overhaul, from 17th April 1951 to 24th May 1951 that boiler No. 9108 was fitted, this having had internal feed water deflector plates fitted during its repair prior to fitting onto 46203, these having been the subject of successful experiments.

Prior to this the L.M.S. taper boilers had been provided with top feed trays to dissipate the feed water on entry into the boiler. Experience had proved that these did not fulfil their design purpose, being exceedingly difficult to clean, having to be withdrawn in sections through the dome opening to be effectively descaled.

A programme of fitting these top-feed plates had been initiated under job No. 5539 issued on 9th November 1949 and the whole of the 'Princess Royal' class were dealt with as the boilers were repaired and interchanged at general repairs, the costs of the modification being charged to maintenance.

For the 'Festival of Britain' in 1951, British Railways inaugurated a new named train, 'The Red Rose', a restaurant car express leaving Euston at 12.30 p.m. and running non-stop to Liverpool, arriving in Lime Street Station at 4.15 p.m. The return working left Lime Street at 5.25 p.m. and in the up direction only called at Crewe, leaving there at 6.15 p.m. and thence running non-stop to Euston arriving there at 9.10 p.m. This arrival time was advanced to 9.00 p.m. from September 1952 giving a 165 minute run from Crewe to Euston (158.1 miles) and

43

'Princess Margaret Rose', in post war black livery and based at Edge Hill m.p.d. (8A) (near Liverpool) at Bourne End signals on 25th March 1950 with the 8.15 a.m. Liverpool (Lime Street) - Euston express consisting of fourteen coaches mainly carmine and cream liveried but with three vehicles still in L.M.S maroon. At 12.11 p.m. the March noon sunshine illuminates the wheels and motion as would evening light later in the year.

E.D. Bruton

At the head of a Liverpool - Euston train 46203 passes King's Langley. The date is prior to 31st July 1950.

Courtesy Fox photos and Ian Allan Library

Crewe station in 1950 is the location as 46203 sweeps through on the centre up road at the head of an express with the driver looking for his signals.

P Ransome Wallis, courtesy National Railway Museum

an overall journey time of 3 hours 25 minutes. 'Princess Margaret Rose' was used regularly on these duties being recorded on 2nd and 4th July 1951 on this train.

46203's sojourn at Edge Hill was interrupted on 22nd September 1951 by a long period on loan to Polmadie shed, accompanied by 46200 'The Princess Royal', which lasted until the 16th May 1953. During this period she was photographed working various trains and regularly the 11.15 a.m. Glasgow to Birmingham train (known colloquially as the 'Birmingham Scot') as far as Crewe, returning the following morning with the 9.25 a.m. train ex Crewe for Glasgow, this working

being the main reason why the two 'Princess Royals' had returned to the Glasgow depot. 'Princess Margaret Rose' was recorded on the morning Glasgow—Birmingham working on both 20th April and 16th August 1952.

During this period 'Princess Margaret Rose' became unique in the whole of the Stanier Pacifics by becoming the first and only locomotive of the type to be sent to other than Crewe Works for heavy repair. 46203 arrived at the former Midland Railway Locomotive Works at Derby for a heavy intermediate repair and modification only just over six months after a heavy general overhaul at Crewe from where she

Fresh from Crewe Works after a heavy general repair and receiving her new blue, livery, (which was to be short-lived) 'Princess Margaret Rose' stands on Crewe North m.p.d. on Saturday 26th May 1951.

J.E. Wilkinson

45

On Crewe North m.p.d. on Sunday 3rd June 1951, 46203 in blue livery, buffers up to the brand new BR Standard class 4-6-2 No. 70014 'Iron Duke' which had been completed in Crewe Works the previous week.
Frank Ashley

46203 in blue livery heads the down 'Merseyside Express' for Liverpool past Wembley Junction signal box on Saturday 30th June 1951.
C.R.L Coles

'Princess Margaret Rose' was transferred to Polmadie motive power depot, Glasgow on 22nd September 1951, where she is seen, still in blue livery, on 4th November 1951 only a few days before being sent to Derby locomotive works for repair.

J.L. Stevenson courtesy A.G. Ellis Collection

ad returned to traffic on 24th May 1951 after spending 32 days on works.

On Tuesday 13th November 1951 she was taken out of service with ɔose cylinders, and after waiting to be shopped for eleven days a deci-ɪon was made that she should be repaired at Derby.

46203 was worked light engine from Camden to Kentish Town shed vhere she awaited a movement over the Midland main line to Derby.

At this point an engine crew from No. 4 Shed at Derby, Driver Stan Mordey and Fireman Jimmy Hanson, who had worked a Black Five ɪp to St.Pancras on a 'Festival of Britain' special and then the train ɪngine light back to Kentish Town Shed, consulted the 'Engine Ar-ɪangements' board at Kentish Town to pick up their return working. They half expected to come back by passenger train 'on the cushions' ɪs riding in the train is known among railwaymen.

"Blimey, we've a light engine working, and that's not a '5X', said Jimmy, "Isn't it a 'Baby Scot'?" "No", replied Stan Mordey, "that's ɪ big un!" Fireman Jimmy Hanson only remembers that there was ɪomething wrong with the engine and his driver going to the shed ɪffice to receive any special instructions as to speed limits etc., and ɪhat they brought 46203 back to Derby and left her on the disposal ɪoad on No. 4 Shed after 'screwing her down' i.e. firmly applying ɪhe handbrake. From No. 4 shed she was moved into the works and ɪhunted up to the 'dead engine' road at Deadman's Lane before being ɪnoved onto the 'Stone Pit' to be emptied of ashes, coal and water ɪnd uncoupled from her tender. She officially entered the works on ɪ0th December 1951.

She was moved into No. 2 Bay and it was soon discovered that there vas insufficient height below the overhead cranes to enable the boiler ɪo be lifted out of the frames. Accordingly she was taken outside again ɪnd re-located in No. 3 Bay where there were two 50 ton overhead ɪranes which could give the necessary clearance. Two men were set ɪn liberating the cab, two on the motion and brakework, and two on ɪhe boiler. The engine was then lifted off its wheels and placed on ɪtands on a side road pit. As Mr.Syd Preston, a boiler-smith in No.

3 Bay at the time, remembers, after removing the boiler cladding, both cranes were brought into use and the special heavy sling, kept for lif-ting off the 'Lickey Banker' (ex-Midland 0-10-0 No. 58100) boiler, was used at one end, and a double sling, pieced together at the other. As the boiler, still complete with smokebox was being slowly lifted, the back end came free but the front end of the engine began to rise off its stands. Upon lowering it was discovered that, although the in-termediate support bracket at the centre of the barrel merely rested on the frame stretcher, the front support just to the rear of the smokebox saddle was secured by three bolts at each side, one of which was hid-den from view and had not been seen by the fitters. Once these were removed the boiler came free and was placed on a boiler trolley to be taken out of the shop.

The engine frames were then placed on stands on a side road at the north end of No. 3 Bay adjacent to the top crossing. It was here that work on correcting the defective loose cylinders began. Mr. Preston recalls that when the bolts securing the cylinders to the frame were tapped with a hammer they were clearly loose and therefore both inside and outside cylinder blocks were removed, each bolt being carefully numbered for later inspection. The holes in the main frames were now clearly seen as being elongated and the only remedy, short of the unsatisfactory and expensive method of welding each one up and re-drilling, was to replace the whole front end section of the main frames, some 16 ft. 3" in length and extending from the bufferbeam to the centre of the leading driving wheel horn gaps. These new frame sections also encompassed a frame fracture on the left hand leading horn gap which had been discovered by Mr J. Sampson who, together with his father had been working on the locomotive frames at this time. New plates, already pre-drilled with the various holes for cylinder fixings, horn guides, frame stretchers, buffer beam gussets were therefore prepared and the existing defective sections of frames were cut off.

However before these new plates for the frame sections had been drilled, 1" wide x 1 ft. 1½" long shear strips had been welded in

47

positions which would leave a nominal gap of one inch between them and the outside cylinder flanges at both front and rear of each outside cylinder. The plates were subsequently annealed and the outer fillet welds machined to a 3" radius to reduce stress.

As this was the first time this major repair had been been carried out on a locomotive of this size, there would have undoubtedly been consultation with the Chief Mechanical Engineer's staff as the work progressed and defects found during the strip down.

This was a major modification designed to prevent movement of the outside cylinders which the class was to become prone to. The then Chief Mechanical Engineer, J.F. Harrison, had become concerned, since any movement between cylinder and frame was leading to leaking joints between the cylinders and the steam passages through the frames, and consequently the problem had to be cured.

Using a double vee butt weld, the carefully prepared edges of the remaining and new frame plates were welded together with a full penetration weld and afterwards dressed flush, removing all visible evidence of the repair, and the welds were then X-rayed to confirm they were sound and free from defects.

As with the construction of new engines, in the areas where the cylinders fitted, the new frames were faced up in the areas of the ports with the frame edges being chamfered in the port passages to facilitate a smooth steam flow.

The cylinders, which in the meantime had been rebored, were then refitted using driving fit bolts, as normal practice, and when these were tightened up keys were welded into the 1" spaces between the front and rear of the cylinder casting flanges and the shear strips (let into the frames) using tack welds top, middle, and bottom to attach them to the shear strips. These keys were made a light interference fit between the cylinder flanges, which themselves had been machined, and the shear strips. These shear strips resisted any tendency for forward and rear movement by the cylinders and also acted as a 'tell tale'. i.e. further movement, however slight, being detected by cracking of the weld. This modification proved to be a satisfactory solution to the problem, seeing out the remaining life of the individual locomotives once each one had been repaired as required.

Shopping 46203 at Derby instead of Crewe raises the question as to why, bearing in mind that Crewe Works had built and repaired these locomotives from new and had the expertise, tooling and special equipment to hand for them. It is likely that the reason 46203 was shopped at Derby was to ensure close technical oversight of the repair and to ensure local availability of specialist metallurgical and X-ray facilities to confirm the procedure in question. It was early in 1942 that the

L.M.S. discovered a growing tendency for locomotive frames of certain larger classes to fracture in certain places particularly in the top corners of the horn gaps, and by 1944 a repair method had been developed using welding, with Derby being at the forefront of research work. Consequently the repair on 'Princess Margaret Rose' involving renewing the front of the frames by welding on a new piece, utilised confirmed methodology. Subsequently similar front end frame replacement was carried out at Crewe Works to 46200, 46201, 46204, 46205, 46206, 46207, 46210, and 46211, between February 1952 and January 1954.

In fact the 'Railway Observer' (journal of the Railway Correspondence and Travel Society (R.C.T.S issue No. 275 of January 1952 recorded under 'Derby Notes' a visit on 10th December 1951:

> "A distinguished stranger was also in the new works bay − in the form of 46203 (66A) − stripped down to the frames. This engine has required new front end frames (16 ft. 3" in length) and has been sent to Derby on the instructions of the mechanical engineer. 46203 only had a general repair in May and great care was taken when the sheeting was removed so as not to scratch the blue paintwork."

The inside and outside cylinders, motion plates, frame stretchers, bufferbeam etc were then attached and re-assembly of the rest of the chassis continued. A point of interest regarding the refitting of the bufferbeam was that the rivetting was done leaving the heads domed, whereas it was normal practice (at Crewe) on the class for them to be flat. Consequently any photographic record taken after her visit to Derby and before further general repairs are easily dated to this period.

'Princess Margaret Rose' was then re-assembled, the bogie and pony truck wheels having been re-tyred in No. 17 Shop and the driving wheels turned, and on 22nd February 1952 the 'Railway Observer' reported that 46203 was complete ready for wheeling after the heavy frame repairs.

The boiler was re-fitted again with great care due to the lack of height in the shop and the lagging and cladding sheeting carefully refixed in place.

Wilf Rogers was given the job of setting the motion and valves, an unusual task since four-cylinder engines were never normally seen in the Derby erecting shop. A reversing gear defect was also rectified having been found during the reassembly.

It was at this time, on 25th February 1952 that one of the co-authors first saw, and photographed 'Princess Margaret Rose' as she stood in the centre road of No. 3 Bay the following day, her blue-liveried boiler

46203 stands in No. 3 bay in Derby locomotive works stripped down and with one new front-end frame plate in position. The centre cylinder block stands in the right foreground and the left-hand outer cylinder is at the bottom left. A removed front end frame plate lies on the shop floor on top of the other new plate for the other side of the engine.

David H Merrifield

'Princess Margaret Rose' now fully re-assembled and with her blue paintwork filled and stopped prior to re-painting, stands in the centre road of No. 3 bay of the Derby erecting shop on Tuesday 26th February 1952.

Brian Radford

cladding sheets and cab refitted and some filling and stopping work already done in preparation for her repaint. She was then taken out of the shop into the 'Stone Pit' area to be re-united with her tender.

46203 was then ready to move into the No. 10 paint shop to be given not a touch up to her blue livery but her new Brunswick Green livery lined out in orange and black. When she arrived at Derby, 'Princess Margaret Rose' had been, as we have recorded, in the 'Caledonian' Blue livery, but in 1951 that livery had been declared to be unsatisfactory in terms of durability and a decision was made to eliminate it and thus re-livery those locomotives which carried it. For the colour change the remaining light blue paint was not stripped off but 'crozzled' areas i.e. those where the surface had been a leather like appearance, were stripped and over-painted. She was then subjected to filling and stopping, a coat of lead primer, more filling and stopping and rubbing down, followed by undercoat and then the top coat of 'Brunswick Green' enamel at which point the B.R. crest and cabside numbers were applied.

She was then picked out and hand lined in black, edged in orange, before being varnished, flatted down and varnished again; this process being repeated as necessary to get a first class finish acceptable to paint shop foreman Bert Hassall. Jim Pick was one of the painters of 46203, and she remained in the paint shop for over two weeks.

She was officially returned to traffic on 17th March 1952 after a rather extended stay of 94 days, making 105 days in all out of use but she was still recorded as being on Derby No. 4 Shed on 21st March 1952 by the 'Railway Observer' during an R.C.T.S. visit.

It was during this time whilst on Derby No. 4 Shed under steam test that 46203 was photographed by a number of people including one of the co-authors who was then an engineering apprentice in Derby Works with B.R. and who in turn was himself unknowingly photographed whilst gazing up at the locomotive in wrapped admiration.

Right: BR Official Photograph of the front of the right-hand outside cylinder of 46203 showing a close up of the wedge plate fastenings highlighted in white, taken on 13th March 1952.

BR Official, Brian Radford collection

46203, now in her new BR standard green livery, stands in the Derby paint shop awaiting the transfer cabside numbers and final coats of finishing varnish in early March 1952
David H Merrifield

Above: On 3rd February 1990 some of the men involved in 46203's unique visit and repair at Derby were invited to Butterley to discuss the event and renew acquaintance with her. Left to right Brian Radford, Arnold Coles, James Hanson, (fireman), Sid Preston, Jim Pick, (painter), Brell Ewart, Bernard Peach and Maurice Wheldon.
Robin Stewart-Smith

Facing Page: 46203 on Derby 4 shed in March 1952. This photograph was sent from Windang, New South Wales, Australia. Detailed analysis of this photograph showed that the young man standing in his overalls without a hat, admiring the locomotive is no other than one of the authors, Brian Radford – a remarkable coincidence considering that although contemporaries, the two individuals do not know each other.
David H. Merrifield

This photograph was taken by Mr. Dave Merrifield, also then an engineering apprentice in No. 8 Erecting Shop, but who now lives in Windang, New South Wales, Australia. He contacted the authors after reading about the writing of this book in the 'Steam Railway' magazine which is sold in Australia as well as in the U.K. and wrote to the authors the following:-

"My friend Mick Braithwaite and I went over to the shed one afternoon with our tea and rock-cakes from the shed canteen. This was highly irregular, but they were the best rock-cakes on B.R.! We settled ourselves on 'Princesss Margaret Rose' which was on the road adjacent to the shed with about 100 lb 'on the clock'. About ten minutes later I heard voices below where I sat in the fireman's seat. Looking down, I realised with horror that it was Mr. (Freddie) Simpson — Works Manager, Mr. (Herbert) Mears — Apprentice Supervisor, and a visitor. I told Mick to blow down his side gauge glass, whilst I grabbed the shovel and laid on six quick rounds before re-gaining my seat. Mr Mears looked up and said, "All right boys?" Receiving an "O.K.", they continued on their inspection. That was a real close shave !"

Following a steaming test after the completion of the repairs and a trial run to Trent, where the locomotive could be turned, she was checked over and any faults or adjustments corrected by fitters from No. 8 shop and then cleared for return to traffic. Driver Harold Coles was called into No. 4 Shed office by Ted Mumford who told him 46203 was ready on the North departure road. "I think we'll get that one out of the way. They've just given it the O.K. from the works."

However it was then around 3.30 in the afternoon and a full hour would be needed for preparing the engine including oiling up. Derby control knew that the locomotive had restrictions over her route back to the West Coast Main Line and came up with the idea of routing her back via the West road to Lichfield and then down the link line to the main Trent Valley Line below. However the locomotive was not allowed to leave Derby until around 6.30 p.m. after the 'rush hour' and Driver Coles therefore didn't get to take 46203 having ended his shift.

However it is understood that she did use this route, almost certainly the only 'Princess Royal' ever to use that piece of line at Lichfield.

After a reported secret check over in Crewe Works by the untrusting erectors and fitters from her home works, to ensure the 'Midland Types' at Derby had done nothing amiss, (the official record card confirms she did in fact pay a short visit to Crewe works from 4th to 8th April) she went back to Polmadie to continue working expresses on the West Coast main line.   The 'Railway Observer' of July 1952

under the location Bonnybridge reported 'Strangers on the 1.45 p.m. Carlisle to Perth include 45527, 46547, 46136, 46200/03/12.'

On 22nd August 1952 'Princess Margaret Rose' was recorded passing Elvanfoot on the 'Up Postal' working, a duty normally allocated to a Polmadie 'Princess Coronation' or a Crewe North allocated 'Princess Royal'.   Whilst at Polmadie 46203 also occasionally found herself in charge of the short four coach formation of the Glasgow (Central) to Edinburgh (Princess Street) services, being recorded by Mr David Anderson on the 1.30 p.m. from Edinburgh on 24th January and 11th April 1953 and on the 7.30 p.m. Edinburgh to Glasgow on 3rd April 1953.

Mr Ron Hill, a senior member and former Chairman of the Scottish Railway Preservation Society also well remembers the 'Princess Royals' on these services. "They didn't half romp along with only four coaches but they stopped at every 'hen-hoose' on the line!" he reported to the authors.

On 28th February 1953 she was in charge of the 9.25 a.m. Crewe to Glasgow Central (and Perth) and worked the train throughout rather than being changed for another locomotive, usually a Kingmoor based Class 5 4-6-0, upon arrival at Carlisle. She was photographed climbing Beattock on this working by Mr J.L. Stevenson (see photograph).

She was re-allocated for a very brief period, again to Edge Hill on 16th May 1953 before moving to Crewe North Shed yet again on 23rd May 1953, a one week transfer.

46203's duties in this next period of her life included working 'The Mid-Day Scot', a Crewe North turn frequently worked by a 'Princess Coronation' Class locomotive. Starting from Glasgow at 1.30 p.m., the up train covered the 73.5 miles from Carstairs to Carlisle in 75 minutes including the climb to Beattock Summit. Stops at Lancaster and Watford gave the arrival time in Euston of 10.00 p.m., a total journey time of some eight and a half hours. In the other direction, departure from Euston was at 1.15 p.m. with a journey time of 8 hours 20 minutes and arrival in Glasgow at 9.35 p.m. This included an 80 minute timing between Euston and Rugby, a distance of 82.5 miles, followed by a more easily timed section of 75.5 miles to Crewe for which 77 minutes were allowed.

The winter timetable saw the addition of a through Blackpool portion which in summer ran separately at 1.30 p.m. as a restaurant car train to meet the holiday traffic requirements.

During the mid 1950s whilst allocated to Crewe North depot 'Princess Margaret Rose' was also regularly used on the morning Birmingham—Glasgow service and was recorded at least twice working the up West Coast Postal train, at that time normally a Polmadie-based 'Princess Coronation' class duty. There is no record of her use

Green Liveried and reasonably clean, 46203 takes water on Dillicar troughs at 60 m.p.h. with the down 11.15 a.m. Birmingham New Street – Glasgow express on Whit-Monday, 2nd June 1952 comprising eleven coaches in the attractive carmine and cream livery. The lovely fells forming the Lune Gorge are dappled in sunshine and shadow.   *Photograph and caption E.D.Bruton*

Eric Bruton writes: Of the four exposures I made of 'Princess Margaret Rose' I think the longer shot from the lower slopes of Loups Fell, overlooking the Dillicar troughs is my favourite. . . . I usually worked within the boundary walls or fences bordering the railway but on this occasion I took to the sloping field lying between the line and the then A685 Tebay – Kendal road which ran high to the right on the lower slopes of Loups Fell. Although the sun was almost ¾ tail-on, leaving the smokebox in the shade, I thought that it would still make a very attractive pictorial shot given that setting, so I did not hesitate in making the exposure. I was pleased that the stock was an unbroken eleven coach rake in the then B.R. Carmine and Cream livery comprising Stanier Period III corridor stock with a Period II 12-wheeled dining car to diagram D1810. . . . I forgot whether the tender was allowed to overflow to any degree before withdrawal of the water picking-up scoop after taking the photo, but I did not want it to do so on this occasion before firing the shutter. I logged the speed at 60 m.p.h. as 46203 swept through against the back pressure of taking up water as the driver and fireman prepared to charge the 1 in 146 gradient from the north end of Dillicar troughs to and beyond the change of gradient to 1 in 75 north of the Lune bridge and through to Shap Summit, heavily curving throughout to boot! One notices in the photo. the darkening at the chimney as what was the first round of almost continual steady firing, until reaching the summit, goes into the firebox. The still rather infant River Lune joins the eastern side of the embankment a little further down, near to the water control gear and 'make-up tank' seen by the dining car (fourth vehicle), and runs alongside the line, at about fifteen feet lower, until point near the start of the sweeping curve round into Dillicar straight, from which point the Lune swings more sharply into the broader valley floor, leaving the railway by some 100 yards or so as the two approach the next curve towards Low Gill. The dark fell beyond the tail of the train is the craggy slope up to Grayrigg Common and to the left the slope is leading to what is locally known as Tebay Mountain. Loups Fell, already mentioned, is behind and to the right of the camera and overlooks Tebay village. Dillicar troughs, of course, were also well known as Tebay troughs, sadly now long gone and this lovely scene is now dominated by overhead wiring and the M6 motorway replaces the high A625 road and scars the whole valley towards Grayrigg, halfway up the right hand slope. Long gone are the lovely peaceful periods of birdsong and the sound of the rushing water as one waited hereabouts for the next train to come through. L-o-n-g waits too on a Sunday! Occasionally a cloud-burst, hailstorm or just gloom and drizzle would mar the scene for a while or longer (like all day on one or two occasions I recall). Oh, happy days!

This photograph shows 'Princess Margaret Rose' storming the 1 in 75 of Shap with a down express dated between February 1952 and March 1953.

Eric Treacy courtesy Midland Railway Trust Archive

Another un-mistakable Treacy shot of 46203 powering her way up Camden bank with a heavy train for the north in the summer of 1953. At this time she was allocated to Crewe North m.p.d.

Eric Treacy courtesy Millbrook House Ltd

on 'The Caledonian' express although other members of the 'Princess Royal' class saw occasional use on this train deputising for the usual 'Princess Coronation', this train being the passenger equivalent of the 'West Coast Postal'. Crewe North 'Princess Royals' were also at this time demoted by being employed on the local passenger workings between Crewe and Manchester (London Road).

Also in the period 46203 regularly worked on the Perth to London (Euston) services as recorded on a B.R. Coal Report dated 9th August 1953 when 'Princess Margaret Rose', working the 9.45 a.m. from Perth, lost five minutes time between Carlisle and Penrith where the train was halted for a further 10 minutes in order to 'blow up' and fill the boiler. A further 10 minutes was lost from Penrith to Shap Summit giving a twenty minute delay.

The locomotive on this day had been re-manned at Carlisle by Driver A. Hodgson and Fireman G. Edmondson of Carlisle Upperby Shed and when 46203 came off the train at Crewe, Driver Hodgson filed a 'bad coal report'. Crewe reported the coal as being 'small and poor' with 'evidence of firebrick' and the state of the fire was found to be

very dirty!. Perth Depot was requested to state the supplier of this coal.

There was a tendency from this time, towards the end of their working lives, for the 'Princess Royals' to be moved north of Crewe and it has been suggested that they were better suited to the hill climbing demands of the route to Glasgow rather than the 'racing grounds' to the south. They could certainly take the steep grades of the route in their stride with heavy train loads and, well handled could equal and in some cases better the performance of the 'Princess Coronations'.

'Princess Margaret Rose' was taken out of traffic on 19th August 1955 and, after waiting for 16 days, entered Crewe works for a heavy general repair which took 36 days. She returned to traffic on 19th October with boiler No. 9101 now fitted and boasting a dome for the first time in her life.

46203 remained at Crewe North for over five years before returning to her old haunts at Edge Hill on 20th September 1958 where she resumed working express passenger trains, frequently working 'The Red Rose', and now sometimes freight trains, on the old link to Euston.

In his book 'Great Locomotives of the LMS', O.S. Nock gives a

'Princess Margaret Rose' bursts from the tunnel at Kensal Green on Saturday 5th June 1954 with the down 'Mid-Day Scot'. *Stanley Creer*

46203 reverses out of Platform 1 of the old Euston station, after arriving with the boat-train from Liverpool – a scene taken in June 1954. The train is being moved to the carriage sidings for exam and servicing as indicated by 'S' on the overhead signal. *Geoff Rixon*

With banking locomotive Fowler 2-6-4T No. 42424 assisting at the rear, 46203 makes a re-start from Tebay onto the 1 in 75 bank to Shap Summit with the 11.25 a.m. Birmingham–Glasgow express on Saturday 31st July 1954.

J.E. Wilkinson

Atmospheric night shot of 46203 as she stands at Crewe station with steam blowing off from her safety valves on Wednesday 28th December 1955 at the head of the 5.15 p.m. sleeping car express from Inverness to London Euston, timetabled to arrive at 8.35 a.m. If the train was running to time it would be about 4.50 a.m. when this shot was taken.   *D.M.C. Hepburne-Scot, courtesy Rail Archive Stephenson*

Period line-up of Stanier locomotives at Carlisle Citadel station on Saturday 23rd July 1955. 'Princess Margaret Rose' stands at the head of W67 express for Glasgow whilst on adjacent tracks stand 'Princess Coronation' class No. 46222 'Queen Mary' and Stanier Class 5 4-6-0s Nos. 45013 and 44786.

D Butterfield

46203, at the head of the eleven coach 'Mid-Day Scot', climbs the northern fells on her way to London Euston about 1956.
W.J. Verdon Anderson, courtesy Rail Archive Stephenson

Evocative scene at Polmadie depot on 22nd April 1956 as 46203 is prepared to work an express to the south as far as Crewe. 'Caley' 0-6-0 57446 and 46246 'City of Manchester' share the scene, the latter later working light with 46203 to Glasgow Central station before the 'Mid-Day Scot' to London Euston. This had also been her diagram the previous day. *David Anderson*

The date is 28th April 1956 as 46203 passes Heaton Norris (Stockport) nearing the end of the journey to Manchester with a down express.
Norman Preedy Collection

Left: 'Princess Margaret Rose' in clean condition stands on Shrewsbury motive power depot in 1956 having worked a local train from Crewe on a 'running in' turn after overhaul.
J.A.G.H. Coltas

Facing Page Upper: Under a threatening sky and piloted by 2-6-4T 42464 which would have been attached at Oxenholme, 'Princess Margaret Rose' climbs past Scout Green on Shap with the 11.15 a.m. Birmingham to Glasgow Central on Saturday 26th January 1957.
J.E. Wilkinson

Left: 46203 backs down from Crewe North depot to attach the through coach from Plymouth prior to taking the down 'Mid-Day Scot' forward to Glasgow in September 1957.
Eric Oldham

Facing Page Lower: Now attached to the Plymouth coach 'Princess Margaret Rose' awaits the arrival of the 'Mid-Day Scot' from the south - a follow-on-shot from the photograph on the left.
Eric Oldham

Below: 'Princess Margaret Rose' quenches her thirst at Camden Shed – Eric Treacy's own caption to this shed scene of 1957 which epitomises the latter days of steam.
Eric Treacy

46203 climbs through the northern fells with an unidentified down express in 1957 or 1958.

W.J. Verden Anderson, courtesy Rail Archive Stephenson

46203 in full flow, attacks the climb to Tring having just passed Cheddington with the up 'Shamrock' express from Liverpool Lime Street to London Euston in May 1959.

Martin Welch

Right: 'Princess Margaret Rose' at Acton Grange on Monday 9th June 1958 at the head of a Glasgow–Birmingham service.

Norman Preedy

Right: 'Princess Margaret Rose' heads up express W48, near Tring. The date must be between 12th August and 29th November 1969 since she carried round-headed front buffers for only that period. *anon*

Below: 46203 on an express approaching Edge Hill with the depot in the distance. The viaduct carried the goods lines to the 'Gridiron' and on to Wavertree. The date is thought to be May 1959. *A.M. Ross*

fine account of 46203's performance between Crewe and London Euston on 'The Red Rose' express on 22nd July 1959 and we will let him take up the story:

"By the year 1959, the English Electric diesels were coming into regular use between Euston and Liverpool, and at the same time the deceleration in train times prior to electrification was also taking effect. The up 'Red Rose' was one of the trains that had been slowed down, with an increased allowance of 170 minutes, non-stop, from Crewe to Euston. In conjunction with signalling work, I was on the line frequently at the time, and returning from Crewe late one afternoon I had an unexpected treat. Arriving on No. 3 Platform only a few minutes before the up 'Red Rose' was due, I was surprised to see it come in from Liverpool headed, not by the expected diesel, but by a 'Lizzie', 'Princess Margaret Rose'. The train was very crowded, and for sometime after we started, and I had clocked the moment of departure, I was still making my way along the corridors trying to find a seat. Gravitating my way towards the front end, I was heartened by the full throated roar of the exhaust beat; and to cut a long and joyous story short, I experienced one of my finest ever runs behind one of those engines, on the eve of their withdrawal for scrapping. It is good to reflect that the engine of what proved to be my own farewell behind one of them was saved for preservation.

The running was top class from the very outset, and the acoustics as we climbed the Madeley Bank, succeeded by the downhill dash towards Stafford on the easy gradients from Standon Bridge, were exhilarating to record, and set the pattern for the whole run. Note should be taken of the uphill work from the Trent Valley, the minimum speeds of 63 m.p.h. at Atherstone, and no less than 67 m.p.h. at Bulkington, and of the sustained high speed to the outskirts of Rugby. There was no let up afterwards either, with further maximum speeds of 80.5 m.p.h. at Weedon and 84 at Castlethorpe. Despite the check at Rugeley the train was 13 minutes inside schedule time at Roade, and would have been still more so but for the severe signal check at Bletchley. The men on 46203 however were proof against any form of discouragement, and their ascent to Tring, with the sustained minimum speed of 66.5 m.p.h. on the 1 in 335 gradient, with an equivalent draw bar horse power of 1,495 was the climax of the run, as far as power output was concerned. The signal stop at Bourne End was very time consuming because it involved a warning to go carefully for some miles ahead in view of a report of possible obstructions on the line. Once clear of this area, the crew resumed their previous style of running and gave us a final burst of high speed from Watford to Willesden. The net time of 143 minutes from Crewe, with its start to stop average of 66.5 m.p.h. is a sufficient commentary on this run in itself. But I can add that it was made in far from ideal footplate conditions, in modern context. By that time, many of the top-link crews at Camden, Crewe North, Longsight, and Edge Hill had a growing experience with the new diesels, and had, no doubt, an appreciation of the relative comfort of their cabs. While some of the tougher spirits among the firemen might feel that the absence of hard physical work would result in their 'getting soft' others were no doubt glad that the end of their days of coal-heaving was in sight. But while I clocked the grand run of 'Princess Margaret Rose', I gave more than a passing thought to the conditions on the footplate; for it was a day of sweltering heat, and instead of driving his engine vigorously to make up lost time which had been incurred north of Crewe, one might have expected rather easier going to ease the labour of firing. But these two worthies, who came from Camden Shed, obviously put their hearts into the job, and turned in a superb piece of work."

Our grateful thanks to O.S. Nock for allowing us to reproduce this account here of a fine performance, which he recorded in his notebook at the time as being 'the run of the year'.

By this period in her life 'Princess Margaret Rose' had been repainted yet again, still in Brunswick Green, but with the second British Railways crest, the work officially recorded as being done on 14th August 1958.

In his article on 'Locomotive Practice and Performance', in the January 1960 issue of 'The Railway Magazine', O.S. Nock also records receiving details of a further run behind 46203 in November 1959 by which date 'The Red Rose' was still normally being worked by English Electric Type 4 1Co-Co1 diesel-electric locomotives. On this occasion however, 'Princess Margaret Rose' set off from Crewe, with 15 coaches including a portion from Manchester added at Crewe, a total load of 506 tons tare (about 545 tons gross).

The Manchester portion arrived late at Crewe and 46203 was ten minutes late leaving as a result. There were four signal checks, two severe, between Crewe and Rugby and by Nuneaton a further 3¾

Date: 22nd July 1959.
Train: 'The Red Rose', Crewe to Euston
Engine: 4-6-2 No. 46203 'Princess Margaret Rose'
Load: 13 Coaches, 456 tons Tare, 495 tons full.

Distance		Sched.	Actual time	Speed
(miles)		(mins)	(m. s.)	(m.p.h.)
0.0	CREWE	0	0 00	—
4.7	Betley Road		8.30	47.5
7.9	Madeley		12 35	46.5
10.5	Whitmore	15	15 36	—
14.6	Standon Bridge		19 23	72
19.2	Norton Bridge	23	22 57	80*
21.2	Great Bridgeford		24 25	83
24.5	Stafford	33	27 05	53
			p.w.s.	
31.0	Colwich		33 29	69
			p.w.s.	15
33.9	Rugeley	43	38 04	—
41.8	Lichfield	50	46 15	72
48.0	Tamworth	56	51 05	80
55.7	Atherstone		57 40	63
60.9	Nuneaton	70	62 10	72
64.6	Bulkington		65 19	67.5
70.0	Brinklow		69 47	76
75.5	Rugby	86	74 50	40
			p.w.s.	
79.3	Kilsby Tunnel North Box		79 52	56
88.4	Weedon	100	88 01	80.5
95.3	Blisworth	106	93 33	70
98.2	Roade	109	96 03	66.5
103.3	Castlethorpe		100 03	84
109.6	m.p. 48.5		104 43	73.5
			signals	10
111.4	Bletchley	121	108 02	—
117.9	Leighton Buzzard		114 53	71
122.0	Cheddington		118 23	68.5
126.4	Tring	137	122 17	66.5
130.1	Berkhamsted		125 19	80
			sig. stop	—
140.6	Watford Junction	150	141 30	72/69
144.8	Hatch End		145 07	72
146.7	Harrow		146 38	76
150.0	Wembley		149 10	79
152.7	Willesden Junction	161	151 13	72
155.7	South Hampstead		153 50	—
			signals	—
158.1	EUSTON	170	159 50	—

* Speed before service slack.

Net time: 143 minutes. Average speed: 66.5 m.p.h.

minutes had been lost.

After this, however, 'Princess Margaret Rose' performed magnificently and the 79.7 miles from Nuneaton to the booked stop at Watford Junction was covered in only 68¾ minutes.

The average speed over the section from Blisworth to Tring, a distance of 31.1. miles, was 73.3 m.p.h. with the result that 46203 brought the train into Watford 2¼ minutes early. A truly magnificent effort reflecting not only great credit on the enginemen but also on the engine itself.

Steam had officially ceased on Liverpool to London (Euston) workings as from 2nd November 1959, but as recorded above, 'Princess Royal' Class locomotive 46203 with sisters 46204, 46208 and 46211 were pressed back into use from storage at the beginning of 1960 until 1961 to deputise for the English Electric Type 4 (later known as Class 40s) 1Co-Co1 locomotives during their teething troubles.

For a further brief period, and in fact for the first time in eighteen years, 'Princess Margaret Rose' was once more allocated on loan to Camden Shed, London on 20th August 1960, this time for just three weeks before returning to Edge Hill again on 10th September.

Work for the 'Princess Royal' Class as a whole was now becoming much less with the availability of more diesel locomotives. The English Electric Type 4 locomotives had by now once again taken over the named trains on the routes formerly the domain of their sisters, the 'Princess Coronation' Class Pacific locomotives. These diesel locomotives were steadily being delivered from early in 1958, mak-

Above: In her short-lived blue livery 46203 is seen here depicted working hard on the ascent of Beattock Bank with a northbound express in the summer of 1951.

From a painting by Colin Wright - Courtesy Brell Ewart

Below: Looking very dirty and in need of a good clean at her home depot of Edge Hill, Liverpool, 'Princess Margaret Rose' passes Winsford, north of Crewe at the head of a rake of coaches in B.R. maroon livery heading the up 'Manxman' to London Euston in August 1959.

Peter Hughes - Courtesy Colour-Rail

46203 winds her way over a maze of lines as she leaves London Euston in 1960 with a down 'Merseyside Express'. Euston Downside carriage sheds are on the top right.
Andrew C Ingram

'Princess Margaret Rose' stands in Euston station on a June day in 1960 having just arrived with an express from the north.
J.F. Clay

Above: Wednesday 15th February 1961 saw 46203, just over one week out of Crewe shops, on the 2.50 p.m. express from Holyhead to Crewe, seen here passing Valley. *A. Chandler*

Right: At the head of the 12.30 p.m. Bangor to London express 46203 stands at Chester General station on Monday 7th August 1961, having changed places with the locomotive that had brought the train on the first leg of its journey to the capital. *S.D. Wainwright*

Below: A scene in the old Euston station in the summer of 1961 (possibly 14th July) as 'Princess Margaret Rose' reverses out of Platform 5, having worked a relief from Blackpool. *Martin Welch*

Above: 46203 'Princess Margaret Rose' sets off from Beattock station at the head of a down Perth express in the summer of 1962 having had a banking engine attached at the rear of the train. *Derek Cross Courtesy Colour-Rail*

Left: A fine study of 46203 as she backs down onto a rake of coaches forming a down express at Carlisle in July 1962. *Neil Thexton Courtesy Colour-Rail*

Left: Backing down towards Carlisle station from Kingmoor motive power depot 'Princess Margaret Rose' is ready to take a northbound express forward on Wednesday 29th August 1962. *Peter J. Fitton*

Right: Two views of 'Princess Margaret Rose' as she stands in the centre road at Carlisle station on Wednesday 29th August 1962 awaiting the arrival of the express from London Euston which she is booked to take forward.

Peter J. Fitton

Below: 46203 gets well into her stride with the Perth express as she passes Floriston, north of Carlisle on the same day. *Peter J. Fitton*

Above: In store at Carnforth on Tuesday 18th April 1961, with chimney covered and nameplates removed 46203 stands next to 46211 on the sidings near the turntable.
W. Ashcroft

Left:'Princess Margaret Rose' speeds north past Quintinshill, Gretna on Saturday 18th August 1962, with the 10.15 a.m. London to Perth express.
R.H. Leslie

Below: In the last fortnight of her BR career 46203 bursts from beneath the bridge at Rockcliffe north of Carlisle with the down **Perth on Monday 27th August 1962.**
Stephen C. Crook

Above: 46203 is pictured on that working later on the same day at Carstairs as she leaves for Perth. *Derek Cross*

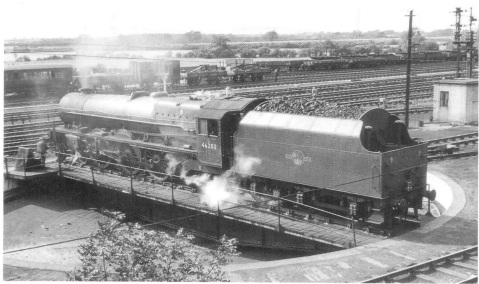

Right: Two days later 46203 is turned on the Kingmoor depot turntable prior to working the 10.00 a.m. London Euston to Perth and Aberdeen forward from Carlisle at 3.49 p.m. on Wednesday 29th August. *Peter J. Fitton*

ing the final demise of the 'Princess Royal' class inevitable within a few years. In early March, 1961 all of the 'Princess Royal' class locomotives were taken out of use and stored.

Accordingly, on 5th March 1961 46203 'Princess Margaret Rose' found herself placed officially 'in store' at Carnforth m.p.d., with her nameplates removed, along with 46200 and 46211. This was despite her only just previously receiving a heavy intermediate repair at Crewe Works, being taking out of traffic on 29th November 1960 and awaiting works attention for 24 days. After 36 days under repair she had been returned to traffic on 9th February 1961.

She was taken out of store on 9th July for limited use and was recorded, carrying a 5A (Crewe North) shedplate, on a variety of trains including the 06.35 Euston—Crewe on 26th July and the 10.05 a.m. Glasgow—Birmingham (Birmingham Scot) on 25th August 1961.

She was again placed in store at Carnforth in serviceable condition on 1st September with 46200. Eight of her sisters were also stored once more, but by now a number of the 'Princess Royal' class were being assembled at Crewe South Shed for what was to be their funereal move into Crewe Works for cutting up commencing with 46204, 46205, 46207, 46210, 46211 and 46212.

The sight of one of these fine classic locomotives being reduced to a pile of scrap metal is surely one of the saddest ever witnessed as steam traction entered its final years on British Railways. A most ignoble end for members of a class regarded by many as one of the finest looking designs of locomotive ever to grace British metals.

However, 46203 was destined, at this eleventh hour, to enjoy a further brief 'Indian Summer' of use with some of her remaining sisters,

for on 24th January 1962 she was taken out of store and transferred to Carlisle Upperby Depot to work a mixture of both fitted freight, parcels, mixed goods, and fish trains. On 5th March 1962 she worked the 09.20 Glasgow (St.Enoch) to London (St.Pancras) as far as Carlisle and on 10th March was observed on the 09.35 Wolverhampton to London (Euston). A fitted freight duty found her on the afternoon service from Willesden to Carlisle on 16th March, and on 21st of that month she worked the Glasgow to Wolverhampton parcels train. Then on 7th April she found herself moved to Kingmoor Shed, from where she began to work some of her former routes with express passenger services having had her nameplates re-fitted. Whilst at Kingmoor she worked the Euston—Aberdeen express forward from Carlisle on 21st and 25th June and on 27th and 30th August. On 31st August she worked the 13.20 Euston Perth forward from Carlisle as far as Perth. She was photographed on Euston—Perth trains in late August, working them all forward from Carlisle and usually working her return trip back to Carlisle on a southbound fish train the following morning.

The reason for this short reprieve was again technical problems with the English Electric Type 4 diesel electric locomotives and in particular with the train heating boilers (for a second successive winter), followed by the Summer timetable requiring additional motive power.

During this period 'Princess Royals' were even recorded working Edinburgh to Aberdeen trains with 46200, 46201 at work with 46203. 46208 was again in use at Edge Hill along with 46206 and 46209 from Camden Shed on top link duties.

As the diesel problems eased, 46203 was again officially placed

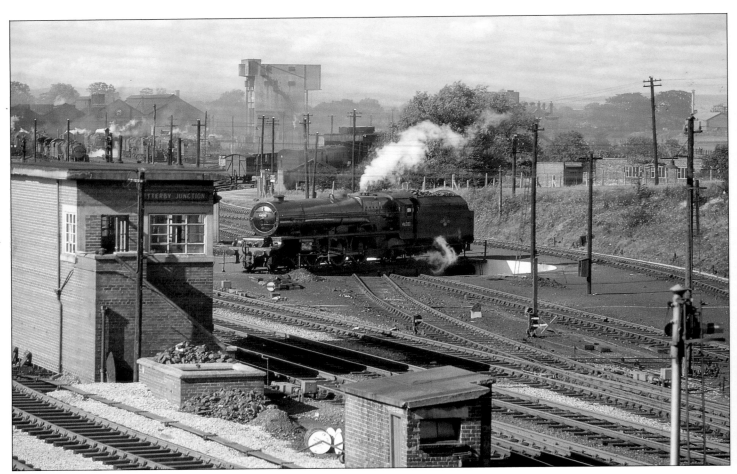

Top: Steam locomotives still fill the roads of Carlisle Kingmoor m.p.d. as 46203 is turned on the turntable to be ready for her next duty hauling an express on Saturday 8th September 1962, her last northbound working. Etterby Junction signal box is to the left of the picture.
Geoff Rixon

Above and Left: 'Princess Margaret Rose' comes off shed at Kingmoor and backs down towards Carlisle station to take over the express from London to Perth. The efforts of Peter Robinson and his friends cleaning 46203 can be seen. They did not manage to finish the task as evidenced by the partially clean tender.
Geoff Rixon

Two studies by David Russell of 6203 'Princess Margaret Rose' standing on Crewe North m.p.d. after her purchase by Billy Butlin and restoration to her old L.M.S. maroon livery. The date is Friday 3rd May 1963 prior her move by rail to the holiday camp at Pwllheli. David Russell is now the B.R. Railfreight Engineer and it was the inspectors in his department that carried out all the exams on the Test Runs with 46203 in 1990 prior her running on B.R. lines.

David F. Russell

'in store', this time at Kingmoor on 9th September 1962 the day after being photographed yet again leaving Carlisle on the outer leg of the Euston-Perth express service. She was put into store in serviceable condition and with nameplates removed once again. Still she was not finished however for she was taken out of store for what turned out to be a brief but final five-day period of duty from 15th October until 20th of that month but research has produced no records or photographs of her workings in these five days. Her use on trains in October 1962 was the last time that she was to be steamed for nearly three decades.

On finally being withdrawn from traffic her official total recorded mileage in service was 1,494,484 miles, which was around the average mileage for members of the class as a whole. Her annual 'recorded mileages' under British Railways ownership were as follows:-

YEAR	MILEAGE
1948	43,695
1949	44,991
1950	57,921
1951	54,428
1952	59,619
1953	53,119
1954	57,967
1955	51,678
1956	54,457
1957	47,713
1958	56,192
1959	51,431
1960	45,469
1961	6,012
1962	not recorded

Total mileage: 684,692.

The total recorded mileage of 1,494,484 miles in L.M.S. and B.R. service clearly does not include some work done up to her storage out of use on 9th September 1961 (for 6,012 miles is very low compared to her known workings) and also excludes all work carried out in 1962 which was not insignificant and certainly exceeded 7,600 miles from known duties and return workings to home shed. Her actual total mileage would therefore have been over the one and a half million mark.

Her sister engine 46201 was also withdrawn in October 1962 leaving only pioneer of the class 46200 and 46206 officially in service until the following month when they too were withdrawn. Interestingly 46206 was the only 'Princess Royal' fitted with a 4000 gallon tender (No. 9816) built for 'Princess Coronation' locomotive No. 6253 in 1946 and of course with a coal pusher. This replaced her original tender No. 9359, also with a coal pusher, paired with the engine from 15th October 1936 except for a period of a year spent attached to No. 6207 from November 1946 to October 1947. 46206 ran with this 'Coronation' tender from 18th October 1962 until withdrawal of the locomotive in the November.

In BR days 'Princess Margaret Rose' had been in Crewe Works for three heavy general repairs as follows:-

TAKEN OUT OF TRAFFIC	RETURNED TO TRAFFIC
17th April 1951	24th May 1951
19th September 1955	19th October 1955
13th June 1958	14th August 1958

She also received five Intermediate Repairs as follows:-

TAKEN OUT OF TRAFFIC	RETURNED TO TRAFFIC
13th November 1951 (Derby)	17th March 1952
29th October 1953	4th December 1953
28th October 1956	21st December 1956
9th September 1959	6th November 1959
29th November 1960	9th February 1961

It is worth noting that in B.R. days she had spent a total of 982 weekdays out of traffic of which in the 1950—61 period alone, 140 of these had been awaiting works and 37 awaiting a repair decision. The longest period on works was spent at Derby, on the dates recorded above, amounting to a total of 105 days out of traffic (94 on works and 11 awaiting works).

In his excellent book 'Stanier Pacifics at Work' John Powell has recorded that the 'Princess Royals' spent rather more time in works than their sister class the 'Princess Coronations', the 'troubles' between heavy general repairs including loose cylinders, leaking joints, superheater header fractures, firebox expansion diaphragm defects and damage caused by overheated big-end bearings.

Extra repairs between general overhauls averaged 2.2 up to 1945 and rose to 3.9 in the 1946—50 period. 'Princess Royals' spent an average 64 weekdays (excluding Sundays) per annum awaiting classified repairs and a further 58.6 days on shed undergoing examination and maintenance. Availability was 60.4% compared with 69.9% for the 'Princess Cornonations' and they were on average available to work 292 miles per weekday compared to 331 for their sister Pacifics, according to Mr. Powell. However working on recorded mileages for 46203 in 1958, and assuming she was available for work on an average of 242 days per year, her actual daily mileage works out at 232.

The withdrawal from service of 46203 'Princess Margaret Rose' by British Railways could easily and quickly have seen the end of this historic locomotive at the hand of the cutters' torch within the precincts of Crewe Works, as with all of her sisters up to that time, but this was not to be.

46200 'The Princess Royal' was cut up at Connell's scrapyard at Coatbridge, Lanarkshire, following arrival there in October 1964. She was the last of the eleven 'Princess Royals' to be broken up for scrap. 46201 'Princess Elizabeth' was due to be preserved by the society of the same name and was therefore destined for a continued existence and preservation which would eventually bring her too even greater fame.

As for 46203 'Princess Margaret Rose' a period of quiet life on static display was about to start.

Facing Page: A few minutes after the lower photograph page 71 was taken 'Princess Margaret Rose' is seen heading northwards out of Carlisle on with the 10.00 a.m. Euston to Perth. *Eric Treacy*

Right: On Thursday 30th August, 46203 heads north past Beattock on the same London–Perth diagram. *Derek Cross*

Right: 'Princess Margaret Rose' on what is believed to be her last working day as she passes Etterby Junction, Carlisle, with the London Euston to Perth express which she worked forward from Carlisle. The date is Saturday 8th September 1962. *Geoff Rixon*

Below: With a banker on the rear, 'Princess Margaret Rose' powers up Beattock bank with this last northbound working on the Euston to Perth. The photographer, Peter Robinson, and some friends had spent time cleaning the locomotive at Kingmoor but had only completed a quarter of the tender side before time ran out. The cleaned portion shows up clearly. *Peter J. Robinson*

Right: 6203, in her special train, arrives at Minffordd station on Sunday 11th May 1975 on her way to Derby as the scene is captured by a bevy of photographers. *Trefor Davies*

Right: A Ffestiniog Railway double Fairlie locomotive was specially posed on the bridge that carries the line over B.R. metals at Minffordd as 'Princess Margaret Rose' passed through the station. This is undoubtedly the only time that these two types of locomotive have been so close together. *Trefor Davies*

Below: The special train skirts the Cambrian coastline before turning inland at Dovey Junction. *Bernard Bartram*

CHAPTER FOUR

SAVED FOR PRESERVATION

'Princess Margaret Rose' languished at Carlisle Kingmoor Shed for a short period, forlorn, uncared for and very vulnerable to the cutters torch as long as her future remained uncertain.

Mr. (later Sir) Billy Butlin, owner of the Butlin Holiday camp empire, had been considering using withdrawn steam locomotives as displayed attractions at various holiday camps throughout Britain, and as such large, prestigious named engines were of interest to him. Several of his camps were rail connected and so movement of any such acquisitions could be done by rail.

At this time, the main classes of locomotives that fell in the category of large, named engines were mainly ex L.M.S., other classes from the other three companies were still required or were ruled out on the basis of loading gauge access by rail.

Four former L.M.S main line express locomotives were duly purchased and restored to their former L.M.S. liveries at Crewe Works prior to being sent to their various destinations for display. From knowledge gained since, the restoration was basically cosmetic, with a number of minor mechanical items being removed to allow easier movement whilst being towed out of steam.

The four main line locomotives were:-

Ex L.M.S. Locomotive	Butlins Holiday Camp
4-6-0 No. 6100 'Royal Scot'	Skegness
4-6-2 No. 6203 'Princess Margaret Rose'	Pwllheli
4-6-2 No. 6229 'Duchess of Hamilton'	Minehead
4-6-2 No. 6233 'Duchess of Sutherland'	Ayr

Three much smaller ex Southern Railway Class A1X 0-6-0T locomotives were also purchased and restored for display at Pwllheli, Ayr and Minehead respectively, together with an ex L. & S.W.R. Class B4 dock tank for the Skegness site.

Butlins were originally interested in ex L.N.E.R. 4-6-2 'Silver Link' which at the time had been withdrawn from service but the then Stores Controller of the Eastern Region was 'less than co-operative' regarding any preservation of withdrawn steam locomotives, whilst the London Midland Region Stores Controller, Mr. A.B.Macleod, his opposite number at the time, was very much in favour.

Mr. A.B.Macleod himself recalls:

"In 1936 No 6201 'Princess Elizabeth', performed her record run from Euston to Glasgow and back which caused much enthusiasm; models of 6201 were made in 'O' gauge, miniature and narrow gauges.

Butlins . . . . . . opened a small passenger line in their camp at Pwllheli; the loco chosen was L.M.S. 6201 'Princess Elizabeth', with a diesel engine in the boiler shell. Butlins then had the ideas that if they could (now) buy the real 6201 as a static exhibit in their camp and have retired L.M.S. railway drivers to tell the public all about the loco, when they climbed up into the cab: it would popularize Butlins camps.

Butlins representatives came to see me to know if I could help them in their idea and sell them 6201. I told them that I had already sold 6201 to the Princess Elizabeth Society in August 1963. I did however have another engine of the same class which was withdrawn and waiting to be scrapped, i.e. No 6203 'Princess

Looking neglected and forlorn 46203 stands in Crewe works minus nameplates and with her chimney covered after being towed south from Kingmoor for preservation. March 1963. The connecting rods have been removed and the cross-heads secured with slats of timber thus allowing movement of the locomotive out of steam to be carried out without creating back pressure in the cylinders and no movement by the cross-heads. The connecting rods are very likely to have been placed in the tender coal space. This photographic evidence shows that she was certainly moved out of steam to Crewe works from Kingmoor depot.

Alan Beck

With livery restored to L.M.S. maroon and her numbers changed to L.M.S. style, she stands in Crewe works prior to being moved to Butlins holiday camp at Pwllheli.

McDonald & Good

Margaret Rose' and would this solve their problem.
The suggestion was accepted by Butlin." We are indebted to Mr. A.B. Macleod for this information which is an important record of the events at the time. By quirk of fate the miniature locomotive mentioned by Mr. Macleod together with another most relevant locomotive are referred to in the footnote at the end of this chapter.

To be strictly accurate the Princess Elizabeth Society record that 6201 was actually purchased on 11th February 1963 with a balance of 25% paid on 9th July 1963. August was the date that the nameplates were collected from Crewe.

It is worth noting that in the 1930s Mr. Macleod held a high rank on the Isle of Wight Railway and that is believed to be the reason that three 'Terrier' Tank locomotives were also selected by Butlins — probably with a little persuasion from Mr. Macleod.

46203 was sold to Messrs. Butlins in April 1963 and 'Princess Margaret Rose' now therefore joined a select company of steam locomotives purchased for that very purpose. She was moved on her own wheels, minus connecting rods, nameplates, shedplate and with the chimney sheeted over, from Carlisle to Crewe Works to be restored to magnificent static display condition in her former L.M.S. Crimson Lake livery with a newly cast replica L.M.S. style smokebox door number-plate '6203' and a 12A (Carlisle Kingmoor) shed plate. Her old number was once again put on the cab side-sheets and the tender lettered L.M.S.

For the move the high pressure cylinder relief valves had their insides removed to prevent a build up of pressure in the cylinders as the locomotive was being hauled from Crewe to Pwllheli.

6203 was seen outside the erecting shop on 17th April 1963 and she emerged from the works at the end of that month looking in excellent external condition (see photo) and on 4th May was hauled dead on her own wheels to the Butlins Camp at Pwllheli via Chester, Bangor, Caernarvon and Afon Wen, there running onto the former Cambrian Coast line for the short haul to the camp which was adjacent to the then open Pen-y-chain Station.

This route had been well used by the 'Princess Royals' as far as Bangor on their trains to Holyhead, and although the route from Bangor down to the camp had previously not been used by such large engines, the distance was not too far and so no great problems of gauge were encountered. She was photographed at Bangor on 4th May 1963 behind Ivatt Class 4 2-6-0 43052 which took on water at this point.

Once at Pen-y-chain she was placed in a siding adjacent to the camp main car park from the end of which, with buffer stop removed, she was later winched along a temporary track laid by B.R. permanent way engineers with her movement controlled by fitters from Crewe works.

This not too easy route had been previously surveyed by B.R. staff and drawings produced to prove that negotiable radii for a locomotive of such large wheelbase could in fact be laid with the railtrack across the car park, alongside the boating lake, and up a sharp slope in order to get to the desired location where a concrete plinth had been prepared some 500 yards from B.R. metals and alongside a children's play area. The movement into position employed some 30 British Railways permanent way and mechanical fitting staff for a whole week, and the location was to remain her home for just over the next decade.

A.B.Macleod remembers;

"I can recollect going up there and spending several days with the District Civil Engineer, and a large group of platelayers. The method employed to move the loco was as follows. The engineer pegged out a route to the plinth and levelled the ground as much as possible. Then about 6 lengths of temporary sleepered track (with a reduced number of sleepers) was laid in turn, and coupled to the end of track and 6203 was uncoupled from the tender and the connecting rods and valve rear removed and placed on the tender. The side (coupling) rods remaining on 6203. She was pinchbarred (car shifter) about a foot at a time onto the bits of temporary track, which was lifted afterwards and brought forward, a most laborious business, until the engine was in position for static

Left: After arrival at Derby Carriage and Wagon Works 'Princess Margaret Rose' was placed on exhibition at the Horticultural Society Show on 16th August 1975 alongside the original gas-turbine driven prototype of the Advanced Passenger Train.   *Brian Radford*

Left: On display at Swanwick Junction soon after the Midland Railways Trust line was opened.   *Brian Radford*

Below Left: The frames of 46203 are positioned on stands with all the wheelsets removed for axlebox metalling. The front bogie truck stands in the foreground. *Howard Routledge*

Below Right: The frames now rewheeled stand in the workshops at Butterley Park together with the tender frames on adjacent road on February 5th 1989.   *Howard Routledge*

display on the plinth. This process was also used to move the tender and couple it to the loco. The motion was replaced by some fitters who came from Crewe for the purpose.

After that I remember supplying Butlins with 2 suits of L.M.S. special uniforms and caps for the engine crews who were retired men from the motive power dept . . . ."

Visitors to the camp during this period were able to climb into the cab of 'Princess Margaret Rose' by means of special timber footsteps and on occasions meet former retired drivers who would explain the workings of the locomotive and reminisce about their days on the footplate of this and other locomotives. These ex-drivers also carried the caretaker duties on 6203 for several years; mechanical parts were oiled and cleaned and she was able to retain a smart appearance thanks to their efforts.

This arrangement could not last forever however and one of the last tasks that these men did was to paint the outside motion with thick aluminium paint knowing that without some protection or regular oiling rust would soon destroy the polished shine. Years later this paint took many hours of hard work to remove but it had certainly done its job well and the motion was in excellent condition underneath.

6203 remained as a visitor attraction at Pwllheli but as time passed her condition deteriorated to such an extent that she had become less of an attraction and was likely to become an expensive maintenance liability within a relatively short period.

We have felt it worth recording here the complete saga of the final disposal of the various Butlins locomotives including 6203, and the particular involvement of the late Geoffrey Sands, former shed master at Stoke and Crewe North M.P.D.s who resigned from B.R. service in 1970 and became manager of Alan Bloom's Bressingham Steam Museum.

During a visit which was suggested by Dr John Scholes, then Curator of Historical Relics for the Transport Commission, to the then recently closed East Lincolnshire line to look for items for Bressingham, he was passing the Butlin Holiday Camp at Skegness where he knew No. 6100 'Royal Scot' was displayed. In his position at Crewe North, No. 6100 was a locomotive he must have had contact with many times and so he thought it a good idea to 'renew old acquaintances'. On speaking to the camp manager he was given the impression that the main line locomotives in Butlins ownership were becoming somewhat of a liability as far as the camp managers were concerned and it was suggested to Geoff Sands that he contact the Board of Directors with a view to release of 'Royal Scot' to Bressingham Museum for display and where it could be looked after by people who 'knew about engines'.

This was duly done and precipitated the decision by Butlins to release all the locomotives in their ownership to appropriate museums.

Following a visit by a Butlin Director to Bressingham, Alan Bloom and Geoff Sands were told they could have their choice for Bressingham.

No. 6100 'Royal Scot' and No. 6233 'Duchess of Sutherland' were selected, they being relatively easy to extract from the camps and of historical interest. With regard to the other six Butlin engines, Alan Bloom suggested that The Transport Trust should be consulted and used to assist in allocating the remaining locomotives.

In the meantime Bressingham set up the removal of Nos. 6100 and 6233 from their respective camps, 'Duchess of Sutherland' being at Ayr in Scotland.

The terms of the agreement between Butlins and Bressingham was agreed as to be the same as the agreements for the locomotives there from the National Collection. These were on a 'permanent loan' basis which had been initiated by John Scholes as a method of safeguarding a number of locomotives in B.R. ownership. This action by him undoubtedly saved a number of locomotives in the 1960s, now thankfully in the national collection, from the cutters torch.

'Royal Scot' was moved to Bressingham to be followed by 'Duchess of Sutherland'. Word had quickly spread about the disposal of locomotives and a problem then arose with 'Duchess of Sutherland' while she was en-route by rail from Ayr to the railhead close to Bressingham, when another interested party tried to gain custodianship. To try and resolve this Butlins offered No. 6203 to Bressingham, but this was declined on the basis that they had an agreement, and in any case No. 6203 was going to be extremely expensive and difficult to extract from Pwllheli; and so No. 6233 eventually arrived at Bressingham.

The interest and clamour created by the enthusiast and preservation movement had taken Butlins by surprise and they quickly realised that these locomotives were extremely valuable assets in the long term and they therefore wanted to change the terms from a permanent free loan to a fixed period loan.

The Bressingham Museum was put under pressure by Butlins to change the terms of the agreement but Alan Bloom stood fast and insisted that Butlins honour their permanent loan agreement with him, which they eventually did, but as for the remaining locomotives, for which the Transport Trust had already invited those interested parties to apply and had arranged inspection, Butlins declined to agree to the permanent loan basis and withdrew the two large locomotives Nos. 6203 and 6229, at Pwllheli and Minehead from disposal.

A permanent loan agreement was signed between Butlins and Alan Bloom in 1970 for the two large locomotives plus an ex-L.S.W.R. B4 Dock Tank from Skegness and L.B.S.C.R. 'Terrier' tank No. 32662 'Martello' from Ayr.

Ivatt 2-6-0 43052 hauls 46203 dead into Caernarvon station on 4th May 1963 on her way to Butlins at Pwllheli.

E.N.Kneale

The same train sets off from Caernarvon, past No. 3 signal box after 43052 had taken water and 6203 had been 'examined' to ensure she was not running hot.
E.N. Kneale

Leaving Caernarvon behind 43052 the specially marshalled train proceeds towards Pwllheli and 6203's new home.
E.N. Kneale

Close-up of one of the nameplates of 'Princess Margaret Rose' which were to remain on the locomotive during the whole of her twelve years at Pwllheli.

D.A. Anderson

After a period in which nothing happened in the early 1970s and the dust was allowed to settle, Mr. David Ward of British Rail, who had been party to the agreements with Bressingham was asked directly by Butlins for advice on the disposal of the remaining locomotives. Butlins Director, Mr. T.H. North, being deputed to sort out this matter, met David Ward at Euston who recommended that No. 6229 go to the National Railway Museum, No. 6203 to the Midland Railway Centre, and 32640 go to an appropriate private railway with a good reputation.

The allocation of No. 6229 to the National Railway Museum raised a storm of protest in Scotland because all the locomotives with Scottish names were going to be based in England. However the protests were in vain and disposal was arranged in accordance with David Ward's recommendations.

Inspections to assess the condition of the locomotives, which by now had all stood in the open, close to the sea with its corrosive elements, in some cases for ten years and more, had been arranged, at David Ward's instigation, with Mr. Bill Harvey former shedmaster at Norwich doing some of these inspections.

The findings were very encouraging, and although a large amount of work was required on most of the locomotives to return them to working order, the appraisal was that this work was within the scope of the railway preservation movement which was rapidly gaining knowledge and expertise at various preservation centres and railway locations.

It was entirely due to Mr. David Ward, and Mr. T.H. North of Butlins that the Midland Railway Company Limited, as the Midland Railway Trust was then known, was formally offered the loan of No. 6203 'Princess Margaret Rose' on 19th April 1974.

The Chairman of the Midland Railway Company, Mr. J. Twells and Vice Chairman, Mr. J.B. Radford (one of the authors of this book) visited the headquarters of Butlins Ltd. in Oxford Street, London in April/May 1974 and the conditions of a free loan of 6203 for a period of twelve years, subject to the M.R. Company bearing the full cost of moving the locomotive from Pwllheli to the Midland Railway Centre at Butterley were approved by the Board of the Midland Railway on 27th June 1974 and eventually formally signed on 13th January 1975

after clarification of some of the terms and conditions.

No. 6229 'Duchess of Hamilton' moved to the National Railway Museum at York and was restored to full working order, subsequently running numerous special trains on the main line following a partial overhaul at the ex-G.W.R. locomotive works at Swindon. This locomotive has recently had a heavy general overhaul carried out at the National Railway Museum's workshop at York, and has now taken up further limited main line duties once more.

As to 'Princess Margaret Rose', her future was about to take a dramatic turn and she was to be taken into the custody of enthusiasts who would look after her every need.

Footnote:

The recollections of Mr. A.B. Macleod in this chapter in respect of the reasons for preserving 46203 are most interesting. During the latter stages of the writing of this book following a large amount of correspondence with many enthusiasts for the gathering of information appertaining to 'Princess Margaret Rose' correspondence was received relating to the 21" gauge locomotives formerly owned by Butlins and mentioned by Mr. A.B. Macleod in his letter. 6201 'Princess Elizabeth' he referred to was one of a pair of locomotives built in 1938 (makers nos. D611 and D612) for Billy Butlin by Messrs Hudswell Clarke & Company Ltd. at their Railway Foundry in Leeds.

The second engine of the two was no other then 6203 'Princess Margaret Rose'! Both were diesel/steam outline representations of their big sisters. i.e. they were not live steam but had diesel engines, in their case 32½ h.p. Dorman diesel engines. Their aesthetic outlines were exceptionally accurate reproductions of 'Princess Royals' to a scale of between half and one third size.

They were originally shown to the public at the Glasgow Empire Exhibition of 1938, where they ran on a half mile track, and advertised the Butlins organisation. After the exhibition 'Princess Elizabeth', painted in L.M.S. red livery, went to Butlins holiday camp at Skegness,

46203 with her motion and coupling rods 'smartened up' with a coat of silver paint, stands on display next to the children's playground at Butlins' holiday camp.
Butlins Ltd

Little and Large - over two and a half decades have passed since the two Princesses were together at Pwllheli as 46203 is re-united with the 21 inch gauge diesel version of her, built in Leeds in 1938 by Messrs Hudswell Clarke & Co. Ltd for Butlins. The photo was taken on 24th February 1991 outside the workshop at Butterley as the diesel engine on the miniature was started for the first time in many years.
Robin Stewart-Smith

whilst 'Princess Margaret Rose' finished untypically in L.N.E.R. green, went to Clacton camp then to Ayr and eventually on to Pwllheli, by which time she had been renamed 'Queen Elizabeth' by applying a thin steel nameplate over the original brass one.

It is therefore now obvious why, having been denied the opportunity to purchase 'Princess Elizabeth' the second choice offered to the then Sir Billy Butlin of 'Princess Margaret Rose' was accepted.

The story of these two 21" gauge engines did not end there however. The correspondent who passed the information to Brell Ewart told him that as far as he knew the two engines had been sent, sometime in the late 1960s/early 1970s for repair to J.H. Rundle, a company in East Anglia who did work for Butlins on a contract basis. On stripping down '6201' an estimate for overhaul costs was prepared and sent to Butlins but apparently because the costs were so high, it was cheaper for Butlins to have some new locomotives made (this time to an American diesel outline we believe) rather than continue with the repair. Butlins relaid their tracks at the same time to 2 ft. gauge. The two 'Princess Royal' locomotives were then dumped 'round the back' in the yard of J.H. Rundle. Here they remained, one in a stripped down state and the other complete, for several more years until a local motor dealer from Whaploade eventually persuaded J.H. Rundle to part with them, the yard having we assume arranged to keep them as part of their deal with Butlins. The motor dealer moved them to his yard in the mid seventies where they remained untouched and rapidly became overgrown with brambles.

Fortunately our correspondent had kept in his records the location of this yard. Following some investigative work, Brell Ewart traced the yard and went to see if they were still there. Amazingly in the front of this yard stood No. 6203 'Princess Margaret Rose' and in a stripped down state in the rear of the vast yard, completely overgrown with nettles and brambles, the dismembered remains of No. 6201 'Princess Elizabeth', partly buried upside down in the mud, together with three passenger carrying vehicles and an amount of rail.

Constructive discussions followed with the owner and, following purchase of the whole lot by Brell Ewart, the two locomotives were moved to the Midland Railway Centre on 23rd/24th February 1991.

After being unloaded by the 10 ton steam crane at Butterley, 6203 was placed on a short length of track outside the main restoration shed where the full size 46203 was in her winter accommodation. That day the locomotive department, who had restored 46203 to working order managed to get the diesel engine running in the 'baby' 6203 a good many years since it last ran.

At the time of writing plans are well in hand for the full restoration of these two historic locomotives and the establishing of a 21 gauge line running around the main Butterley Park site.

Brell Ewart later described the finding of the 21" gauge 'Princess Margaret Rose' as "like uncovering a miniature Picasso painting in the loft".

It is a quite remarkable story which only developed as a result of the research being carried out for this book, and it is amazing that the two engines, so closely related, should have taken turns in the course of time to save each other from extinction and it must be a unique event in the annals of railway locomotive lore.

CHAPTER FIVE

6203 COMES TO THE MIDLAND RAILWAY CENTRE

Now that an agreement had been reached between Butlins and the Midland Railway Company there came the difficult organisation of the operation to recover 6203 from Pwllheli and get her to the Midland Railway Centre.

During her time at Pwllheli she had not moved from the concrete plinth which had been her resting place for over ten years. Initial appraisal of the task outlined two alternatives, one by road and the other by rail.

Within the camp, although movement by road transporter was impossible, it was still possible to reverse the movements made when the locomotive had been delivered in 1963, by laying temporary track in sections from the plinth, along a route past the boating lake and across the car park to a position where a temporary connection could be made to the main line at the former Pen-y-chain station, by now out of use and with the former loop at the station removed. This involved a move of some 500 yards.

However, for the move to Derby over British Railways tracks, a return over the original route to Crewe via Afon Wen and Caernarvon was no longer possible since during the intervening period the line had been closed by B.R. One alternative route only was available which involved the line to Barmouth, Dovey Junction, Machynlleth, Welshpool, Shrewsbury, and Crewe and from there to Derby via Stoke-on-Trent.

B.R. were approached and the Divisional Manager at Stoke-on-Trent agreed to look at this route and the need to split and slew the line at Pen-y-chain, which would have to be done early on a Sunday morning in order for 'Princess Margaret Rose' to regain B.R. metals without interruption to normal B.R. services. Mr Tom Carr, the Divisional Freight Officer at Stoke was the main contact, but the Divisional Civil Engineer, Mr Noel Glennon, and the Divisional Planning Manager, Mr Joe Cairns were also deeply involved. Apart from the slewing, other problems involved the clearances at the various sta-

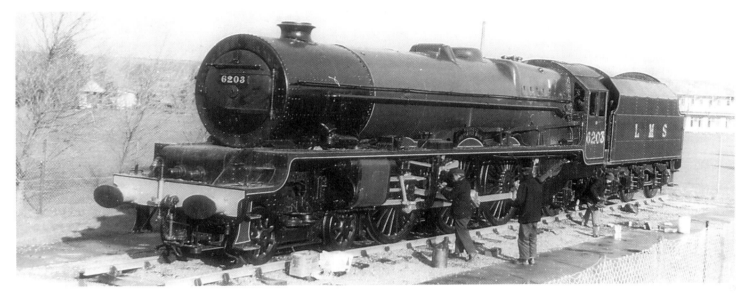

Above: The first working party begins the onerous task of recovering 6203 from the plinth at Butlins Pwllheli holiday camp on 25th January 1975.   *Joe Carver*

Left: The end of the first day as the working party pose in front of 6203 having recovered the nameplates and front numberplate for safe keeping.   *Brian Radford*

tions and tunnels particularly at Aberdovey (Penhelig), and the axle loading on various overbridges and structures such as the wooden viaduct at Barmouth. In addition the overhead 25 kV wires in the Crewe and Stoke areas would have to isolated, because of insufficient overhead clearances, whilst the locomotive passed.

In all the move was fraught with difficulties and it would have been easily justifiable for B.R. to have said that the only available route by rail was not possible due to the engineering problems. However, the decision was made that the move over the route could go ahead, and the enormous task of planning it with B.R began.

So far as the move through the camp was concerned the Midland Railway Company initially approached the management at Crewe Works for assistance with the locomotive mechanical part of the exercise, it being Crewe who had carried out this duty when 6203 originally went to Pwllheli, and the 275 Squadron of the Central Volunteer H.Q., Royal Corps of Transport at Bedford were asked if they could help in the actual recovery. Both found themselves unable to help, the latter because the exercise would have taken longer than the four days at their disposal, and so the Midland Railway Company had the problem to solve all by themselves.

During the period that 6203 had stood on the plinth at Pwllheli, copper thieves had cut off some of the lubrication pipework and undone and removed others. Evidence of this was found in the nuts, studs, and pipeclips left on the plinth where they had fallen during the illicit operation. Thankfully the original nameplates, which had remained on 6203 during the whole of her time at Pwllheli, were left untouched. Had the thieves known the value of these they would undoubtedly have been the first items to disappear.

The B.R. requirements for the preparation of the locomotive were determined and on 25th January 1975 a party of ten volunteers from the Midland Railway Company journeyed to Pwllheli to confirm that the company could in fact move the locomotive using its own volunteers, and during the visit the preparation of 6203 for her journey began.

Naturally one of the main concerns of the B.R. Mechanical Inspectors was the lubrication of moving parts: the last thing that anyone wanted was for 6203 to 'run hot' on her journey, and so assessment of temporary replacement pipework had to be made. Axles and axleboxes were found to be in good condition and by using small jacks and 'Atlas' movers, the locomotive was gradually and so slowly moved over a distance of some 8½ inches in the afternoon. Still 495 yards, 27½", or thereabouts to go!

Concentrating on lubrication, the axlebox lubricator was removed for overhaul in Derby and both nameplates were taken off for safe keeping. After the compulsory group photos the group returned to Derby, tired but elated with the knowledge that, although difficult, the job could actually be done by themselves.

On the second visit on 8th February all axlebox underkeeps were removed, oilpads cleaned, inspected and serviced and the axlebox lubricator refitted after its Derby overhaul. Liberal quantities of oil and grease were then fed to all parts of the locomotive including the motion until evidence of its arrival at crucial locations showed up. Another essential requirement for the move was an operational handbrake, and so the tender brake was stripped and made serviceable again.

For the next visit, the temporary track panels, eight in number and twenty feet long, had to be made up at the Midland Railway Centre at Butterley and delivered to site by 9 a.m. on 22nd February where they were unloaded. Two panels placed behind the locomotive enabled the locomotive to be moved backwards by hand in order to enable the track on her plinth to be slewed to the correct direction of movement before further panels were added to it to take the tightly curved alignment necessary to miss the edge of the boating lake and align 6203 with the main camp through road.

Upon moving the locomotive forward again the piston valves refused to move; unbeknown to the team of volunteers, some of the thousands of children that must have climbed all over her in the years at Pwllheli had put handfuls of ballast and other loose fittings such as the

Inches at a time, 6203 is moved forward on the temporary track laid by volunteers on 22nd February 1975, haulage being provided by a tractor.

M.R. Trust Archive

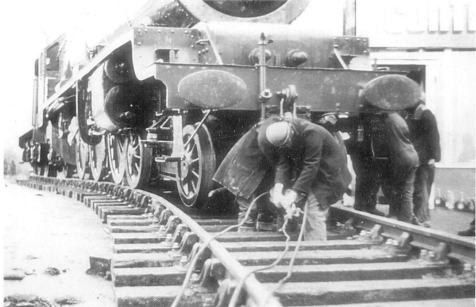

Above: 6203 is eased past the side of the Empire Theatre on the temporary track laid along the main road through the camp.
M.R. Trust Archive

Left: Slight hitch as the volunteers endeavour to re-rail the leading bogie wheel which had become derailed the weekend before.
Peter M. Stanley

Below: 6203 is hauled slowly past the Regency Bar on her way to the main car park of the camp.
M.R. Trust Archive

6203 reaches the main car park and the slewed track begins to turn her to the tender first position as required for the move back onto B.R. metals.

M.R. Trust Archive

smokebox dart and handles down the blastpipe and they had entered the steam chest jamming the valve. The first sign of this problem was when one of the combination levers achieved a somewhat curved posture, and so parts of the motion had to be stripped to facilitate further movement by isolating them. Bearing in mid that many Stanier locomotives had needle roller bearings in the motion joints, it was not suprising that the stripping of these, in a holiday camp, in the middle of winter resulted in the loss of a number of these minute rollers. This would be a replacement problem to be solved at some future date.

Two other problems arose; soft ground proved too difficult for the hand winch to overcome and also some rather thick tree branches, which had seemingly grown way beyond normal tree growth since 6203 passed down this route in 1962, fouled the required clearance necessary for passing. The latter was soon overcome by some rather delicate but deliberate woodcraft. The soft ground resulted in a change of plan and for the next working party on 1st/2nd March, two Fordson tractors with rear winches were relieved of local beach duties and hired to enable further movement of the locomotive to proceed. Proceed it did, and on a 1 in 7 downward slope this method proved the working party's undoing, for a few unwatchable seconds 6203 quite gracefully proceeded, slowly gaining momentum directly towards the boating lake, until she derailed her leading bogie wheels. It is unlikely that a Stanier Pacific had ever become derailed at a more opportune moment.

A phone call to the Midland Railway Company Locomotive Superintendent, Mr Eric Riley, was answered by the assurance that one and a half hours work would see her on the track again and so it was to prove, for on the following weekend 6203 was re-railed after only twenty minutes, and after easing the slope by jacking and secure packing of the track panel, she was on the move again, one tractor at the rear and one at the front, slowly reeling her in!

Each time a wheel looked like unloading itself and mounting the rail, the track was jacked up to meet the tread once more. As the locomotive moved slowly forwards of course, the track panels behind had to be dismantled and then reassembled in front; a time consum-

ing task indeed. By close of play on Sunday, 9th March 'Princess Margaret Rose' had reached the crossroads where the road from the camp entrance passed over a humped back bridge over the boating lake and then crossed 6203's route and on into the camp at right angles.

While 6203 remained in this position between the weekend movement periods, a most amusing incident occurred. Each Tuesday, the Pwllheli Fire Brigade, all part-timers, held a practice in the area to check time from call out to arrival on the site of the supposed fire. Unbeknown to the M.R. Co., the location chosen for 11th March was Butlins Red Camp, on the seaward side of the road that 6203 was on. It takes little imagination to picture the scene as said the fire brigade aboard their fire engine, bell ringing, approached the hump-backed bridge at a high rate of knots and, breasting the brow of the bridge, the driver suddenly became aware of one of the largest and heaviest steam locomotives to run of British Railways in the shape of a Stanier 'Princess Royal' class Pacific named 'Princess Margaret Rose', blocking his route! "Hell, there's an engine coming over the level crossing!" he shouted, braking violently and throwing his fellow firemen unceremoniously in the direction of the front of their vehicle.

He soon saw however that there was in fact no track in front of 6203 and that she was stationary, and with remarkable presence of mind, he accelerated around her front end and reached the practice destination with little actual delay. An unlikely tale for them to relate to their children and possibly grandchildren one presumes.

Overall the volunteers felt that progress was good, but further obstacles were in store, for at a further meeting between the M.R. Company and B.R Representatives at Stoke, it was requested that the locomotive be turned through 180 degrees before being presented to the B.R. track thus being tender first to B.R. and smokebox first for hauling away from Pen-y-chain. Although a fairly simple and understandable request, this presented the volunteers with a large problem, but without complaint on 15th/16th March, the laborious operation of turning her commenced, using the camp car park as the working area.

By laying the track panels on a curve to the remotest corner of the

car park and then by slewing the track behind her and subseqently pulling her back and forth, she was slowly turned through the required angle to finish up parallel to the fencing separating the camp from the B.R. mainline. After each for and aft move the sections of rail had to be unkeyed and the sleepers re-aligned to enable the track to be curved in the opposite direction, a short piece of rail having to be trimmed off the curve at each end (which of course had been the longer outside rail on the preceding move!). It was during one of these shunts that the buffers of the locomotive were almost inside the camp indoor swimming pool in order to maximise the length of curved track available in the car park.

It was certainly a long and tedious operation with progress measured in degrees rather than the usual distance, but by Sunday 13th April 6203 was in her final position ready for the B.R. connection and movement.

She had been moved only a distance of some 500 yards through the camp, but had actually travelled over 1,200 yards due to her constant shunting backwards and forwards involving in all some 1,300 man hours of work. This had been a colossal undertaking for a small group of volunteers and was made all the more praiseworthy by the fact that the cost had been reduced from an estimated £3,000 to just £950, most of which had been expended on the hire of the Fordson Tractors.

The movement to Derby was scheduled to commence at 08.00 on Sunday, May 11th, but some final preparation work was needed laying the final link-up section of temporary track to receive the slewed end of the B.R. mainline, the connection being due to take place at 04.00 that day. The final working party on Saturday busied themselves with this work before retiring into the camp accommodation ready to be woken at the unearthly hour of 3.45 a.m.!

By 04.00 the early morning light found a large gang of volunteers working alongside the B.R. permanent way gang clearing away ballast and slewing across the track. A short section had been left out of the temporary track and when the last two lengths had been bolted to the B.R. track these make-up pieces were cut and laid in.

By 06.00 all was ready and Class 24 diesel No. 24053 which had arrived at Pwllheli the previous day with the wagons and brakevans, coupled on to 6203 with one tube wagon and a brakevan between the locomotives, and with no fuss 'Princess Margaret Rose' was hauled backwards onto the B.R. tracks and moved into the station platform at Pen-y-chain so that the task of slewing the main line back again could begin. The job was to then dismantle the temporary track, cut it into sections and reinstate the ground levels and boundary fence. With the main line now intact again, the class 24 propelled 6203 together with the tube wagon and brakevan forwards to join up with

A brief check around 6203 after the train had been re-marshalled at Cricceth and the train locomotive, 24053, positioned at the front with a freight brakevan and with a further tubewagon and brakevan at the rear.
Peter M. Stanley

The train passes Minffordd with one of the Ffestiniog Railway's double Fairlie locomotives posed on the overbridge that carries their line over the B.R. lines. *Peter M. Stanley*

The special train skirts the Cambrian coastline south of Barmouth on the way to Towyn.
Peter M. Stanley

the other tube wagon and brakevan standing to the south of the point of disconnection to complete the formation of the special '9X98' train.

One minute late, at 08.01, the diesel set off propelling the train, with 6203 now between the tube wagons and brakevans, towards Cricceth where the diesel was to run round ready to haul the train all the way to Shrewsbury.

6203 had so far moved without any problems, but there was still a very long way to go before Derby was reached.

The train left Cricceth at 08.51, nine minutes early and continued towards Portmadoc where one of the Ffestiniog Railway's double Fairlies was posed on the overbridge, making a very noticeable contrast in the relative sizes of the two locomotives.

On now over a few bridges which B.R. were obviously concerned about judging by the presence of civil engineering staff lurking on the banks of streams passing under the line which had hitherto only carried G.W.R. 'Manor' class locomotives as an absolute limit in axle loadings and weights.

Along the coast skirting Harlech Castle the train ran nine minutes early, until it came to a dead stand at Barmouth for a further examination at 10.16. One of the main concerns with 6203 having stood for such a long time in the camp, outside, open to the elements and without regular attention, was the lubrication of moving parts and B.R. were concerned not to let her 'run hot'; and such regular stops were to be made for mechanical inspection and a 'feel' round. The inspection

Above: Passing through Barmouth shortly before a stop for an examination of 6203.
Alan Bullock

Left: Just beyond Barmouth station 6203 receives a careful exam to ensure that all is well. Further oil was applied at each stop to ensure continued good running.
Brian Radford

at Barmouth revealed all was well and she was running cool with no problems.

Off again at 10.40 along the coastline towards Barmouth Viaduct which was the object of some understandable concern with its wooden piling and with wooden ties and planking for most of its considerable length. However apart from some creaking and groaning emanating from beneath, 6203 slowly inched her way at 5 m.p.h. across the viaduct and safely reached Morfa Mawddach on the other shore.

Then followed a fine run along the coast through Fairbourne, Llwyngwril, Llangelynin, Torfanau, and on to Tywyn, home of the Talyllyn Railway where a crowd had gathered and cheered as 'Princess

Margaret Rose' sneaked under a very low bridge which was under repair with rather less than a comfortable clearance.

The Aberdovey tunnels, four in all, presented the next clearance problem, and here again 5 miles an hour was the order of the day. Viewed from the leading brakevan it did rather look like threading a big cork through the neck of only a slightly larger bottle!. All was well however and 6203 emerged into the sunlight at the end of the last tunnel still intact and having cleared the walls by at least an inch or two. It should perhaps be mentioned that the line is single track and therefore tunnel clearances are not quite so generous as on double track lines.

A group of four scenes showing 6203 on her way to Derby:

Top: After leaving Barmouth No.6203 edges past a house before crossing the estuary.　　　　　　　　　　　*Brian Radford*

Bottom: Running along the picturesque coastline near Penhelig before turning inland and through Dovey Junction.　　　　　　*Brian Radford*

On along the beautiful coast with its superb scenery, through Penhelig, Abertafol, and Gogarth to where the line curves inland to join the line from Aberystwyth at Dovey Junction, passed only four minutes behind booked time. On then without a pause to Machynlleth to a rousing welcome from about a hundred or so locals including a Sunday School party, local railwaymen and children of all ages from five to fifty-five and more! Here the footplate was again invaded by a constant stream of young enthusiasts all keen to savour a footplate visit on this titan of the tracks.

6203 was again examined for warm bearings and a clean bill of health was given by B.R. which reflected well on the Midland Railway team under the leadership of Locomotive Superintendent Eric Riley.

Whilst here the party took the opportunity to view at close quarters the M.R. Company President's Midland carriage parked in the carriage shed. This was one of the two rail motors built in 1904 for the Morecambe—Heysham line, and converted later to a General Superintendents Service Saloon. This vehicle is now in the National Railway Museum at York.

Back to 6203 and off exactly to time after an oil up and check round the locomotive. Talerddig Bank was the next passing point and the inclines here played havoc with the motive power which had been under almost constant load since 08.00 at an unusually low speed. No. 24053 showed a marked unwillingness to pull hard up the bank and before reaching Caersws the train came to a dead stand while the train crew attempted to reset the regulator trips. The problem was solved with assistance from a B.R. fitter in the Midland Railway team who rectified the problem and 24053 sprang back into life.

After a pause of some fifteen minutes, the train moved off and Welshpool was reached some eighteen minutes behind schedule where a further stop for mechanical examination to 6203 again revealed the 'Princess' to be running trouble free. Again well-wishers had gathered to witness what was likely to be the one and only visit of a 'Princess Royal' class on the line.

Seven minutes later the train set off again heading through Westbury and on to Sutton Bridge Junction via the Shrewsbury loop line into Abbey Foregate, where 24053 finally decided to give up the struggle

for the time being in spite of the road being set up to cross the main line with all signals pulled off!

The driver left to seek a replacement while the second man, with some assistance from one of the Midland railway party, endeavoured to get power again. Just in time 24053 saved her bacon, power was restored and, after a twenty minute delay, the train crossed into the sidings for the locomotive to run round for the haul tender first on to Crewe.

Away again, the special passed the station platform full of spectators, some twenty one minutes late, and ran through the station and on to Yorton, Wem, Prees, and Whitchurch to Willaston where the train came to a stand to await confirmation of the isolation of the overhead 25 kV electrified lines into Crewe Basford Hall sidings. Here, arrival was timed at 20.08, only some eight minutes late, after a journey of some 158 miles and over 12 hours, a superb achievement.

Here a reception party from Crewe Diesel Depot arrived to 'Check over' this local product and to ensure that she was being treated correctly by these 'Derby types'. Again 6203 was examined and then oiled round and greased, all to the immense satisfaction of the Crewe men. The whole ensemble then took the opportunity to visit the B.R. Staff Association club for a quick bite to eat and a welcome pint of best bitter.

24053, having done sterling work, had left the train on arrival at Basford Hall sidings, and shortly before the final leg of the journey was to commence, Class 25 Bo-Bo diesel-electric locomotive No. 25267 arrived with a fresh crew and was coupled up.

The train was moved down to Basford Hall south sidings ready to pass under the 'dumps', a line going under the main line and joining the Crewe—Derby line to the south of the carriage sheds. Prompt at 22.50 the train moved off, threading its way across the sidings, underneath the main West Coast main line, and onto the North Stafford line where good time was made to Kidsgrove and a further halt was necessary to ensure the overhead wires were again switched out and isolated through Stoke.

On now through Kidsgrove and Etruria to Stoke-on-Trent, where the darkness was punctuated by the flashbulbs from a bevy of onlookers

gathered on the platform as the special passed along the middle road, and then on to Caverswall for the final stop and examination. Coming to a stand in total darkness the night was suddenly lit up by more flashbulbs from linesiders still intent on witnessing this historic event and recording it for their own personal collections; even at nearly mid-night such was the interest in this famous locomotive. Those on the train only hoped that the photographers could see something of what they were photographing as the night was ink black.

Cresswell and Uttoxeter were next on the itinerary, the latter being passed at 00.42, with a solitary figure witnessing the event, followed by Tutbury (01.02), North Stafford Junction (01.36), L.N.W. Junction (01.20), Derby London Road Junction at 01.36 and the down goods

lines at the back of Derby Station to a welcome from a solitary figure racing along Platform 6.

The train was then propelled directly into Derby Carriage and Wagon Works, and with a quick collection of all belongings, all the party piled into the rear cab of 25267 for a trip across the lines to Derby No. 4 Shed and the end of a truly excellent day which would be remembered by all for many years to come. Eight weary people and two nameplates then disappeared to make their way home.

This complex operation could not have been carried out at all without the splendid co-operation from Messrs Butlins in respect of movements and facilities given within the camp at Pwllheli, and the various departments of British Railways particularly the freight of-

Facing page top: Another exam in progress at
Machynlleth before the climb up the bank to
Welshpool.   *Brian Radford*

Right: It is now four o'clock in the afternoon
as 6203 pauses yet again, this time at
Welshpool, to ensure all bearings are cool and
to apply even more oil!   *Brian Radford*

Right: 6203, now being hauled tender first by
24053, approaches Shrewsbury station, the
platform end being crowded with enthusiasts.
                            Brian Radford

Facing page bottom: Partway up Talerddig
Bank the train locomotive decided to give up
the struggle having hauled 6203 at quite a
slow speed all the way from Pen-y-chain. She
was coaxed back into life by fitters in the M.R.
group.   *Brian Radford*

ficer of Stoke Division, Tom Carr, the planning officer Joe Cairns,
and Noel Glennon of the civil engineer's department at Shrewsbury,
and also the permanent way gang who left their beds at an unearthly
hour and travelled by road to Pen-y-chain to carry out the slewing which
proceeded the official movement itself.

The total cost of the operation to the Midland Railway Company,
including inspection fees and overhead isolation was £1,818.99. A complete record of this historic journey forms appendix 7.

'Princess Margaret Rose' remained in Derby Carriage and Wagon
works and was on show there on 16th August 1975 at the annual works
horticultural society show and was then moved for display at the
Locomotive Works for their 29th horticultural society open day on

30th August 1975.

6203 was eventually moved to the Midland Railway Centre, Butterley in two stages, being towed from Derby to Toton by Class 25
Bo-Bo No. 25163 on 4th November 1975 and on the following day
she completed the journey from Toton to Butterley behind class 20
Bo-Bo No. 20076.

Once on MRT metals she was moved from Codnor Park Junction
up the line to Butterley Station using the Butterley Works shunter named 'Teucer'.

She was now at her new home after a truly epic journey and a new
chapter of her life was about to start, some forty years after she had
first entered service.

CHAPTER SIX

RETURN TO STEAM

At the Midland Railway Centre 6203 created much interest and she was put on static display, still in L.M.S. livery but with dummy painted nameplates on in lieu of the highly valued originals which were securely stored away.

Having the locomotive at homebase permitted a much closer examination, and allowed the locomotive department time to carry out some repair work to the tender and boiler cladding, the upkeep of the locomotive being part of the agreement between the Midland Railway Company and Butlins.

On 31st July 1976, 6203 was visited at Butterley by an old acquaintance, Bishop Eric Treacy, who had accepted an invitation to open the Midland Railway's 'Rail-Ex 76' at Gregory's Rose Gardens, Stapleford. He pronounced himself delighted with the opportunity to once more sit on the footplate of a locomotive he had travelled on and photographed in action quite brilliantly during her active life with the L.M.S. and B.R., and he used the opportunity to take another of his inimitable shots. In a letter to Brian Radford on 7th August 1976 he wrote, "I was glad to meet the lads at Butterley who keep an eye on things." He enclosed a photograph taken on his visit and gave his permission for his action photographs of 'Princess Margaret Rose' to be used by the Trust without a reproduction fee.

During this period 6203 was fitted with replacements for some of the parts that had been stolen since her last steaming, some thirteen years earlier, cab windows and seats being among these. The smokebox had been patched on top in her last years on B.R. this being a stop-gap repair to see her through the final months of service. Close inspection revealed that this large item would have to be replaced with a new one before any steaming could be contemplated.

All this work made 6203 very presentable and she proved to be a good attraction for the visitors to Butterley.

The term of the free loan was for twelve years and with the expiry

A beaming Bishop Eric Treacy leans out of the cab of 'Princess Margaret Rose' as he had done on a number of times before, but this time she was a static exhibit at Butterley station. *Brian Radford*

He then took a typical 'Treacy study' of her after chatting to 'the lads who look after her'. The date is 31st July 1976 and sadly this was to be their last meeting. *Eric Treacy*

Johnson and Stanier - a comparison of front ends, as Midland 4-2-2 673 built at Derby in 1897 lines up with Stanier 4-6-2 6203 'Princess Margaret Rose' built at Crewe in 1935, at the Midland Railway Centre in 1979.
Richard Stevens

date in the distant future little thought was given at this time to the outcome on the expiry of the agreement with Butlins except that the London Branch of the Trust opened a special bank account in support of the eventual purchase of the locomotive if and when that was offered.

Gradually, over a period of time, spent mainly in the carriage shed at Swanwick, 6203 lost her shine and became ready for a repaint, and in order to satisfy some demand, and also for a change, she was repainted in 1985 in unlined Brunswick Green with the B.R. No. 46203.

From the time she had arrived at Butterley in the custodianship of the Midland Railway Trust, it had always been the hope that one day 'Princess Margaret Rose' would be offered for sale by Butlins to the Trust, but being aware that she could easily be snatched from that custody by a very high financial bid, the Board of Directors of the Midland Railway Trust elected to remain publicly silent on this subject and hope that Butlins would honour their agreement and offer the Trust first refusal if and when the time came.

In November 1985 this happened. Butlins, who had now become part of Rank Holdings and Recreation, offered the Midland Railway Trust, as the Midland Railway Company had now become, an extension to the loan period until 28th January 1992 or alternatively a second option which was for the Trust to purchase the locomotive outright. The Trust were very keen to pursue the latter but it was not until September 1986 that Rank placed a value of £60,000 on their locomotive, it being their assessment of a fair market price taking into account all the work expended by the Trust and the cost and effort in getting the locomotive from Pwllheli to Butterley.

Rank had seemingly taken the trouble to consider their position carefully, as not only were they selling 6203 but also all of the other locomotives that had been acquired by Butlins some thirteen years earlier. During this intervening period the railway preservation scene had grown from a mere handful of sites and museums to a large widespread movement controlled in some cases by million pound plus plc companies, albeit these organisations not being integrated to any degree.

Rank realised that they owned, in these locomotives, assets which if put on the open market could realise a vast sum of money, but in doing this they would likely see the locomotives purchased as investments and the question had to be asked 'was this what they wanted ?' Also there were the agreements with the custodians, who had been selected very carefully in the early 1970s as being most suitable, which indicated that they would have first refusal should disposal by Butlins be considered.

It was therefore to the great credit of the Rank Organisation who

stood by their inherited agreements, in spite of tremendous pressure being applied by individuals, organisations and other interested parties, as well as the railway enthusiast press, that they offered first options to purchase to all the custodians. Those for 6203 and 6229 were accepted sometime before the ones for 6100 and 6233 which were more complex, both being at the same site on a permanent loan (as opposed to a fixed term loan), and having had large sums of money spent on them by Alan Bloom and the Bressingham Steam Museum.

However back to 6203, and following a meeting of the Midland Railway Trust Board of Directors, who had made a decision to purchase 6203, a formal letter of acceptance was sent to Messrs. Rank Organisation.

The Trust had requested a staged payment for the locomotive which Butlins had generously agreed to, further indicating their fair play in the matter, and a deposit of £10,000 was paid.

The Trust, who were by no means flush with money, then set about raising the balance of £50,000 which had to be paid to Rank no later than the end of October 1988. Despite a good start, with appeals to members of the Trust, enthusiasts and local business, it became clear that the amount required was not going to be forthcoming within the required timescale. The Trust's financial policy of no large-scale borrowing, which it had used and controlled its finances with since conceptio, was put under severe test, but the Board of Directors held firm and it looked as if 'Princess Margaret Rose' may well have to be foregone in the interests of the Trust as a whole until Brell Ewart, a Director of the Trust and long-time member offered to take over the purchase. Following the approval of Rank (who had insisted on protective clauses in the sales of the locomotives to prevent quick-resale and the potential of realising quick, large profits for the vendors), it was agreed that Brell Ewart take over the agreement with the proviso that 6203 should be permanently based at The Midland Railway Centre. As Brell Ewart had been a regular volunteer in the Trust's Locomotive Department and was part owner of British Railways standard tank Locomotive No. 80080, this condition was already the wish of Mr. Ewart, and was thus readily met.

The sale of the 'Butlins engines' had been greeted with considerable interest by railway enthusiasts and therefore when it became known that restoration to working order was going to start on 'Princess Margaret Rose', a new influx of additional volunteers joined the group of volunteers in the Locomotive Department at the Midland Railway Centre with a view to working specifically on her.

The work involved in returning 6203 to steam, the last of the Stanier Pacifics preserved by Butlins to be so dealt with, was a full heavy general overhaul i.e. a complete mechanical strip down with the boiler lifted off. Since the arrival of 6203 at the centre in 1975, cosmetic

Run past of locomotive stock heading for the carriage shed at Swanwick Junction and secure covered accommodation after an open day at Butterley, Midland Railway Centre in 1977. The locomotives are Fowler 0-6-0T 16440 in L.M.S. red livery, ex-Midland Railway Kirtley 2-4-0 No. 158A dating from 1866, and 'Princess Margaret Rose'.

Frank Ashley

repairs only had been done, the basic mechanical items had been kept cleaned and oiled but no other major work had been done. In the late seventies and throughout the eighties the Trust's locomotive department had been involved in the restoration of several ex-scrapyard locomotives which had been rebuilt and restored to a very high standard and allowed to run over B.R. metals. The experience gained on these would now prove invaluable in the work to be carried out on the largest project yet tackled — the restoration of 'Princess Margaret Rose'.

The locomotive department at the trust was based in Butterley Station Yard until the winter of 1987 when the move was made into new facilities at Swanwick, now called Butterley Park motive power depot. Here a new machine shop annexed onto a two road restoration shop, both constructed in new modern materials and fully insulated, complete with mess room, superintendent's office and locker room, was the new home for the department.

This machine shop has since been named 'The Richard Levick Machine Shop' in memory of Richard Levick, a gifted engineer and highly valued member of the Midland Railway Trust, who had been in the team that had recovered 6203 from Pwllheli and who had machined many of the items during the early stages of her restoration to working order. He tragically lost his life in a machine shop accident on 17th August 1989.

Although this was to be the location for the overhaul, the first item of work to be done on the 'Princess' was carried out in the large museum building where she had stood for some twelve months after being moved from the carriage shed which had been her home since arrival at the centre. This was the removal of the asbestos lagging from the outside of the boiler barrel which insulated the boiler. 6203 was standing on the adjacent road to ex-L.M.S. Class 4F 0-6-0 locomotive No. 4027, which also required the same treatment. A specialist firm was engaged to carry out this work, which had to be done under very strictly controlled conditions, and necessitated the erection of a large polythene cocoon round the boilers of the two engines.

When the asbestos was removed, close examination of the external condition of the boiler barrel was possible for the first time since 1958, when the boiler was fitted to the locomotive. The examination found it to be in excellent condition. The superheater elements and all tubes were removed from the boiler while the locomotive remained in the main museum building, the elements being in such good condition that they looked brand new, the makers name still readable on them. It seemed likely that these had been replaced at the last works visit and so had only seen a few thousand miles of traffic use.

In September 1988, the locomotive was moved from the museum building onto the ash pit to allow the tender to be split off, no easy task as it had last been separated from the engine in 1963 for the move through Butlin's camp at Pwllheli.

The engine was then moved into the new restoration shop to enable work to commence completely stripping the locomotive down to its frames — the first task once work starts on a heavy general overhaul. With 6203 this was much easier than compared with ex-Barry Scrapyard locomotives which had been left for many years open to the elements in a hostile atmosphere without any attention whatsoever, although 6203 herself had of course been in a seaside environment in the Butlins Camp.

The history of 6203 was always in the minds of the dedicated team, under the leadership of Mr. Eric Riley, the Trust's locomotive superintendent, as work progressed and certain items were looked for. The shear strips adjacent to the outside cylinders from the 1951/2 Derby repair were clearly visible. Traces of the fixing for the mechanical cylinder drain cocks replaced in 1956 by steam ones, were found, together with a number of platework repairs in the cab, smokebox and running plate, as would be expected on a locomotive of her age and mileage.

All of the platework on the cab and other individual items removed from the locomotive were shot-blasted down, revealing many layers of paint, but surprisingly no blue, for the maroon paint applied in the Crewe works paint shop prior to the movement to Pwllheli was the only paint found beneath those coats applied by the Midland Railway Trust during the 1985 re-livery to Brunswick Green.

The boiler was lifted off on 12th November 1988 using the Cowans Sheldon 50 ton crane No. RS1001/50 which is owned by the trust. This was the first time this boiler had been off since 1958 and the first time that a 'Princess Royal' boiler had been off since their main line careers had finished with British Railways.

The frames of 6203 were finally stripped by the end of 1988, and it was then very evident, that the locomotive was in remarkably good condition. The frames needed repairs only in the dragbox area, with only minor platework requiring replacement on the running plate. Many 'Lyons Maid' ice cream cartons and a number of sixpences were found under the cab floor, these being souvenirs that she had brought back from Pwllheli and her holiday camp days.

The tyres were measured and found to be almost brand new, and when cleaned by shotblasting they revealed a manufacturing date of August 1960 at the Steel Peach and Tozer's mill in Sheffield. These had been fitted to the wheelsets in late 1960 during the heavy intermediate overhaul and again from records have only officially done some few thousand traffic miles.

It was now clear that the whole condition of 6203 was exceptionally good, but this really is not surprising when analysed.

'Princess Margaret Rose' had been withdrawn from traffic early in the British Railways programme for steam displacement, being surplus to requirement even though having officially run only 6,000 miles since a heavy intermediate overhaul in Crewe works. This was basically due to her size and axle loadings thus limiting the route availability of the class as a whole for other lines and routes, and so she, like her sisters, was withdrawn as there was nowhere for them to be put to work, together with the fact that in any case the class had almost reached the end of its economic life of 30 years in accountancy terms.

The excellent condition extended to all mechanical items on the locomotive, and can be judged by the fact that the only mechanical parts requiring replacement were piston and piston valve rings, and seals in the cylinder drain cocks, the latter having hardened through age.

Several items were fitted new to replace missing items, these being some needle rollers from valve gear bearings which were probably lost at Pwllheli when part of the motion was stripped, and also springs in the cylinder relief valves which had been removed prior to the movement from Crewe works in 1963 to negate back pressure in the cylinders when she was being towed out of steam.

The whistle was another item which did not survive the period of time at Pwllheli, it being missing when 6203 arrived at Butterley. Fortunately soon after her arrival into the Midland Railway Trust's custodianship the whistle from No. 6206 'Princess Marie Louise' was donated by a Trust member.

The opportunity of re-metalling all the white metal bearing surfaces was taken in order that the locomotive would re-enter traffic with all bearings in new condition on the same date, even though some were in good condition having seen little traffic use.

On close inspection of the bogie truck when stripped, the white metal bearing surface on the left hand trailing axlebox showed that it had run hot at sometime. It was thought that this had happened during the move from Crewe to Pwllheli in 1963, as no overheating had been found during inspections on the return trip in 1975 and she was unlikely to have been running like that during her last days on B.R.

The tender tank had been lifted off the tender frames on the same day as the boiler had come off the engine frames, and this revealed a rather thin inner skirting on the inner frames and very poor front dragbox.

In today's theatre of operations for steam locomotives on the main lines of British Railways, examinations are carried out by British Rail Inspectors which allow the locomotive to run for the succeeding six months, with a full internal examination of the boiler in addition every seven years, this necessitating the removal of all tubes and fittings from the boiler and in most cases the removal of the boiler from the frames as well. This occasion gives opportunity for mechanical overhaul and other renewals to be carried out with the aim of keeping the locomotive within main line standards for the next seven years when further heavy maintenance can be carried out. So the decisions for renewal and maintenance of items are therefore related to whether the said item will last in acceptable condition for another seven years in service. In addition, it is often the case that if a particular item shows the need for possible replacement in the future, it is replaced when the locomotive is stripped because of ease of access and also saving time at a later date when the locomotive may be in service within its seven year certificate.

In the case of the tender the decision was taken to replace the inner skirts and this was best done by turning the frames upside down with the wheelsets removed, to allow easier access for rivetting the new skirts in place. This again involved the use of the 50 Ton Cowans Sheldon crane and when the initial lift was complete it revealed that replacement of the front drag box and brakeshaft bracket was also necessary. The original item in each case had been complicated steel castings, but it was not feasible to replace then with new castings which would have involved new patterns at very high cost and so fabricated steel items were made, the drag box being fabricated and welded in situ.

In service days most steam locomotive tender frames and associated steelwork were very prone to wastage due to the regular soaking receiv-

Now under new ownership, the restoration of 6203 begins in the Butterley Park museum building at Swanwick as the asbestos boiler clothing is removed, along with that on ex-L.M.S. 0-6-0 44027, by the specialist firm Asbestos Insulation Removers in September 1988.

Derby Evening Telegraph

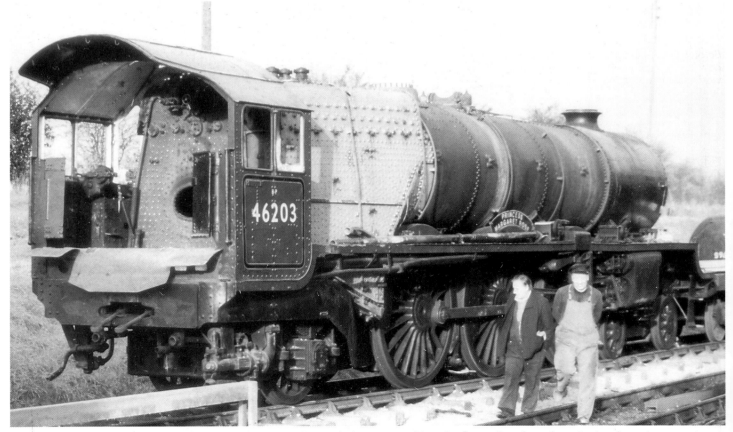

46203, now split from her tender, stands on the ash pit roads prior to being moved into the restoration shops for stripping down into constituent parts. The Trust's locomotive superintendent, Eric Riley and member Alan Porter walk thoughtfully away, perhaps contemplating the size of the task!

Brell Ewart

Above: The tender tank of 46203 is lifted clear of the frames so that the replacement work on the chassis can be done. *Brell Ewart*

Right: The boiler, now undergoing major repair, stands minus both its smokebox and front tubeplate so that essential work can be carried out. *Brell Ewart*

Below: The locomotive frames stand in the new heavy repair shop at Butterley Park as work on them continues in the summer of 1989. *Brell Ewart*

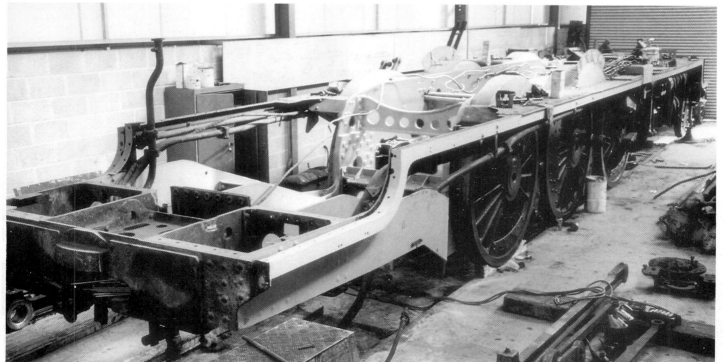

Left: The overhauled front bogie is positioned under the front end of 46203 so that the centre pin can be carefully guided into its location as the frames are lowered.
Robin Stewart-Smith

Facing Page Top: In the heavy repair shop the tender, now complete, stands ready for finishing off and the addition of the extra water tank, whilst to the right the shotblasted and primed cab stands ready to be re-united with the engine. *Chris Milner*

Left: The trailing truck, now also refurbished, is moved forward so that it too can be located in its position underneath the rear end of the engine. *Robin Stewart-Smith*

Facing Page Bottom: All re-tubing works is now complete and the superheater header refitted as the new smokebox is carefully craned into position. *Robin Stewart-Smith*

Left: The tubing gang hard at work inserting the new superheater flues into the boiler.
Brian Radford

ed each time water was picked up over water troughs.

With 'Princess Margaret Rose's' tender, which had remained with the locomotive since 1937, this had obviously been a major contributing factor in getting to this poor condition. When the new items had been completed, the whole of the tender chassis was shotblasted and prim-

ed with special etching paint for long lasting protection, and when reassembled it gave the wonderful appearance of being brand new, especially with the tyre thickness on the wheelsets being so good.

Consideration was given at this time to increasing the tender water capacity as water is only available on the main line today at pre-

Above: Two views of the chassis, primed and repainted red and with a large number of lubrication pipes re-installed, nearing completion.
Brian Radford

Below: Two views of the business end of the boiler as the re-fitting of the various cab fittings near completion with Eric Riley doing the fitting up.
Robin Stewart-Smith

Right: An historic moment as the completed chassis is pulled out of the heavy repair shop to be re-united with the boiler.
Brian Radford

Below: For the first time in almost thirty years a 'Princess Royal' boiler is re-united with the frames of a locomotive of that class, as boiler No. 9100 is gently lowered into position on 24th March, 1990 using the Midland Railway Trust's 50 ton steam crane. The crane itself is one of a batch of three ordered by Stanier in 1930 and built in 1931 with a 36 ton lifting capacity but rebuilt by makers Cowans Sheldon & Co Ltd. in 1938 to 50 tons capacity in order to cater for the heavier locomotives such as the 'Princess Royals' *Brian Radford*

arranged places whereas in the days when steam traction was predominant it was available at all main stations and many other locations in the form of water troughs. Today it is better to carry more water even at the expense of sacrificing some coal space in the tender particularly when remembering that some coal may be carried 'in reserve' in support vehicles on the train but water cannot. A supplementary tank was therefore designed to fit on top of the water tank in the tender, utilizing the void at the rear of the coal trimming plate and the tank itself. This was carefully designed and fitted so as not to disturb the classic lines of the Stanier tender and when completed less than half a ton of coal had been sacrificed with the gain of 750 gallons of water. It is interesting to remember that in 1937 the 'Princess Royal' class were fitted with the new and specially designed tenders in order to carry 10 tons of coal instead of 9 to avoid running out of coal on the long non-stop runs, and now in 1990, one of the only two remaining 'Princess Royal' tenders is modified again, this time to avoid running out of water!

The cab, which had been taken off at the same time as the boiler lift, revealed a number of repairs from earlier days, some of which were in need of further attention. This work was carried out initially at Ashbourne where the cab could remain undercover after being shotblasted and primed.

On the boiler it was known that the firebox stays were nearly all monel metal and thus it was hoped that very little work would be required in this area. This turned out to be the case, with just the renewal of the stay nuts, albeit over 2,500 in total, which were all made in the machine shop at Butterley. With the boiler work, the option was also taken to remove the front steel tubeplate from the boiler on the boiler inspector's advice. Once out, the tubeplate was straightened in a large press after having the thin areas built up with weld to regain full thickness. Although this whole operation was a big job, which had not been undertaken by the locomotive department at Butterley before, it was preferable to do it at this time, when the tubeplate was easily accessible with the smokebox already off, rather than in seven years time when the boiler may be able to remain in the frames during the seven year overhaul and also preventing the necessary removal of a smokebox which would only be seven years old. Some thirty new rivets were fitted by the boilersmiths in the combustion chamber flanges and new steel studs to all boiler fittings, dome cover and top

feed cover as well as the superheater header which was also removed for work to be carried out on the tubeplate. The new boiler flues came from West Germany, as a matter of interest from Wuppertal which is the home of the world famous overhead railway, and the small tubes were supplied by British Steel.

When 6203 had come to the Midland Railway Trust a number of copper feed pipes and lubrication pipes had been missing. Replacements for all these deficient items were made in the workshops at Butterley Park. During the re-assembly of the locomotive the opportunity was taken to slightly modify and improve the lubrication layout by introducing a central greasing point for part of the inside motion, thus reducing the need for reaching inside the frames to less accessible parts.

The smokebox door was repaired and the opportunity was taken to have a new one spun using the existing as a pattern while it remained off the locomotive. The new one is now 'in stores'.

By Christmas 1989, the restoration of 6203 was progressing well and some thought was naturally turning towards her initial runs both at the Midland Railway Centre and on B.R. From the commencement of the restoration the S.L.O.A. (Steam Locomotive Operators Association) management committee had been kept informed of progress and a likely steaming date had been forecast by the restoration team. Early in 1990 a proposal to run a main line steam-hauled special as a memorial train for Richard Levick had been accepted by the management committee and Mr. David Ward of B.R. The date for this, which had to be fixed with several months notice, had been set for Saturday June 2nd 1990 using No. 46203 for motive power — if she was ready. The challenge was therefore thrown down!

During the weeks and months leading up to this date the impetus of work grew. The main frames had been substantially complete for sometime and so the main concentration of work was put onto the boiler. The new smokebox was rivetted to the boiler barrel and the boiler steam tested off the locomotive on Friday 9th March. Two weeks later on Saturday 24th March the boiler was reunited with the frames having had her new ashpan fitted at the same time. The work grew increasingly intense as the calendar ticked by. From what had seemed months to go to the 2nd of June, was suddenly only eight weeks away. The boiler cladding was proving to be a difficult item as the only sheets available from the steel suppliers were too small to fit round

Right: 46203,now basically complete stands ready to be moved back into the heavy repair shop for the addition of boiler cladding and other remaining work. *Robin Stewart-Smith*

Facing Page Left: Another view of 46203's boiler being lowered into position using the Trust's 50 ton crane. *Brian Radford*

Facing Page Right: Later that day the cab is lowered into position to complete the basic parts of the engine. *Robin Stewart-Smith*

Below: Boiler cladding now complete and in a new coat of red undercoat, the engine stands ready to be given her finishing coat of B.R. maroon paint. *Brian Radford*

the circumference of the barrel. Thus began one of the most awkward jobs of all — to weld barrel cladding without the welds being visible.

This difficult operation was eventually completed, but valuable time had slipped by. The painters were waiting to come in and start their preparation work with the selected livery and colour being kept secret thus creating interest. It was kept this way until the last possible moment, making it a talking point right up to the first steaming. Not many locomotive classes can boast four different livery colours with a further four varieties on these; such was the choice available.

Behind the scenes the colour had been selected and paint bought some months earlier, even so the secret was well kept and one railway periodical managed to announce she was in B.R. Brunswick Green even after she had been steamed and displayed publicly in red !

The final choice of livery was B.R. maroon lined out in black and straw and using the earliest version of B.R. smokebox door numberplate with L.M.S. style numbers '46203'. Photographic evidence confirmed that the locomotive had carried this style of plate in the early days of British Railways although she had never been turned out in the particular paint livery during her service with B.R.

The painting was substantially completed during the first week in May, with the minor outstanding items for steaming being fitted at the same time. Many long hours were worked in the period and great commitment shown by those members of the restoration team as the culmination of over twenty months work drew nearer.

A small fire was lit in her, for the first time as a completed engine, on Tuesday 8th May and gradually built up over the next three days to get steam up to working pressure thus allowing for final adjustments of safety valves on 11th May at the same time as the B.R. mechanical and 'in steam' examination. Though it would have been desirable to have had a trial run with her before the official examination on Fri-

day 11th May, time had beaten the team, the main culprit being the boiler barrel sheeting which had consumed so many valuable days of time to make and fit.

However confidence was high. Mr. Colin Wood, the B.R. mechanical inspector, and Mr. Sam Foster the boiler inspector, spent the morning of the 11th checking the locomotive over as boiler pressure was steadily raised to 250 lb/sq.in. thus allowing the four safety valves to be finally set and checked. In the early afternoon the moment of truth arrived; with Colin Wood at the regulator, cylinder drain taps open, tender handbrake wound off, she was wound into full forward gear and given a breadth of steam into the steam chests and cylinders for the first time since October 1962. With jets of steam issuing forth with a deafening 'Ssshhh' from the opened drain cocks, she eased forward. No Champagne, no speeches, just satisfying smiles of a job well done and summed up beautifully by Eric Riley who said, "No matter how long engines stand, they never forget how to chuff."

Over the next three days 'Princess Margaret Rose' ran light engine between Swanwick and Ironville on the Trust's line, to 'run her in', with 100 miles being covered over the period. Apart from initial teething problems with the injectors and top feeds on the boiler, nothing else required attention. This reflected the high quality of work carried out by the Locomotive Department of the Midland Railway Trust.

On the 15th and 17th May, the light and loaded test runs had been programmed by B.R., with the locomotive to be weighed on the weightable in the B.R. Technical Centre on London Road, Derby on the 16th.

So on 15th May after the customary photographs alongside the engine, and with Driver Arthur Roberts, Fireman Terry Green and Traction Inspector David Thompson, all from Toton depot, No. 46203 turned out from Codnor Park Junction onto B.R. metals. Driver Roberts had visited 'Princess Margaret Rose' at the Midland Railway

Left: Great care was taken to ensure that 46203 was in every way correct in her livery detail which was done to the original drawing. In these two views members of the painting gang are carefully doing the lining out of the engine.
Brian Radford

Right: Later that day 46203 makes her first acquaintance with the former Ais Gill signal-box as she stands at Butterley station yard on the first of her many trial runs prior to her official B.R. test run, due on 15th May, just four days away! *Melvyn Hopwood*

Below: In steam again! The historic occasion as on 11th May 1990, 46203 moves slowly away under her own steam for the first time since 1962. *Robin Stewart-Smith*

Right: 'Ready for the off' -B.R. and M.R. Trust staff pose beside 46203 L-R. Brian Radford, Boiler Inspector Sam Foster, the B.R. guard, Melvyn Chamberlain, B.R. Mechanical Inspector Colin Wood, Barry Wheatley, John Riley, M.R.T. Locomotive Superintendent Eric Riley, B.R. Traction Inspector David Thompson, Mick Boothby, Chief Traction Inspector Don Tennant, Fireman Terry Green, Driver Arthur Roberts, Brell Ewart and Terry Thorpe.
Stephen Radford

Centre many times, the first occasion soon after her arrival, and had vowed that if she ever returned to the main line his would be the hand on the regulator on that 'red letter' day. And so it proved to be.

During the writing of this book, some weeks after the date of his run with No. 46203, Driver Arthur Roberts was taken off the roster for steam duties having failed an eyesight test without wearing spectacles at a routine medical examination. His runs with 'Princess Margaret Rose' were his last as driver on any steam locomotive on the main line.

Due to the very low overbridge at Langley Mill (Bridge No. 41) which affects the up slow line, a reversal back to Pye Bridge in order to gain access onto the up fast line was necessary before setting forth to Derby. A speed restriction of 35 m.p.h. had been placed on the first run to Sheffield and so gentle running was the order of the day initially. The arrival at Toton where a stop was necessary for the depositing of the Annetts key (part of the interlocking for access from Butterley (MRT) to BR) enabled a quick 'feel round' at all bearings and axles — all was well.

The route past Trent, Sheet Stores Junction, and Spondon into Derby was taken in similar genteel manner with a further stop to the rear of Derby Station and although speed was still restricted the four

cylinder beat of the 'Princess Royal' was easily discernible. Further inspection at Derby revealed all was still in order and the speed restriction, placed on her by Inspector Colin Wood, was raised to 50 m.p.h. at his discretion.

Even though her livery was still incomplete she looked magnificent in the spring sunshine which accompanied her as she rolled up the miles along the old North Midland Main Line to Chesterfield where a number of well informed enthusiasts witnessed her passing as she slowed down for the crossover to the 'Old Road' at Tapton Junction (Chesterfield). Several permanent way speed restrictions and a signal stop at Whittington prevented any purposeful running until Woodhouse Bank which was climbed with ease by the one coach special before coasting down into Platform 8 at Sheffield Midland Station.

Following further inspection and a top up with water, the signal changed to green. The guard gave the 'right-a-way' and the exhaust from 'Princess Margaret Rose' barked sharply as she disappeared into the short tunnels and up the 1 in 100 gradient towards Bradway Tunnel.

Maximum speed attained was no higher than a brief 60 mph burst just south of Duffield as she returned to Derby without incident. She was bedded down on Etches Park Depot for the first night away from

Proud owner Brell Ewart looks out from the cab of 'Princess Margaret Rose' on 10th May 1990, the day before her trial run.

Melvyn Hopwood

B.R. Driver Arthur Roberts and Fireman Terry Green await the signal to move out onto the M.R. Trust's main line on the first leg of her light test run on 15th May 1990, whilst Eric Riley stands by looking justly delighted at the successful outcome of many months hard work.

Brian Radford

46203, with 'Midland Railway Centre' headboard, coasts through Spondon station on her way to Derby during her light test run on 15th May 1990.

Melvyn Hopwood

Butterley in 15 years.

Early morning of the 16th saw a Class 08 diesel shunter take the 'Princess', still in light steam, across the main line and position her on the electronic weigh-table. Following a morning of slight adjustments to the springs on the locomotive and tender all was pronounced well and following lunch she was returned to Etches Park for preparations to begin the following day.

The principal reason for B.R. requiring test trains to be run for newly restored steam locomotives is to subject them to the maximum conditions reasonably anticipated for the work they will be expected to carry out hauling the special trains. The locomotive is therefore given a large load, several gradients to climb and also a turn of speed up to the maximum and probably slightly over that officially laid down for steam haulage on passenger trains. The route often used for these trains, Derby to Sheffield and return, is ideally suited to all these conditions. During the test run the locomotive is carefully monitored from the footplate by the mechanical inspector for riding characteristics, ability to create sufficient output from the boiler, and on completion a check to ensure that all mechanical parts have performed without any overheating or failure; without doubt as severe a test as can be reasonably given in today's diesel and electric orientated railway world.

The morning of the 17th May 1990 was a beautiful spring morning and with several members of the support crew having stayed with the locomotive overnight, she was showing 200 lb/sq.in. with a good fire at 9.15 a.m. when Driver Reg White, Fireman Lindsay Shelton and Inspector Harry Leyland arrived from Derby 4 Shed. Mechanical Inspector Colin Wood and Boiler Inspector Sam Foster were there to oversee the run and the locomotive support crew were Mick Boothby, John Cook, Brell Ewart, John Riley, Barry Wheatley, and Eric Riley with Brian Radford also on board to take detailed timings for the record of the run which is reproduced as Appendix 11 of this book. It had been decided by Brell Ewart that the train would run with the 'Red Rose' headboard on, after all she was a red engine, with rose in her name and she had recorded some outstanding performances on this train over many years in B.R.service.

The departure time was scheduled for 10.10 but at the appointed time the empty stock had not arrived and so 'Princess Margaret Rose' sat quietly on Etches Park Depot bathing in the sun and looking every bit the large elegant and powerful locomotive that she is.

After some two and a half hours delay due to movement difficulties encountered by B.R., 46203 backed onto the empty stock at the south end of Platform 4 Derby Station. As soon as the train had been coupled up and the compulsory brake test completed, the signal turned to green and with a blast from the Stanier hooter 'The Red Rose' departed. A slight wheelslip on the maze of points and crossings at the south of the station saw the regulator shut off until clear of the junction, this being followed by the locomotive being worked hard and the exhaust being heard fully for the first time. The acceleration of the train could be distinctly felt as it sped through Spondon with a slowing for Sheet Stores Junction and then Trent. Due to the lateness of the train many would-be photographers, a good number of whom had squeezed extended lunch hours from their employers had returned to work assuming locomotive failure or some other mishap — failure indeed — the word was never contemplated by the team. From Trent 46203 was given the gun and as Toton yard and motive power depot were passed at speed working hard, the depot workforce was assembled to salute the passing of 'Princess Margaret Rose' on 'The Red Rose' in full cry.

By now the footplate crew were gaining confidence in their steed with every mile passed although it has to be said that this Derby team handled the locomotive as though they drove the class every working day in their normal link, for one would never have known that this was the first time any of them had been on a 'Princess Royal'.

Hard running continued up the continuous rising grade to Morton followed by a signal check and then a stop at a red signal just south of Clay Cross. A little anxiety on remaining water was dispelled during this brief stop as the fireman looked into the water tank from the rear of the tender through the filler lid, his anxiety caused through the locomotive coming to stand on a severe cant in the track and with the tender water indicator on the high side of the camber a false reading was being given. A green light soon saw a quick restart and progress towards Chesterfield, the locomotive owner's home town in his schoolboy days. This was the place where his interest in steam locomotives was nurtured and who would have ever dreamt that just over twenty years later he would be travelling behind his own preserved and restored 'Princess Royal' Class Pacific No. 46203 through places where he had stood on countless occasions watching the Jubilees, Royal Scots, and other ex-LMS classes pass by; a dream come true.

The speed slowed through Hasland and Chesterfield down to 15 m.p.h to allow the cross over at Tapton Junction to be taken, thus gaining the route of the 'old road' - so named as this was the original North Midland route between Derby and Leeds via Beighton constructed before the modern-day route for main line trains through Bradway Tunnel and via Sheffield.

Once clear of the crossing she was opened up again and speed once again restored as the train sped through Whittington, past Barrow Hill depot and through the former site of Barrow Hill station where the train was saluted by raised glasses of the liquid variety from the balcony of the Working Mens Club. As on the occasion two days earlier, permanent way slacks cut the speed through Killamarsh and soon the train was crossing over the famous level crossing at Beighton (the only one on the G.C.R. route between Sheffield Victoria and Marylebone) much to the delight of waiting drivers. The train was now at the foot of Woodhouse Bank and the crew gave of their best as 'Princess Margaret Rose' stormed up the incline. To say the sound was quite loud in the support coach would be a dramatic understatement as the speed actually increased during the climb from 40 m.p.h. at the foot of the bank to 46 m.p.h. at the top — the only locomotive up to that date to do that on a test run. Once at the summit the speed was eased, as the remnants of Darnall Steam Shed were passed, before dropping down through Nunnery Junction and into Platform 6 at Sheffield Midland Station to be greeted by an enthusiastic but somewhat small and obviously numerically depleted posse of enthusiasts.

46203 had covered the 52.2 miles from Derby in a shade over 88 minutes, achieving a maximum speed of 72 m.p.h. just beyond Beighton Junction.

At Sheffield, Eric Riley and Inspector Colin Wood were quickly down at track level feeling round the motion and axles while other members of the support crew attended to filling the tender with water and pushing the coal forward. The inspection revealed that all was "as cool as a cucumber" in the words of Eric Riley, and so in view of the late running as soon as the tender was full with water the signalman was informed and the train was 'given the road'.

On departure from Sheffield, with an exhaust beat as loud as any yet heard, she stormed out of the station and disappeared into the short tunnels as the 1 in 100 climb for the next four miles was commenced. With speed gradually increasing and Driver White slowly winding back the reverser, the bark from the chimney became more intense with every half mile covered and the sound echoed loudly from tall buildings close to the line as 46203 dug in her heels with calculated aplomb. People working in nearby works yards froze as this 158 ton machine stormed past in a crescendo of sound with a volcanic emission issuing forth from its furnace via the chimney. Millhouses park saw a tennis match stop to witness the passing of the Royal Name before finally the curvature of the track brought the now skeletal remains of that well known station and junction of Dore and Totley into view and where several photographers witnessed the event. The noise from the locomotive was so loud that in the support coach any effort to converse had to be done by shouting through cupped hands. Bradway Tunnel was entered and pitch darkness blanketed out any visual effects other then dramatic 'Roman Candle' displays passing the windows from the continuous chimney emissions with the regulator still wide open all the way through the tunnel on the still rising grade. Out of the southern end where the 1 in 100 summit was breasted, exceptionally quick acceleration followed and Dronfield Station sped by on the down grade with the locomotive still being worked hard. Unstone and Sheepbridge followed in even faster vein although the 'Princess' was now shut off, but as the curve of Tapton Junction was rounded the power was applied again with a roar. Spectators on Chesterfield Station were treated to what must have been a tremendous sight of a 'Princess Royal' bearing down, on a rising grade, regulator wide open and whistle blowing as she sped 'The Red Rose' by them.

Lines from 'Speeding North With The Royal Scot' came to mind - 'tearing through Tebay at 75' and 'the inhabitants of these parts set their clocks and watches as the Royal Scot passed by'. Probably a good job that Cestrefeldians did not set their timepieces with this test train, running some ninety minutes ahead.

Hasland and Avenue Carbonisation Plant were passed in similar style with further salutes from a small group of photographers on the site of the famous Clay Cross Station as 46203 took the tracks to the right and headed for Ambergate and Derby. Storming into Clay Cross Tunnel, an area well traversed by George Stephenson in a bygone era, the train was again plunged into darkness tempered only by the swirling smoke and steam entering the support coach from every window which were all open to savour the occasion to the full. Speed was now on the increase again on the down grade as the train sped through the south portal of Clay Cross Tunnel and charged on towards Wingfield, passing lush green fields in the Amber Valley and the trackbed remains of the Ashover Light Railway. A slight slowing of speed for the restriction at Ambergate was followed by further power

Fine action shot of 46203 as she storms out of Sheffield Midland station on the return leg of her loaded test run on 17th May 1990.

David Wilcock

Above: Now fully restored after a general overhaul at the Butterley Park shops of the Midland Railway Trust, 46203 stands in steam prior to the test run on 15th May 1990 with preserved Class 5 4-6-0 44932 standing behind. The B.R. maroon livery was never carried by 46203 in B.R. days.   *Brian Radford*

Left: 'Princess Margaret Rose' stands on the weigh-bridge at the Railway Technical Centre, Derby in order to record the axle loads on each wheelset and adjust them if necessary.   *Brian Radford*

Right: Inside the control room of the weigh-bridge as the weights shown by each load-cell are monitored and the springs are adjusted to give the correct axle weights on all wheelsets.   *Brian Radford*

Below: A scene of activity at Sheffield Midland Station as 46203 is examined after the outward leg of the loaded test run on 17th May 1990.   *Brian Radford*

'Princess Margaret Rose' bursts from the south portal of Clay Cross Tunnel at 75 m.p.h. nearing the end of her highly successful loaded test-run to Sheffield and back on 17th May 1990.

Robin Stewart-Smith

application through Broadholme and Belper with a high speed burst reaching a maximum of 85 mph through Duffield and Little Eaton. The tower of Derby Cathedral indicated the train's destination and with one final burst of speed 46203 coasted to a stand at a red signal on the outskirts of Derby by St Mary's Goods Yard. After several minutes delay 'Princess Margaret Rose' moved the train slowly into the Derby Station complex on the goods roads to the rear of the station platforms where she came to a stand.

'Princess Margaret Rose' had covered the 36.4 miles from Sheffield to Derby in 41 Minutes 12 seconds at a start to stop average speed of 52.78 miles per hour. Maximum speeds of 84 m.p.h. and 85 m.p.h. had been achieved at Wingfield and Little Eaton respectively.

Further examination by the mechanical men which found nothing amiss concluded the test and after uncoupling the support coach from the empty stock and a change of footplate crew, and having said cheerios to Colin Wood and Sam Foster, 46203 with support coach moved off for the return to Butterley.

Sitting in the support coach on the return to Butterley, comparisons were immediately made with O.S.Nock's logged run behind 46203 on 'The Red Rose' in 1959, which is detailed in Chapter 4 of this book, and described by him in his own hand as 'the run of the year'. This had certainly been the run of the year for those on the train.

Arrival back at Butterley saw 'Princess Margaret Rose' facing the opposite way round as she entered the Midland Railway Trust line smokebox first. After being allowed to cool down over two days the firegrate was cleaned and a close inspection made of the locomotive. Other than a small number of very minor weeps from tubes in the firebox she was in perfect order. She was however rather dirty and grimy having collected large amounts of soot and dirt from the tunnels passed through on the run. Once cool she was returned to the workshop to allow the painters to finish their lining and transfer work and also to allow the mechanical staff to complete several minor outstanding items, in particular the plumbing to the auxiliary water tank on the tender which at this time was still not in operation. It was also the wish of all concerned to turn 46203 out in pristine condition on Saturday 2nd June 1990 for 'The Richard Levick Memorial' train to be run as her first public outing in memory of a colleague. The two-week period remaining allowed perfect time to prepare and complete her.

The weather in the two weeks prior to the 2nd June had been very hot with very little rainfall, and as such the ground was tinder dry. However, in the immediate days before, the weather broke and showery weather prevailed thus allaying any fears of cancellation due to fire risk.

And so the day of the first revenue earning train hauled by 'Princess Margaret Rose' had come, some 27 years and 7 months after her last one in October 1962 when steam traction was still regular motive power on British Railways.

With 46203 having returned from the test running on B.R. facing smokebox first into the Midland Railway Trust's line at Codnor Park Junction, as no turning facilities are yet available at the centre, the locomotive had to leave tender-first hauling the maroon support coach displaying coachboards carrying the train name 'THE RICHARD LEVICK MEMORIAL'. The route out onto B.R. metals followed the same procedure as that 18 days earlier in setting-back down the 'down' goods line to Pye Bridge in order to cross over onto the 'up' fast in order to make her way onwards to Derby. On the morning of Saturday 2nd June a number of trains were being delayed in the area by a bridge reported as being in a possibly dangerous state at Chesterfield having been struck by a lorry. Because of delays, the timetabled path to Derby was lost and so arrival by 46203 into Derby was some 90 minutes late and after the arrival from St. Pancras of the diesel-hauled leg of the train. Water was swiftly taken and after remarshalling of the support coach by the class 08 shunter onto the train, 'Princess Margaret Rose' duly backed onto the train and 'The Richard Levick Memorial' headboard was fitted aloft onto the top lamp bracket on the smokebox door. A proud, memorable and sad moment. The B.R. crew were Driver Tom Blakeman, Fireman Alan Porter, who had been a leading member of the restoration team from the start in 1988, and Traction Inspector Ron Dye, with Fireman Alec McPherson as second fireman.

This being the first outing on a public train for 'Princess Margaret Rose' as was to be expected large crowds of enthusiasts and photographers were at every vantage point throughout the day and the departure from Derby saw Platform 1 lined to capacity along the southern end.

With sanders on, 46203 left Derby in fine style in the hands of Driver Blakeman and, with 14 vehicles behind she accelerated away, crossing over the maze of tracks without slipping even though the rails were wet with the heavy rain that was falling at the time. The usual gallery of spectators and cameramen witnessed the early stages of the

run past the Technical College grounds at Wilmorton but soon after the train slowed and came to an unscheduled stop approaching Spondon. After the Inspector had spoken to the signalman from the lineside telephone the train was soon away again and accelerating smartly towards Beeston and Sheet Stores Junction where speed was curtailed to allow the junction and the complex track at Trent to be negotiated. With the customary wave to the inhabitants of Trent Power Box who would monitor the train's progress as far as Tapton Junction, the regulator was opened up and again the 'Princess' got into her stride with the 560 ton train.

Every vantage point saw lineside spectators standing, all there to view and witness the return of the 'Princess' who had lain dormant for too many years but who was now back where she belonged — on the main line hauling heavy express passenger trains.

On the rising gradient, following the valley of the River Erewash and past the end of the Trust's line from whence she had departed some two hours earlier, she gave a long whistle in salute to a friend who had given so much to steam locomotive preservation and restoration and in whose memory the very train itself was being run.

The train ran straight through Alfreton and Mansfield Parkway Station omitting the timetabled photographic stop to the surprise of the expectant waiting crowd and on towards Clay Cross Junction, where the engine could be heard working hard as she rounded the curve and commenced the downhill run into Chesterfield. The route again took 46203 across the ladder junction at Tapton and a magnificent sight the train looked as it snaked slowly at 15 m.p.h. from the down fast to the down slow and thus taking the 'old road' via the Rother Valley to Sheffield. Once clear of Tapton she was again opened up fully and continued on towards Whittington and Barrow Hill where once again she was toasted with raised glasses from the balcony of the Working Mens Club by the well informed group. With permanent way restrictions still in force speed was again reduced near Killamarsh and through Beighton Junction. Woodhouse bank was heavily populated with spectators, many of whom were adorned with a considerable variety, and in some cases a number of cameras. They were met by a 'Princess Royal' locomotive in full cry charging up the bank and emitting noise of deafening proportions and even with 560 tons behind her, maintaining constant speed from bottom to top. Through Woodhouse Station and Darnall followed by the drop down through Nunnery Main Line Junction she arrived in Sheffield Midland Station at Platform 6, to be greeted by yet another capacity viewing audience as the train drew to a stand against the watering point. Due to the delayed departure from Derby, the train was running sometime behind schedule, but a long timetabled stop at Sheffield allowed plenty of recovery time and advantage of this was fully taken.

With this occasion being the first time the auxiliary water tank had been used, a quick check revealed that it was working to perfection and so the quantity of water required to be taken at Sheffield was 750 gallons less. With the support crew carrying out their watering and coaling shoveling duties, Eric Riley, Barry Wheatley and Mick Boothby inspected the motion and axleboxes. All was pronounced well. The Derby crew were delighted with the locomotive's performance and undoubtedly enjoyed the glory of the moment as cameras clicked and flashed at them from all directions — all very reminiscent of the arrival of 'Princess Elizabeth' at Glasgow in November 1936 having run non-stop from London in record time.

With several blasts on the whistle indicating imminent departure, the passengers, many of whom had gathered round the locomotive, entrained, and with the green signal given, the guard blew his whistle and Driver Blakeman gave a hoot on 46203's whistle and opened the regulator.

'Princess Margaret Rose' responded in style by issuing forth slow, deliberate, and very load blasts from the chimney, emitting a vertical column of steam and smoke as the pace of the beat quickened as she increased speed and quickly enveloped herself into the tunnel. With over four miles in front of her at a gradient of 1 in 100, a good start was essential. With sanders on 'Princess Margaret Rose' was about to prove and confirm what she and members of her class were designed and built for, and could do as well as any other large passenger engine ever built — climb hills.

The train stormed through Heeley with the continuous bark from the chimney echoing from all sides. Heads peeped out of every window along the train to witness this outpouring of immense power. Past the site of the former steam shed at Millhouses and the site of the station there, blasting under the many overbridges on this section of the line. Passengers and lineside spectators all watching the voluminous clouds of steam dissipate into the dense and swaying foliage of the lineside trees, and still the deafening blast of the locomotive as she forged upwards towards the junction at that evocatively named station of Dore and Totley where yet another host of onlookers witnessed

Above: 46203 storms up the 1 in 100 gradient at Heeley on the return loaded test run on 17th May 1990.   *Peter Fox*

Below: After a splendid outward portion of the first 'Richard Levick Memorial Special' on 2nd June 1990, Driver Tom Blakeman receives the congratulations of the crowd on the platform at Sheffield Midland Station and signs autographs as owner Brell Ewart, somewhat blackened, leaves the footplate.

Brian Radford

Above: Ready for action 'Princess Margaret Rose' displays the classic lines of a Stanier pacific as her highly varnished paint finish reflects the adjacent scene on 2nd June 1990.

Brian Radford

Left: Generations of boys over the years have been thrilled by the sight of steam locomotives. A young boy and his grandfather have come to see 46203 as she stands at Sheffield Midland on 2nd June 1990.   *Brian Radford*

Right: Under the road bridges and short tunnels, 46203 storms out of Sheffield in a crescendo of sound and she heads south with the return leg of 'The White Rose' special on 15th September 1990.

J.H. Cooper-Smith

Below: 46203 speeds from Milford Tunnel, just north of Duffield, on the 'White Rose' special return leg back to Derby from Sheffield.

Chris Milner

'Princess Margaret Rose' runs through the centre road at Nottingham Midland Station, on the evening of 10th November 1991 after working the return leg of 'The Red Rose' excursion to the Great Western Society's railway centre at Didcot.

Mike Purslowe

46203 heads the first leg of 'The Richard Levick Memorial' special out of Derby on 2nd June 1990 with her load of fourteen coaches.

Robin Stewart-Smith

the momentous return of 'Princess Margaret Rose' as she rounded the curve and gave another long salute on her whistle to an absent friend who originated from these parts close by to this location.

The entry into the tunnel at Bradway under the Derbyshire Hills saw no letting up as the engine forged on towards the summit. Bursting out of the southern end of the tunnel a brief toot on the whistle indicated the summit and the train now accelerated on the falling grade very quickly. Speeding through Dronfield Station still accelerating appreciably with Unstone quickly passed the regulator was eased, and the steam and smoke was reduced to a trail clinging to the top of the locomotive and coaches as speed still increased to what was undoubtedly a maximum speed for the run of 75 mph at Sheepbridge. Past Whittington Moor on the high embankment, round the curve onto Tapton Junction and then, with Chesterfield in full view, the regulator was opened fully. The train roared towards Chesterfield Station and must have given the onlookers and passengers waiting on the platforms a fine sight as 46203 tore through, powering her train on towards Hasland on the rising gradient. Again all vantage points were occupied with what seemed from the train to be armies of photographers standing in rows on embankments, all festooned with a variety of cameras, video and sound equipment, and all out to record for posterity this historic occasion with the locomotive performing to perfection to a totally enthralled audience both on and off the train.

Continuing on up the rising grade no respite for the locomotive or the stoker came until Clay Cross Tunnel was entered and then, on a falling grade far less firing was required as the fire had built up and with a stop over at Derby now only some twenty minutes away. However speed was still high as the train raced past the remains of Wingfield Station at 69 m.p.h. and on through the pastures of the Amber Valley towards Ambergate with its 60 m.p.h. speed limit through the short Toadmoor Tunnel and the junction with the Matlock Branch. Once clear of these power was reapplied and further good running was again the order of the day through Belper at 69 m.p.h.

and then Duffield until the outskirts of the city of Derby were reached when speed was allowed to drop before the train entered Derby Station and 'Princess Margaret Rose' came off the train to replenish her supplies of coal and water.

46203 had made the run from Sheffield to Derby in 46 minutes 10 seconds as against a booked time of 57 minutes — a gain of almost eleven minutes over 36.4 miles, a masterly piece of running on her first revenue earning trip at an average speed of 47.3 m.p.h. start to stop.

The second circuit of the day was run a little harder by the crew as far as Sheffield. This is explained by the fact that the first run had been taken at an easy pace to keep any possible risk of lineside fires down to a minimum, but as the rain had been fairly steady for several hours all risk of this had gone and so the locomotive could be worked harder. With all seats again fully sold the train was again packed to capacity, many of the passengers having booked for the whole day determined to witness every moment of this momentous occasion.

From Derby to Sheffield the same route was taken and the train was again greeted by many thousands of spectators. Sheffield was again the watering point with another long timetabled stop allowing any lost time to be made up.

This second outward run was made in 88 minutes against a booked time of 81 minutes, a signal stop at Nunnery main Line Junction of almost 2 minutes and a number of other signal checks causing the lost time. A top speed of 67 m.p.h. was recorded at Draycott and Breaston.

At the due departure time from Sheffield, the train was held due to the late running of the 15.04 York—Bristol HST service which was some twenty minutes down and would have left before the 'Princess' if on time. However when it arrived at Sheffield some fault was apparent on a power car on this train and 'Princess Margaret Rose' was hurriedly given the green signal for departure ahead of it.

46203's departure from Sheffield was again spectacular and the locomotive, being handled superbly by Driver Blakeman, stormed away and onto the 1 in 100 climb. After a very short distance a yellow signal dictated a slowing of speed and the train was 'put inside' on the Woodseats Road loop drawing to a stand at the red signal adjacent to an overbridge well patronised with onlookers. Cameras clicked and whirred as the 'Princess' stood there like an athlete on her starting blocks while Inspector John Sumner, who had taken over from Inspector Ron Dye for the second circuit, climbed down from the footplate to the trackside telephone to enquire from the signalman the reason for the detour and delay. He was told that the fault on York—Bristol HST had been corrected and so it had been decided that this train should be allowed to overtake as soon as possible . Within minutes the HST came past the standing Pullman train, its power cars working at full output on the stiff grade.

With eager anticipation the crowd on the bridge readied their cameras as 'Princess Margaret Rose' was given the green signal and indicated her intentions with a blast on the whistle. The regulator was opened but she stood there as if glued to the spot. With a broad smile on his face Driver Blakeman closed the regulator, wound her into reverse, allowed her to rollback and in the same movement wound her into full forward gear and re-opened the regulator. With a single emphatic 'chuff' she moved forward. 'Chuff-chuff-chuff-chuff' she eased from the loop and momentarily slipped on the nose of the point as she regained the main line. The regulator was fully opened and the rake of Pullman coaches duly snaked out behind the 'Princess' as she gathered momentum. A classic piece of handling this, by Driver Blakeman, with the locomotive proving itself master of its job in being able to restart a train of 560 tons on a 1 in 100 incline.

The journey continued in much the same vein as the first run some hours earlier with Unstone, Sheepbridge, and Chesterfield being taken at speed. However north of Ambergate a yellow signal followed by another yellow with a feather indicator routed the train inside the loop at Broadholme where on reaching the southern end of the loop a train hauled by a class 47 diesel came into view standing on the main line apparently having failed. Luckily, or by good judgement, its driver had been able to get his train to a position where following trains could pass with minimal delays. With speed reduced 'Princess Margaret Rose' regained the main line having run through the loop at a measured 15 m.p.h. and again she was opened up, but by now, with momentum lost, the top speed was well down from that of the earlier run.

On this second run, a maximum speed of 74 had been reached at

milepost 149 and Sheepbridge, only slightly less than the maximum of the first run at that same location. However because of the delays the overall time to Derby was 1 hour and 38 seconds compared with the booked time of 57 minutes.

Derby Station saw 46203 uncoupled with support coach and run round for further replenishment of water thus allowing the Class 47 diesel to couple up to the Pullman Stock for the return to St. Pancras. The majority of passengers, having detrained, followed their hero of the day to the north bay for a final farewell as with tender now full again 'Princess Margaret Rose' reversed out of the bay and with a last salute ran through the station en-route for Coalville and the open day on the morrow. Driver Blakeman later wrote to Brell Ewart :

"It really was a fitting tribute to Richard (Levick) . . . . . also the superb condition of 46203 was a tribute in itself. Truly superb. The photos that I have seen up to now, taken in places where she was working hard, there is not a blow from the piston glands, valve spindle glands, or cylinder drains — all the places where it is possible under heavy steaming to get blows. . . . . a truly superb machine and certainly the best engine in preservation today *par excellence*. Harry Leyland who was the loco inspector on the test run told me in his own opinion it was the best engine he had ever been on in his life. Coming from a 'dyed in the wool' Gresley man, that is praise indeed."

46203 was on display in steam all day at the Coalville Open day returning to Butterley late on Sunday 3rd June when her fire was eventually dropped. After being allowed to cool down for a further day she was returned to covered accommodation in the restoration shed where in the following days a further modification was made to the tender to allow it to be filled from ground level through hose connection made through the space formerly occupied by the water scoop.

'Princess Margaret Rose' had now joined the small number of locomotives passed for hauling passenger trains on B.R. metals and as such she was allocated work in the S.L.O.A. / Flying Scotsman Services steam charter market, her first outing being yet a further trip round the Sheffield circuit on the Northern end of 'The White Rose' train which had been hauled from the London suburbs by ex-L.N.E.R. Pacific No. 4472 'Flying Scotsman' as far as Derby.

A slight adjustment had been made to the valve gear of 46203 by the team from Butterley following close aural analysis on earlier runs and so her performance on this train was eagerly awaited. True to earlier form another excellent performance was given.

'Princess Margaret Rose' takes her inaugural main line tour past the south end of Toton yard on 2nd June 1990.

Chris Milner

Above: The Settle–Carlisle line makes a magnificent backdrop to this picture of 'Princess Margaret Rose' crossing Smardale viaduct with 'The Midlander' train from Leicester on 4th July 1991. 46203 worked from Blackburn through to Carlisle, this being the first time she had worked into Carlisle station since September 1962.   *J.H. Cooper-Smith*

Below: 'Princess Margaret Rose' storming up the gradient close to Ais Gill summit, on Saturday 24th August 1991 with 'The Appleby Round Table Expresss' (see page 124).   *J.H. Cooper-Smith*

Right: For the first time in preservation and after a 28 year break, the two remaining 'Princess Royal' class pacifics meet at Appleby station, the changeover place for the locomotives on 'The Cumbrian Mountain Express' diagram. The date is 22nd June 1991 and 'Princess Elizabeth' has worked the train from the south as 'Princess Margaret Rose' waits to take it back. The sight of two 'Princess Royals' in steam together on the main line is something that most enthusiasts thought they would never see. *Howard Routledge*

Below: Displaying 'The Royal Scot' headboard, 46203 is turned on the 70 ft. turntable at Steamtown, Carnforth on Sunday 7th July 1991.
J.H. Cooper-Smith

Below: Being prepared to work 'The Cumbrian Coast Express' from Carnforth to Workington on Saturday 17th August 1991.
J.H. Cooper-Smith

Below: New ground for 'Princess Margaret Rose' as she crosses Leven Viaduct near Ulverston on Saturday 17th August 1991 hauling 'The Cumbrian Coast Express,*
John F. Stiles

46203 was still limited to certain routes due to her height being above that acceptable to go 'under the wires'. i.e. underneath overhead electrified wires. This ruled out any work from Crewe and work into Carlisle over the Settle and Carlisle line. A winter workshop operation was therefore planned to make the necessary modifications to the cab, dome, top feed and tender.

In the meantime a private charter was organised by the team who looked after her this being run from Nottingham to Didcot and back and taking the name of 'The Red Rose'. This was chosen as it was on the train of the same name that O.S. Nock recorded the magnificent performance in 1959 (which is also detailed in this book), and it being somewhat synonymous to the rebirth of a red engine with 'Rose' in her name.

This train ran on Saturday November 10th and this was the day of a few 'firsts'.

It was the first time a 'Princess Royal' had hauled a train from Nottingham Station, and the first time 46203 had traversed the Great Western Route from Birmingham to Didcot. The lasting memory of this day was the return run from Landor Street Junction to Burton on Trent, all in the hours of darkness, with Driver Malcolm Butler of Toton Depot, who is also a regular driver at the Midland Railway Centre, at the regulator. With departure some twenty minutes late from Saltley all effort was made to pull the time back and all the passegers were treated to the audible spectacle of a 'Princess Royal' in full cry.

The 1990/91 winter was spent in the workshop at Swanwick having the adjustments made to the height of the locomotive and also fitting the A.W.S. apparatus which was taken out of store to be re-fitted. This allowed 'Princess Margaret Rose' to be certified by the BR Inspec-

torate for 75 m.p.h. running in anticipation of the raising of the maximum speed limit from 60 to 75 m.p.h. for approved locomotives. The fitting of this apparatus also necessitated holding mutual improvement classes for the support crew on the full operating procedures for this equipment.

The new year of 1991 saw 46203 with all her modifications completed and the allotting of locomotives to operations for the summer season by the SLOA management committee was keenly awaited.

The programme, announced in February 1991 allocated 46203 to the north of England, to be based at Carnforth and Carlisle Upperby depots to work over the Settle to Carlisle and Cumbrian Coast lines with the highlight being paired with sister locomotive 6201 'Princess Elizabeth'.

The first steaming of 1991 was on 30th March when she was steamed up for the Easter visitors and completed two light engine runs down the Midland Railway Centre's line to Ironville.

The British Railways inspection was completed on 24th May and on 25th May she hauled three preserved mainline diesels from the Midland Railway Centre to Coalville for what was to be the last open day at that Depot. The other steam locomotive at the open day was ex. L.N.E.R. Pacific No. 4472 'Flying Scotsman' thus displaying the thoroughbreads of both L.N.E.R. and L.M.S. side by side. The move north from Butterley took place on Friday 31st May when 46203 moved in steam with the support coach to Carnforth in preparation for hauling the northbound 'Cumbrian Mountain Express' from Blackburn to Appleby on 1st June. This was the first time that the locomotive had ever worked over the Settle to Carlisle line and although in places she was eased back due to the extreme risk of linside fires, for there

With 46203 about to sound her whistle in tribute to Richard Levick the first 'Memorial' special pounds past the end of the 'Midland Railway Trusts' line at Codnor Park Junction at 50 m.p.h.

Robin Stewart-Smith

Above: In full cry 46203 sweeps the special train through Barrow Hill and on towards Sheffield on 2nd June 1990.
Chris Milner

Right: Admirers gather round 46203 as the support crew cast their eye over her at Sheffield Midland before commencing the return leg of the first 'Richard Levick Memorial' special on 2nd June 1990.
Brian Radford

had been no rain for several weeks, she proved that she was a very powerful engine and given the right conditions was capable of some high class performances over this very demanding route.

The first southbound run from Carlisle to Blackburn was certainly a 'red letter' or to be more precise a 'red engine' day; for this was the day that 6201 'Princess Elizabeth' worked the northbound leg and so the only two 'Princess Royals' in existence were to meet at Appleby. The B.R. crews on the two locomotives were all from Carlisle and well used to handling L.M.S. pacifics from B.R. steam days. They are also very enthusiastic about steam traction and so the two 'Princesses' were posed to allow the moment to recorded for posterity. It was 30 years since they were last togther.

Between 22nd June and 7th September 46203 worked six times between the two depots hauling trains over both the Settle Carlisle and Cumbrian Coast routes, with the northbound trains of 4th July

named 'The Midlander' being worked right through to Carlisle Citadel. This was the first time since 1962 that she had worked a train into Carlisle Station and it was a very proud occasion for all concerned to return to a location she had graced on countless occasions in earlier times.

Her final southbound run of 1991 over the Settle−Carlisle line was on 4th October when she hauled 'The Westmorelander' train from Carlisle through to Crewe. This train was planned as a means of moving the locomotive down to Crewe for her to work the Crewe to Holyhead train, 'The Ynys Mon' on 12th October in place of ex L.N.E.R. pacific No. 4498 'Sir Nigel Gresley', which had still not returned to traffic from its seven year overhaul.

The route to be taken to get to Crewe involved a circuituous route round Manchester and over to Chester when a reversal was necessary in order to turn to reach Crewe. The train had been sold out for several

Above: 46203 powers her way up the 1 in 100 gradient on her way to the summit at Ais Gill on Saturday 24th August 1991 with 'The Appleby Round Table Express' headboard displayed on her top lamp bracket in recognition of the opening that day of the new watering facility at Appleby provided by Appleby Round Table. *Anne Stiles*

Facing Page Top: On 7th September 1991 'The Cumbrian Mountain Express' was once again hauled by 46203 on the northbound leg from Farringdon Junction to Appleby. She is seen here at Garsdale during a water and photographic stop surrounded by admirers. *Howard Routledge*

Left: A water stop at Long Preston, north of Hellifield, on Saturday 24th August 1991 as 46203, with a 66A (Polmadie) shedplate and 'Caledonian' headboard on, stands carefully positioned below the road bridge to take water from the road tanker above. *Howard Routledge*

Facing Page Centre: A line-up of contrasts at Carlisle station on Friday 4th October 1991 as 46203, shortly to take over 'The Westmorelander' stands alongside a Civil Engineer's liveried Class 47 diesel locomotive and Class 82 driving van trailer No. 82127 which is on the front of an express to London Euston. *Brian Radford*

Left: A fireman's eye view from the footplate of 'Princess Margaret Rose' as she approaches Garsdale with 'The Cumbrian Mountain Express' on Saturday 24th August 1991. *Howard Routledge*

Facing Page Bottom: The tender tank is replenished at Garsdale on 4th October 1991. 46203 had run from Appleby to Ais Gill summit in 23 minutes 10 seconds in less than perfect conditions. The support crew can be seen trimming the coal and servicing the engine. *Brian Radford*

weeks and an eager audience greeted the 'Princess' as she backed on-to the Pullman train in Carlisle ready for the 11.13 departure.

The run up to Appleby was tempered with speed restrictions although a spirited run through Armathwaite Station was greeted by the whole of the infant school and playgroup who lined both platforms to the delight of the passengers.

From Appleby she was opened up by Driver Kenny Stubbs with enthusiatic support from Inspector Jimmy Boyle and Fireman Paul Kane. The climb to the summit at Ais Gill was completed in 22 minutes in conditions less than perfect. If not the fastest ever, this must have been one of the noisiest and was well appreciated by the enthralled passengers as they were given an exhibition of L.M.S. pacific power par excellence.

Water was taken at Garsdale where 46203 posed for photographs after this epic climb. Further water stops were taken at Blackburn and Manchester Victoria. This was followed by a charge through Manchester Victoria Station in the teatime rush hour in order to get a run at Miles Platting bank. A lasting memory of this deafening climb will be of the small boy stood on the parapet of an overbridge close to the summit waving a stick as though conducting the 'last night of the proms' all to the beat of the locomotive as she slowed to breast the summit at 15 m.p.h.

The train then ran through the Manchester suburbs and eventally across the viaduct at Stockport, a route she had often traversed in times long past.

Chester Station was run past in the dark to allow a reversal to be made before a further spirited run to the locomotives destination at Crewe some 9½ hours after leaving Carlisle.

Saturday 12th October was yet another day of firsts in an already memorable year for 'Princess Margaret Rose', as she departed from Crewe Station hauling the 'Ynys Mon Express' to Llandudno Junction and on to Holyhead. During the week long stay over prior to this

run she had been stabled on the Crewe Heritage Centre where she had been joined by 'Princess Elizabeth' this being the fifth time that the two 'Princesses' had been together since June. After almost 30 years apart it seemed the two had almost become inseparable.

On return from Holyhead on 12th October 46203 moved onto the Heritage Centre to replenish the water in her tender before moving off being hauled by a diesel pilot along the former North Stafford-shire Line, the same route she had traversed on the epic run from Pwllheli in 1975, but this time in full working order and in light steam. The diesel pilot left soon after Stoke and 'Princess Margaret Rose' ran to Derby and then along the Erewash Valley to Butterley and back home.

In her first full season on the main line she had hauled nine trains and covered 1912 miles. She had put up some superb performances and had been well received by all the B.R. crews who handled her.

Thus 'Princess Margaret Rose' had made a triumphant return to steam after one of the longest 'out of steam' periods for any Class 8P locomotive. For her to run immediately following shopping at The Midland Railway Centre for major overhaul without problems of any significance fully reflected the skill, dedication and commitment, that has been a hallmark of the Midland Railway Trust Locomotive Department since its conception.

It is good to know that skill of this quality still exists today, some twenty two years after the end of steam traction on British Railways, and that No. 46203 'Princess Margaret Rose' will be based where she will be well cared for in years to come — the essential ingredient for further extension of her running life some 55 years after being built. And who knows? In years to come perhaps further chapters of this book will have to be written as 'Princess Margaret Rose' now looks forward to several years of main line activity and the distinct possibility of lining up alongside two other preserved Stanier Pacifics; a thought indeed to relish.

'Remember the good old days of steam' - two friends stand and admire 'Princess Margaret Rose' as she powers her way out of Sheffield up the 1 in 100 gradient on 2nd June 1990.

Robin Stewart-Smith

Above: 46203 finds an oasis of sunshine against a dark sky as she storms up the incline past Orgreave on the second memorial run on 2nd June 1990.
Chris Milner

Right: Well-wishers and admirers crowd around the cab of 'Princess Margaret Rose' as she stands at Derby station at the end of the second 'Memorial' special with Driver Tom Blakeman of Derby 4 shed signing autographs and Fireman Alan Porter surveying the memorable scene.
Brian Radford

Below: The following day 46203 was the star attraction at the Coalville open day where this fine broadside study was taken by Nick Hopkins.

Left: The final mainline duty for 46203 in 1991 was working 'The Ynys Mon Express' from Crewe to Holyhead and return, thus again covering ground in preservation on what were some of her former routes. She is seen here at Holyhead station on Saturday 12th October 1991. *Howard Routledge*

Left: Back at her home depot once more, 46203's final working in 1991 was on 17th November, when thanks to special permission from the Department of Transport, she worked trains on the Midland Railways Trust's line from Hammersmith to Riddings Junction. This was a typical November day with foggy patches. She is seen here at Butterley station with 'The Shamrock' headboard on in company with ex L.M.S. 0-6-0T 47357 before the start of the days work. Interestingly these two locomotives were both at one time allocated to Edge Hill depot and so had met before. *Brian Radford*

Below: 46203 leaves Chester on 23rd August 1992 with the North West Coast Express from Crewe to Holyhead. *Hugh Ballantyne*

Right: The first time that a 'Princess Royal' engine had hauled a train out of Nottingham was on 10th November 1990. 46203 is seen at the head of 'The Red Rose' special to Didcot.
T. Bailey Forman Newspapers

Below: 1st June 1991 saw 46203 on the Settle–Carlisle line working the 'Cumbrian Mountain Express'. She is seen here northbound passing Blea Moor loops.
Robin Stewart-Smith

46203 at the head of 'The Midlander' passing Barron Wood in beautiful summer weather on Friday 5th July 1991.

Rhys Jones

APPENDIX 1

THE SERVICE RECORD CARDS

This appendix comprises re-productions of the L.M.S. and B.R. service record cards of 'Princess Margaret Rose'. An explanation of the various classes of repair is necessary in order to enable the reader to understand what was involved.

Repairs were divided into one of two categories, scheduled or casual. Under these, they were then sub-divided into a heavy or light type. On the record cards for 'Princess Margaret Rose' the following codes are used :

L.C.	Light Casual	N.C.	Not Classified
L.S.	Light Service	H.S.	Heavy Service
L.O.	Light Overhaul	H.O.	Heavy Overhaul
L.I.	Light Intermediate	H.G.	Heavy General

Heavy repairs generally depended on the condition of the boiler and the tyres with General repairs being carried out at pre-determined intervals depending on mileage and number of days in traffic. For the 'Princess Royals' the mileage between this type of repair was about 250,000 with the time span about every two years in the earlier part of their working life and then increasing to about a three yearly cycle as the annual mileage covered became less.

A service repair was carried out at some mid-point between these general repairs to enable the locomotive to run until the next scheduled general repair.

Depending on the amount of work listed on the 'Shopping Proposal Form', which was sent in from the Depot where the engine was allocated, the shopping controller would categorise the level of repair in advance of the locomotive arriving at works. Mileage records were considered together with previous repair work carried out. This enabled the works to maintain a controlled workload and also to ensure that there were not too many locomotives of the same class out of traffic at the same time.

Service or casual repairs could fall into any category — light or heavy with casual repairs being done on an ad-hoc basis to correct some defect or damage. A repair was classified in the Heavy category if it involved any one of the following items of work :-
  Re-boilering
  Boiler to be removed from the frames
  New tyres to four or more wheels
or any two of the following items:-
  New cylinders
  New axles
  Retubing boiler
  Turning wheels
  Re-fitting axleboxes
  Overhaul motion or brakework
  Boiler repair whilst in the frames involving not less than 15% of the stays

At a general repair the boiler was always lifted out. On all types of locomotives the maximum time between these was about five years to be in compliance of the conditions set out by the Board of Trade relating to steam locomotive boilers. At a heavy general overhaul the intention was to return the locomotive to 'as new' condition whilst the service repair was intended to permit the locomotive to run to the next general repair.

A light repair involved work in any of the following areas:-
  New cylinders
  New axles
  Replacing more than 50% of the boiler tubes
  Turning four or more wheels
  Refitting axleboxes
  Overhauling motion
  Fitting a patch to the boiler
  Re-lagging boiler
  Fitting four or more new axleboxes
  Welding, patching or straightening frames
  Re-boring cylinders and re-facing ports
  Removal and repair of tanks.

46203 'Princess Margaret Rose' heads 'The White Rose' through Duffield with the Sheffield – Derby leg of the railtour on 15th September 1990.

Rhys Jones

LMS ENGINE HISTORY CARD. C.R.1A.   "PRINCESS MARGARET ROSE"

(CME)

DIVISION ~~WESTERN NORTHERN~~ 8/10/35 WESTERN NUMBER 6203

29.2.36

PASSENGER TENDER ~~SHUNTING~~ SUPERHEATER   CLASS (MP) 7   NAME OR No OF TYPE STANDARD

~~GOODS TANK NON SUPERHEATER~~   WHEEL TYPE 4-6-2   WHEEL BASE (E & T) 63' 10"

EMPTY WEIGHT 94 – 7   WORKING WEIGHT 104 – 10   DIA OF DRIVING WHEELS 6' 6'

CYLINDERS No 4   DIA 16¼'   STROKE 28'   OVERALL LENGTH OVER BUFFERS (E & T) 74' 4¼"

100 NS

CLASS of BOILER BELPAIRE TAPER   TUBES No ~~112 × 32~~ (REVISED OFFICIAL 1935)   STEEL   COPPER   BOILER PRESSURE 250 Lbs
(19/1/37) 112 × 32 A/crad 22/12/37

FIREBOX GRATE AREA 45 Sq ft   TRACTIVE POWER AT 85% 40300 lbs

BRAKES VACUUM (Pump Ejector) STEAM   VALVES PISTON ~~SLIDE~~   MOTION (TYPE) WALSCHAERT   CARRIAGE WARMING WITH ~~WITHOUT~~

BUILT BY CREWE   DATE BUILT 1ST JULY 1935

ENGINE incldg. Fitting £ 574 = 544 £ 58)   CHARGED TO Renewals M&EE minute 147   DATE "IMPROVED" × 6'-4-36 Ⓧ 19/1/37.
COST £ 8538
TENDER £ 1154 incldg. Patens £ T = 544 745   Total COST OF "IMPROVED" ENGINE £
COST OF "IMPROVEMENT" £9-16-18   CHARGED TO × See Below   × See below
10.19.5 ×£277

DATE REPLACED & TRANSFERRED TO DUPLICATE STOCK   REPLACED By No.

AMOUNT TRANSFERRED £   FROM   A/c To   A/c

DATE TAKEN OUT OF TRAFFIC   DATE BROKEN UP   SCRAP VALUE

CREDITED TO   A/c   MILEAGE UP TO DEC. 31ST. 1926   ✓

BOILER CHANGES   144,061

| DATE | PARTICULARS OF BOILERS FITTED | | | | | PARTICULARS OF BOILERS TAKEN OUT | | | | |
	VALUE	FROM	DATE NEW	MILEAGE	Belpaire or Round Top	Belpaire or Round Top	HOW DISPOSED OF	RECOVERED VALUE	MILEAGE	COST OF REPR
15.12.36	603	464	6202	June 1935	45,668	B(9100) No 9100	B(9100) No 9101	6209	460	316 144,061	52

× Fitting Steam Sanding Gear   Capital Revenue Total
£31-6-8   0-9-9   29-16-5
② DWO. 4403 Gangway doors steps & name plates   £ 44-19-0   34.1.7   10.17.5
NWO 4616 Hinged Smokebox Door bar   £ 1-9-1   14-1   1-3.2
£ 13-4-7   18-5   14-3-0
also   £ 14.13.8   £ 2.12.6   £ 17.6.2
Ⓧ 4 ton in place of 3 now elements - - - 70-0-0
Crewe A/W.S. 3912 ? 38
AA 486/30

RENEWAL PROVISIONS.

| YEAR | COST PER TON | REPLACEMENT COSTS | | | | | | LIFE | | ANNUAL PROVISION | |
| | | ENGINE INCLUDING BOILER | | | ~~BOILER~~ R | | ENGINE EXCL DG | | | | |
		GROSS COST	NETT RES DL. VALUE	NETT COST	GROSS COST	NETT RES DL. VALUE	NETT COST	ENGINE REPLACENT COG	ENGINE EXCL BOILER	ENGINE EXCL DG BOILER	BOILER
1935	£ 92.33	£ 8712	£ 369	£ 8343	£ 1902	£ 155	£ 1747	6596	30 YRS	10 YRS	220	175

DISTINCTIVE TENDER No.

NUMBER	DATE FITTED
~~9393~~	1.7.35
9374 Crewe A/1.5/3-7-35	19-1-37

PAT. NOS. 303754-22. 320082-23.

HEAVY REPAIRS						6203 LOCOMOTIVE ALLOTTED TO:—		
DATE TAKEN OUT OF TRAFFIC	DATE PUT BACK INTO TRAFFIC	MILEAGE SINCE LAST HEAVY REPAIR	COST OF REPAIR		REV. FOR N.W. INC.	DISTRICT	DATE FROM	DATE TO
			REF. TO COST A/C.	AMOUNT £				
6. 8. 36	14. 8. 36	109 567	ho. 1249	1339 622 3		Camden	6 . 4 . 35	
30 .11. 36	19. 1. 37	34 494	H. 68.	75.x		Polmadie	24 . 8 . 35	
						Camden	29 . 2 . 36	

LIGHT REPAIRS					REV. FOR N.W. INCL.			
DATE TAKEN OUT OF TRAFFIC	DATE PUT BACK INTO TRAFFIC	MILEAGE SINCE LAST HEAVY OR LIGHT REPAIR	COST OF REPAIR					
			REF. TO COST A/C.	AMOUNT £				
19-3-36	6-4-36	76 409	LS. 499	348 68	16			
8-4-36	18-4-36	76 611	LO. 0.520	73	6			
15-6-36	19-6-36	92 932	L 996	84	5			

SUMMARY

YEAR	EXPENDITURE				MILEAGE	COAL-ISSUED (TONS)	WEEK DAYS OUT OF SERVICE			
	HEAVY REPAIRS £	LIGHT REPAIRS £	RUNNING REPAIRS AND SHED EXAMINATIONS £	TOTAL £			HEAVY AND LIGHT REPAIRS	SHED REPAIRS AND EXAMINATIONS	NOT REQUIRED	TOTAL
1935	–	–	224	224	48 585	1125 52	UR. –	12 2	9	23
1936	622	463	511	1596	95 476	2353 55	60	31 1	1 –	93

L M S   ENGINE HISTORY CARD.

E.R.O. 3666
O.P. 4/7

PASSENGER TENDER ~~SHUNTING~~ SUPERHEATED
~~FREIGHT-TANK-NON-SUPERHEATED~~ (1-1-51) CLASS M.P. **8 X** WHEEL TYPE 4-6-2 NAME OF TYPE Princess Std.

"PRINCESS MARGARET ROSE"

C.M.E. COSTING GROUP No.

ENGINE NUMBER
46203 / 46203

EMPTY WEIGHT	94 - 7	WORKING WEIGHT	104 - 10	DIAMETER OF DRIVING WHEELS 6 - 6	WHEEL BASE (E. & T.) 63 - 10

CYLINDERS No. 4 DIAMETER 16½ STROKE 28 OVERALL LENGTH OVER BUFFERS (E. & T.) 74 - 4

BOILER No. REV No. W43 DIVNL REFCE. 1 Taper BELPAIRE OR ROUND TOP 1 B TUBES No. 171 & 24 STEEL BOILER PRESSURE 250 LBS.

Std 100 ns
28.11.39

FIREBOX GRATE AREA 45 SQ. FT.

TRACTIVE POWER AT 85% B.P. 40,300 LBS.

C.A. COSTS REFCE. No.

BRAKES { VACUUM EJECTOR STEAM } VALVES { PISTON } MOTION WALSCHAERT CARRIAGE WARMING { WITH WITHOUT }

1 A
ALLOCATION (DIVISION & DATE)

BUILT BY L.M.S. Crewe DATE BUILT 1ST JULY 1935

W.

TOTAL COST £ 1184 PATTERNS, INCLUDED 4 £ 394 SUPTCE. INCLUDED £ 45 CHARGED TO M. & E.E. MIN. No. 534 DATE 1934

MILEAGE AT DEC. 1936 144,061 TOTAL (LIFE) SINCE LAST GENERAL REPAIR

DATE TAKEN OUT OF TRAFFIC FOR BREAKING UP | DATE ACTUALLY BROKEN UP | SCRAP VALUE. GROSS £ | COST OF CUTTING UP £ | NET £ | DATE CREDITED COMPLETE RENEWALS

NOTES:— Previously 6203, re-numbered 46203, W.E.8.5.48

{ 754417
57921 } = 1940

IMPROVEMENTS, ETC.

DATE	ORDER No. (N.W. &c.)	PARTICULARS	CAPITAL £ s. d.	REVENUE £ s. d.	SUPTCE. £ s. d.	TOTAL £ s. d.
10.9.37	3098		10 0	5 10 0	—	6 0 0
28.1.39	X4851	Sug. 3858	87.6.0	1 4	—	87.4 3
7.9.40	H 181		70 0 0			70.0.0
27.12.41	X6802	& X7348 & 429 & 3868 & Misc	84-14-8	17-14-7		102-9-3
4.9.43	71881	& T.I. Fed blackout connections	21-0-0	2 10 0		103-10-0
25.12.43	7769	& Misc	11-0-0	82.10.0	—	93-10-0
5.8.44	7630	Water Scoop for Blr Top. Feed Trays	4 0	1.16.0	—	2 0 0
2.9.44	6319	(26/7/44)	115-6-0	3.12.0	—	118-18-0
P.E. 19/5/45	3868	and 5495. (6/8/44)	30-0-0			30-0-0
P.E.14.7.45	5275	Steel in lieu of copper tube + ejector exhaust pipes	1-5-0	1-6-7	—	52-11-7
P.E.27.12.47	5470	bw53 & X9953.	9-11-0	20 6 0		30-16-0

TECHNICAL ALTERATIONS ETC.

RENEWAL PROVISION (Section No.............)

REPLACEMENT COSTS

YEAR	GROSS REP. COST PER TON	ENGINE (INCLUDING BOILER) GROSS REP. COST	NET RESIDUAL VALUE	NET REP. COST	BOILER GROSS REP. COST	NET RESIDUAL VALUE	NET REP. COST	ENGINE (EXC. BOILER) NET REP. COST	LIFE ENGINE (EXCLDG BOILER) Yrs.	BOILER Yrs.	ANNUAL PROVISION ENGINE (EXCLDG BOILER)	BOILER
1937	91.85	8666	633	8033	2166	273	1893	6140	30	10	205	189
1938	87.65	8,270	516	7,754	2,035	217	1,818	5,936	30	10	198	182
1939	93.58	8829	579	8,250	2,136	250	1,886	6,364	30	10	212	189
1940	109.444	10,326	730	9,596	2,540	313	2,227	7,369	"	"	246	223
1941	114.91	10,842	733	10,109	2,406	309	2,097	8,012	"	"	267	210
1942	124.16	11,714	734	10,980	2,572	319	2253	8727	"	"	291	225
1943	129.80	12,246	731	11,515	2,774	314	2,460	9,055	"	"	302	246
1944	135.91	12,823	705	12,118	2,823	292	2,531	9,587	"	"	320	253
1945	140.34	13,241	631	12,610	2,817	242	2,575	10,035	"	"	334	258
1946	146.89	13,859	672	13,187	2,912	294	2,618	10,569	"	"	352	262

ORIGINAL COST	YEAR OF DEPRECIATION	STANDARD LIFE
ENGINE £ 8,119	FIRST 19	30 YEARS
TENDER £ 1,153		
TOTAL £ 9,272	1965	

TENDER

PREFIX	No.	DATE ATTACHED
LMS CREWE "1ST/ATT" 2/3/35	9124	1.7.35
	9374	19.1.37

46203

Engine Number 6203

BOILERS

	FITTED												TAKEN OUT				
DATE FITTED	REG'D No.	ECON. STOCK REF'CE	BELT. or R.T.	VALUE SHELL	VALUE FIREBOX	FROM	DATE NEW SHELL	DATE NEW FIREBOX	MILEAGE SHELL	MILEAGE FIREBOX		DATE RECOVERED	DISPOSAL	VALUE SHELL	VALUE FIREBOX	MILEAGE SHELL	MILEAGE FIREBOX
15-12-36 / 3-12-38	9100	100NS	B	603	462	6202	1935	1935	45668	45668		5·11·38	Stock	473	260	194626	194626
20-12-41	9101	100NS	B	432	347	6208	1935	1935	270338	270338		20-12-41	6207	353	155	446249	446249
26-7-44	9106			580	307	6209	July 1935	1935	395696	395696		26·7·44	6210	82	159	542067	542067
8·12·47	9102	100NS	B	199	517	6211			542315	542315							
24·5·51	9106	100NS	B			6210											
	9108	100NS	B			46204											

HEAVY AND LIGHT REPAIRS

DATE TAKEN OUT OF TRAFFIC	DATE RETURNED TO TRAFFIC	No. OF WEEKDAYS OUT OF TRAFFIC	CLASS OF REPAIR	MILEAGE SINCE PREVIOUS HEAVY REPAIR HEAVY	MILEAGE SINCE PREVIOUS HEAVY REPAIR LIGHT	BOILER *	REF'CE TO COST A/C	COST OF REPAIRS TOTAL (R.R.O.3578)	REVENUE PORTION N.W. INCLUDED	NET ENGINE (EXCLUDG N.W. REV. & BOILER)	RECOV'D BOILER (EXCLUDG T. & M.)	TOTAL (ENGINE AND BOILER)
	19-1-37	43	H.G.①		–			1398 / 7952		3		1100
5·8·37	10·9·37	32	H.S.	54,581		4	1526	642	6	529	107	636
29·11·37	13·12·37	13	L.O.		17,496	4	2124	125	–	125		125
28·10·38	12·1·39	67	H.G.②	94,377		2	2	1373	–	1327	163	1490
28·12·39	13·1·40	15	L.S.		77,423	4	5	X426		X426		X426
14·9·40	12·10·40	19	L.O.		121,388	4	67	224		224		224
25·1·41	22·2·41	22	H.C.	134,764		4	5	323	–	275	48	323
15·11·41	20·12·41	31	H.G.③	37,147		2	35	1266	18	849	212	1061
28·3·42	16·4·42	7	L.O.		14,809	4	18	164	···			164
13·11·42	15·12·42	28	H.S.	56,795		4	54	610	–	524	86	610
27·7·43	18·8·43	20	H.S.	38,712		4	35	1,032	83	864	84	948
21·9·43	30·9·43	9	L.O.		5,000	4	43	98	5			98
11·8·44	26·7·44	39	H.G.④	50,664		2	30	2366 / 1825	1826	366	2192
21·5·45	30·6·45	36	H.S.	52,764		4	42	1318	1	1107	210	1317
26·10·45	16·11·45	19	L.O.	32,792	26,504	4	76	102	–			102
24·12·45	9·2·46	41	H.O.	33,767		4	13	938	–	860	78	938
29·7·46	7·9·46	36	L.S.		38,847	4	49	1,471	–			1,471
18·1·47	19·2·47	28	L.O.		68,499	4C	8	660	–	–	–	660
21·2·47	20·3·47	24	L.O.		68,910	4C	13A	210	–	–	–	210

				MILEAGE SINCE PREVIOUS HEAVY REPAIR	MILEAGE SINCE LAST TO SHOPPED							
18·9·47	8·12·47	71	H.G.⑤	32,976	43,833 / 43,000	2C						
26·2·48	5·5·48	59 / 33	H.O.	14,243	12,486	C						
16· · 11·48	23 12·48	40	L.S.	30,710	43,196	C						
				SINCE PREVIOUS GEN. OR LHT								
18·2·49	13·5·49	72	H.C.	12,623	12,124	C						
5·8·49	15·9·49	36	L.C.	28,436	27,937	C						
16·10·49	28·10·49	11	M.C.	31,932	31,433	C						
2·6·50	3·7·50	26	L.I.	67,282	21,792	C						
17·4·51	24·5·51	32	H.G.	58,214	22,085	2 C						

X *Incomplete*

* BOILER
1 – NEW. 2 – CHANGED.
3 – LIFTED AND PUT BACK.
4 – REPAIRED ON FRAMES.

DISTRICT ALLOCATION

SHED	DATE
Camden	29·2·36
Edge Hill	21·10·39
Holyhead	6·4·40
Crewe	28·9·40
H Elyn ed.	2·11·40
Edge Hill	9·11·40
Camden	26·12·42
Edge Hill	3·4·43
Crewe Loan	9·10·43
Crewe	27·11·43
Edge Hill	20·5·44
Crewe L. Loan	18·10·47
Edge Hill	14·2·48
Polmadie (loan)	22·9·51

STORED

SERVICEABLE or UNSERV.	DATE IN	OUT

SUMMARY

YEAR	REPAIRS EXPENDITURE HEAVY	LIGHT	RUNNING REPAIRS & SHED EXAMS.	TOTAL	MILEAGE	COAL ISSUED TONS	LBS. PER MILE	WEEKDAYS OUT OF SERVICE HEAVY & LIGHT REPAIRS	RUNNING REPAIRS & EXAMS.	OTHER PURPOSES	NOT REQUIRED	STORED SERVICE-ABLE	UNSERV-ICEABLE	TOTAL
1937	1981	125	485	2591	74,941	1,741	52	65	68	–	1	–	–	134
1938 (36 wks)		520			57,390									
(53 wks)					74,014	1,735	53	56	67	–	–	–	–	123
1939					83,612			14	55	–	–	–	–	69
1940					57,999			29	37	–	11	–	–	77
1941					40,375			56	94	–	1	–	–	151
1942					58,884			45	58	–	–	–	–	103
1943					57,016			29	32	–	–	–	–	61
1944					51,086			39	83	–	7	–	–	129
1945					49,777			60	69	–	–	–	–	129
1946					67,436			72	38	–	3	–	–	113
1947					45,690			123	36	–	1	–	–	160
1948					43,695			92	53	–	–	–	–	145
1949					44,991			108	42	–	1	–	–	151
1950			57,721					76	43	–	–	–	–	119

PASSENGER ~~FREIGHT MIXED TRAFFIC~~ "PRINCESS MARGARET ROSE"

TENDER ~~TANK~~ SUPERHEATED ~~NON SUPERHEATED~~

DIESEL ~~ELECTRIC MECHANICAL~~

ENGINE NUMBER **46203**

CLASS M.P.	8	WHEEL TYPE	4-6-2	NAME OF TYPE	PRINCESS STD. (TAPER)

	T.	C.		T.	C.					
EMPTY WEIGHT	94	7	WORKING WEIGHT	104	10	DIAMETER OF DRIVING WHEELS	6	6	WHEEL BASE (E. & T.) 63 10	

CYLINDERS—No. 4 DIAMETER 16¼ STROKE 28 OVERALL LENGTH OVER BUFFERS (E. & T.) 74 4¼

C.A. COSTS REFCE. N° **1A**

BOILER—E.S. REF. No. 100 N° DIVN'L REFCE 1 BELPAIRE OR ROUND TOP B TUBES. No. (14.8.58) 112 & 32 123 & 32 STEEL COPPER BOILER PRESSURE 250 lbs.

BEARINGS, ROLLER—(Make) — FIREBOX—GRATE AREA 45 SQ. FT. TRACTIVE POWER AT 85% B.P. 40,300 lbs.

BRAKES (VACUUM PUMP EJECTOR) ~~WESTINGHOUSE~~ ~~STEAM~~ VALVES (PISTON ~~SLIDE~~) MOTION WALSCHAERT ~~XXXXX~~ CARRIAGE WARMING WITH ~~WITHOUT~~

SPECIAL FEATURES :- Electric Light, Self-Cleaning Smokebox, Rocking Firegrate, Self-Emptying Ashpan, Manganese Steel Axlebox Liners.

DATE BUILT 1ST JULY 1935

BUILT BY L.M.S. , CREWE LOT No. REN'L PROG. AUTHORITY :—Min. No. 534 DATE JUNE 1934

MILEAGE AT 31.12.50 956,399 TOTAL (LIFE) 1,494,484 SINCE LAST GENERAL REPAIR

DATE TAKEN OUT OF TRAFFIC FOR BREAKING UP, ETC DATE ACTUALLY BROKEN-UP SOLD TO MESSRS. BUTLIN'S LTD. APRIL 1963

NOTES :— *Withdrawn.* W.E. 20/10/62. (L.M.R. Outside Authorised Prog.)

ALLOCATION: L.M.R. / L.M. W. / Region / Divn. / Date / Region / Divn. / Date

IMPROVEMENTS, ETC.

DATE	ORDER No. (N.W. &c.)	PARTICULARS	CAPITAL £ s. d.	REVENUE £ s. d.	TOTAL £ s. d.
PE 26.12.53	R 1013	Fttg. Tell-tale device	1. 19. 6		1. 19. 6
	E 2212	Prov. of cast steel inside Cylinders	357. 6. 4	345. 13. 8	703. 0. 0
5.11.55	E 780 & R. 3335 — Inversion from Smokebox to Dome regulator. Provision of new style hinge pins.		142. 3. 4	116. 19. 6	259. 5. 10
PE 29.12.56	E 3869	Fttg. Strengthened Axlebox Guides (attention to boxes)	36. 8. 6	134. 18. 9	171. 7. 3
7.9.57	R. 7461	Prov. of Speed Indicators. (Larger carriage)	126. 16. 10	24. 15. 2	151. 12. 0
6.9.58	R. 3135 & E. 4196 — Provision & fitting of steam operated by-pass valves — Provision of metaflex joints.		36. 18. 4	72. 6. 2	109. 4. 6
PE 13.6.59	E. 4983	A.T.C.	302. 9. 0		302. 9. 0
3.52		Fitting of shear strips to front of cylinder castings (Derby)			

DISTRICT ALLOCATION				ORIGINAL COST		YEAR OF DEPRECIATION	STANDARD LIFE	TENDER		
M.P. DEPOT	DATE	M.P. DEPOT	DATE					Prefix	No.	Date attached
EDGE HILL	14.2.48	Carlisle U	27-1-62	ENGINE £ 8119		FIRST :— 19 ___		LMS	9374	19.1.37.
POLMADIE (LOAN)	22.9.51	Carlisle K	7-4-62	TENDER £ 1153			30 Years			
EDGE HILL	16.5.53			TOTAL £ 9272		FINAL :— 19 65				
CREWE N	23.5.53			Above information used for Depreciation purposes on and from 1/1/48.						
EDGE HILL	29.9.58									
Camden	20.8.60									
Edge Hill	10.9.60				N/LE					
Carnforth	11.3.61									
Crewe N	15.7.61									
Carnforth	9.9.61									

E.R.O. 3666 Back

CLASSIFIED REPAIRS (WORKSHOP AND M.P. DEPOT)
(* BOILER:—A = Changed, B = Lifted out and put back, C = Repaired on frames)

ENGINE NUMBER **46203**

DATE		WEEKDAYS OUT OF SERVICE				Class of Repair	Where repaired	MILEAGE		* Boiler	Cost Form Serial No.	COST OF REPAIR (Excludes barrel and firebox where boiler repaired to Stores Order)	
Taken out of traffic	Returned to traffic	Waiting Repair Decision	Waiting Works	On Works	Total			Since previous General or Intermediate repair.	Jan. 1st to date shopped			TOTAL as per cost form £	Revenue Portion of New Works Included £
	8·12·47					HG	C			A			
26·2·48	5·5·48				59	HC	a	14,243	12,486		•		
16·11·48	23·12·48				33	LS	c	44,953	43,196				
19·2·49	13·5·49				72	HC	c	12,623	12,124				
5·8·49	15·9·49				36	LC	c	28,436	27,937				
16·10·49	28·10·49				11	NC	c	31,932	31,433				
2·6·50	3·7·50	-	2	24	26	L.I	c	61,282	21,792				
17·4·51	24·5·51	-	-	32	32	HG	c	58,214	22,089	A	-79·51		
13·11·51	17·3·52	-	11	94	105	H.I.	Derby	32,343	54,428	B.			
4·4·52	4·4·52	-	-	1	1	NC(EO)	Brent	1,874	1,874	"			
8·4·52	10·4·52	-	-	2	2	NC(Rect)EC	"	1,874	1,874	"			
29·4·53	15·5·53	6	1	7	14	LC	"	83,869	24,250				
20·8·53	24·9·53	5	4	21	30	HC	"	26,557	44,601				
29·10·53	4·12·53	-	6	25	31	HI	"	110,302	50,682				
22·2·54	19·3·54	-	3	19	22	HC(EO)	"	13,250	6,814				
8·9·54	16·10·54	-	7	26	33	HC(EO)	"	46,341	43,935				
19·9·55	19·10·55	5	11	36	52	H.G.	101,749	55,071	41,009	A			
29·10·55	10·11·55	-	2	8	10	NC(Red)EO.	"	333	21,424				
9·2·56	23·3·56	5	5	19	29	L.C.(EO)	"	19,239	8,906.				
18·10·56	21·12·56	1	17	58	46	HI.	"	64,146	538·44				
1·6·57	3·8·57	-	16	38	54	L.C. (EO)	"	31,133	30,520				
23·9·57	26·9·57	-	-	3	3	NC(EO)	"	41,445	40,832				
18·10·57	7·12·57	-	6	37	43	L.C. (EO)	"	44,205	43,592				
13·6·58	14·8·58	-	5	48	53	HG.	"	78,738	30,409	2..			
13·4·59	22·5·59	4	5	25	34	L.C.	"	46,167	26,384				
9·9·59	6·11·59	11	8	31	50	HI.	"	102,178	44,495				
14·6·60	12·8·60	-	7	44	51	HC(EO)	"	33,498	26,562				
29·11·60	9·2·61	-	24	36	60	HI	"	52,405	45,469				

ANNUAL STATISTICS

Year	Mileage	Fuel Oil Issued (Gallons)	WEEKDAYS OUT OF SERVICE									
			CLASSIFIED REPAIRS				Running Repairs & Exams.	Not Required	STORED		Total
			Waiting Repair Decision	Waiting Works	On Works	Total			Serviceable	Unserviceable	
1951	54,428		-	11	60	71	36	1			108
1952	55,311	59,619	·	·	68	68	43				141
1953	53,119		11	11	53	75	52	2	-	-	129
1954	57,967.		-	10	45	55	37	1	-	-	93
1955	51,678		5	13	44	62	51	13	-	-	126
1956	54,457		6	22	47	75	51	2	-	-	128
1957	47,713		-	22	75	97	47	-	-	-	144
1958	56,192			5	48	53	66				119
1959	51,431		15	13	56	84					
1960	45,469										
1961	6,012										
1962	—										

BOILER CHANGES

Date fitted	Registered No.	New or Repaired	Economic Stock Reference	Belpaire or Round Top
24·5·51	9108	R	100NS	B.
19·10·55	9101	R	100NS	B.
14·8·58	9100	R	100NS	B.

STORED (SERVICEABLE OR UNSERVICEABLE)

S. or U.S.	DATE		S. or U.S.	DATE	
	In	Out		In	Out
S	5·3·61	9·7·61			
S	1·9·61	24·1·62			
S	9/9/62	15/10/62			

TECHNICAL MODIFICATIONS

Part 1. MAJOR TECHNICAL MODIFICATIONS TO 'PRINCESS MARGARET ROSE'

Date of completion	Order No.	Description
6th April 1936		Fitting of steam sanding gear in lieu of gravity fed.
19th January 1937	AA484/30	Boiler heating surface modified from 3 row (24) to 4 row (32) superheater elements and small tubes reduced from 141 to 112.
	DWO 4403	Gangway (cab) doors, steps and sideplates.
	NWO 4616	Hinged smokebox door bar. Tender No. 9374 attached with 10 tons coal capacity in lieu of Tender No.9124 (9 tons).
5th August 1944	NWO 7630	Water scoop for boiler feed top trays.
14th July 1945	5275	Steel in lieu of copper tube used for ejector exhaust pipe.
March 1952	Special	Fitting of shear strips to outside cylinders.
26th December 1953	E2212	Provision of cast steel inside cylinders. Fitting of tell-tale device to inside big-ends.
November 1955	E780	Conversion from smokebox to domed regulator (boiler No. 9101 done and fitted to 46203).
5th November 1955	R3335	Provision of new brake hanger pins and alteration of brake hanger carriers. 29th December 1956
7th September 1957	R7461	Provision of speed indicator equipment.
6th September 1958	E3135	Provision and fitting of steam operated cylinder cocks.
	E4176	Provision of 'Metaflex' joints.
p.e. 13th June 1959	E4983	Fitting of automatic train control equipment.

Part 2

JOB NUMBERS ISSUED RELATING TO 6203 AND REQUIRING MODIFICATIONS TO THE LOCOMOTIVE

New work orders (N.W.O.) were allocated where the value of reclaimed material was negligible. Displaced work orders (D.W.O.) covered modifications where a significant value of material was involved. An 'X' suffix indicated work of an experimental nature.

Special note: Some modifications were carried out before the issue of the official Job Number documents which commenced at No. 5030. Earlier modifications were allocated an earlier number counting downwards without any relevant sequence. Dates given are the dates on which the documents were first issued.

Job No. Issue Date, Job No. and Work Content.

14th November 1935: Job No. 5012 (amendment).
Ferrobestos pads on pony truck bolster slides.

11th December 1935: Job No. 4982.
Main steam pipe joint clips to be 4 bolt type as engines pass through for general repair.

16th September 1936: Job No. 5019: New work Order X4714
Steam sanding gear in place of trickle sanding. (6203 done 6th April 1936 according to engine record card).

Date unknown: Job No 5025: New work Order No. X4851
Alterations to 4-6-2 engines. No details available. (6203 done 28th January 1939).

11th August 1937: Job No. 4959
Cab window glass: Window thickened from 3/16" to ¼" using new glass for classes 6,7,8. Classes 5 and below to use glass reclaimed from carriages.

1st January 1938: Job No. 5053
All valve spindle crossheads for standard taper boiler engines to be cast iron split into top and bottom section. - at renewals as required (charged to maintenance).

3rd February 1938: Job No 5031
Cab window fastenings, handles and catches in place of springs.

22nd March 1938: Job No 5059
Stops to be fitted on regulator stuffing boxes and catches to regulator handles as engines pass through shops for repairs.

14th May 1938: Job No. 4968
N.V.nuts not to be perpetuated on horn clips - replaced by nut and cotter as previously.

9th August 1938: Job No. 4970
Modified spring link bracket.

18th August 1938: Job No. 5088: New work Order No. 5149
Removal of vacuum pumps. Reason:- combined ejectors function satisfactorily without the need for pumps, plus pumps are thought to be a contributory factor in the cases of fracture in the L.H. piston rods in the crosshead. (M. & E.E. minute No. 1455 27th July 1938).

26th January 1939: Job No. 4991: New work Order No. K7116
New bronze link coupling in regulator to prevent sticking. Ditto for domed regulator.

16th March 1939: Job No. 5123
Independent lubricating pipe to tender brake cylinder.

10th May 1939: Job No. 5115/1: New work Order No. X6802
Fitting of coned joints to sandbox extension pipes altered to flanged joints. (Extension of original job no. issued 16th February 1939 to cover Princess Royals and Coronations) (6203 done 27th December 1941).

14th May 1939: Job No. 5139
Mushroom type cylinder lubrication check valves replaced with ball type plus stronger spring to retain oil against vacuum leakage when engine standing. All phosphor bronze check valves on axleboxes. (at repairs in shops) (6203 done 28th January 1939).

28th June 1939: Job No. 4983: New work Order No. K8334
Gland fitted to outside steam pipe to prevent movement and steam leakage.

25th August 1939: Job No 5141
Fitting of non-ferrous firebox stays in the extended areas in triangular area at top corners of the lowest firebox sideplates. (Job closed 13th November 1962).

1st September 1939: Job No. 5146/1
Stiffening brackets for cab backing plates to prevent fractures.

1st September 1939: Job No 5152
Standardisation of brake blocks and mods. to brake hangers to suit (Drawing No. 33/13114). (all locos).

27th March 1940: Job No. 5189
Provision of rocking washers on spring gear of engine and tender (as renewals). (All done and Job closed 15th February 1957).

2nd April 1940: Job No. 5207
Adjustment of bolster pads to compensate for differences in thickness of bogie or pony truck tyres by more than ¼" from those of the coupled wheels.

8th April 1940: Job No. 5208
Fitting of drain cocks to Class H exhaust injectors to prevent freezing in cold weather. (Fitted at repairs to all spares) (Costs charged to maintenance).

5th July 1940: Job No. 5043 (part): New work Order No 4832
Removal of Hasler Speed recorder equipment and fitting of BTH speed indicators. (6200/1 and 6203 – 6212 had Hasler).

17th July 1940: Job No. 5155
Increased bogie side play to 'Princess Royal' class (except 6202) to enable them to negotiate curves more easily (as engines pass through shops).

26th Febrauary 1941: Job No. 5240
Modifications to gangway door springs and guides to prevent loss in service (renewals and replacements).

3rd July 1941: Job No. 5255: New work Order No X7348
Fitting of sand gun to keep tubeplate as clean as possible. (when next in shops for General repair - Princess Royals only (excluded 6202) Modified on 4th April 1944 to provide flexible connecting pipe which can be removed from the sand hopper when not in use. Included 6202 (6203 done 27th December 1941).

1st August 1941: Job No. 5256
Additional ventilation by means of modified front window fastening to give air flow when air raid precaution fireglow screens are fitted.

12th December 1941: Job No 5276: New work Order No. X7630
Separate water scoop for top feed tray in boilers displacing combined scoop and deflector. (Drg D37/15162, D34/13849) Modified drawing issued 26 June 1942 showing changes to original scoop fitted. (6203 done 5th August 1944).

9th January 1942: Job No. 5281
Removal of spark deflector plates for storage during war time. (Drawing No. NF 1000.00-D35/13924) - as engines pass through works.

5th February 1942: Job No. 5285
Clip for detonator case in cabs to prevent deterioration when housed in engine toolboxes in damp conditions. Costs charged to maintenance.

27th February 1942: Job No. 5274
New standard brick arches using standard firebricks (Drawing D41-16324).

27th March 1942: Job No. 5292
Replacement of combined boiler support, frame stretcher and spring bracket casting for leading coupled wheels with separate boiler support and spring bracket/frame stretcher castings to prevent fractures found to occur. (as repairs are required). Costs charged to maintenance.

11th April 1942: Job No. 5297
Extension of lugs on regulator stuffingbox to prevent overtravel of regulator handle causing sliding grid type of regulator in smokebox lifting off its seat and remaining open. (Incident caused and casualty).

5th August 1942: Job No. 5305
Provision of larger injector steam valves (1 1/7'' instead of 1½'' diameter).

9th September 1942: Job No. 5309
Top feed clackbox connections.

16th September 1942: Job No. 5317
Alteration to water gauge bottom frames to remove integral drain cock.

7th December 1942: Job No. 5236
All 'Princess Royals' to have ashpan sidedoor locking arrangement as fitted to No. 6210 plus eyebolts and hooks to hold doors open.

16th February 1943: Job No. 5239
Fitting improved piston head and rod (involving new front cylinder covers) in which rod is secured to piston by new nuts. Engines to be called in specially when material available.

16th July 1943: Job No. 5351
New design of air relief valves on standard engines. (Steel valves & cast iron to replace aluminium alloy).

6th August 1943: Job No. 5354
Extension to fall plate sections to prevent falling between engine and tender on sharp curves.

1st December 1943: Job No. 5357
Clip for brake hanger top pins to replace split pins found to break.

6th June 1944: Job No. 5043 (part): New work Order No. 4832
BTH speed indicating equipment to be removed due to difficulty of maintaining same in satifactory condition plus difficulty in obtaining parts. - work undertaken in shops and MPDs and equipment stored.

15th February 1945: Job No. 5403: New work Order No. X8594
Deflector plate for exhaust injector overflow on RH side of tenders fitted to all 4-6-2 engines. (Water and steam blowing back onto tender wheel and axlebox causing fouling of oil)

3rd May 1945: Job No. 5413
Provision of stronger bogie control springs and lubricated bolster pads. (Princess Royal and Princess Coronation classes).

Not Issued: Job No 5428
Providing rocking grate and self cleaning grate on five 4-6-2 passenger engines.

3rd April 1946: Job No. 5391: New work Order No. 6453
Two additional washout plugs at front end of barrel to facilitate dirt and scale removal. (all taper boiler engines) (6203 done 27th December 1947).

6th December 1946: Job No. 5472: New work Order No. 7071
Fitting of external water strainer on each tender to 46 4-6-2s to exclude foreign matter. (6203's tender No. 9374 fitted p.e. 25th December 1948).

8th January 1948: Job No. 5491: New work Order No. X9953
Provision of new spring detail, safety clips, and bottom frame bar to bogies. (due to failures) (6203 done p.e. 27th December 1947).

8th August 1949: Job No. 5537
BTH speed indicators and modified drive mounting. (18 7P 4-6-2 engines) (Not known if 46203 included).

9th November 1949: Job No. 5539
Fitting of top feed deflector plates in lieu of top feed trays which do not fulfil design purpose owing to difficulty in cleaning.

4th January 1950: Job No. 5542: New work Order E780
Conversion from smokebox to dome type regulator in boilers in order to reduce maintenance. (6200/1 altered in 1935 under DWO 3868). 10 engines plus one spare. Job extended to cover spare boiler for 6200/1 on 20th July 1950. Job completed by 19th August 1958.

9th May 1950: Job No. 5555: New work Order No R1013
Fitting of tell-tale device to give warning of excessive heating on inside big-ends. (Job completed 16 March 1954). 46203 done during H.I. overhaul 29th October 1953 – 4th December 1953 with the cost of £1-19-6d charged to Capital.

16th May 1952: Job No. 5663: New work Order No. E2194
Removal of sand guns and equipment.

6th June 1952: Job No. 5665: New work Order No. E2212
Provision of cast steel inside cylinders of modified design to replace exisiting cast iron due to frequent fractures - To be done when they require renewing. (all done by 4th January 1957). 46203 done during H.I. overhaul 29th October 1953 – 4th December 1953 at a cost of £703-0-0d with £357-6-4d charged to Capital and £3345-13-8d charged to Revenue.

27th January 1954: Job No. 5686: New work Order No. R3135
Provision and fitting of steam operated cylinder cocks. (12 Princess Royal Locomotives). Job suspended on 6th June 1961 ; only 46204 not then fitted.

6th February 1956: Job No. 5755: New work Order No. E3689
Fitting strengthened axlebox guides at first and second driving axle positions. (Trouble with broken guides). To be done at general repairs. All locomoives completed by 16th June 1960. 46203 done at Heavy Intermediate Overhaul 28th October 1956 - 21st December 1956. Cost - £171-7-3d with £36-8-6d charged to Capital and £134-18-9d charged to Revenue.

20th August 1957: Job No. 5794: New work Order No. R7461
In view of the number of high speed trains now operating in the L.M. Region it was decided to fit speed indicators as quickly as possible to the ex.L.M.S. Class 8P 4-6-2 locomotives. Locomotives to be taken to Crewe Works specially to be fitted. (All complete by 10 september 1958). 46203 fitted 7th September 1957 at a cost of £151-12-0d with £126-16-10d charged to Capital and £24-15-2d charged to Revenue.

14th March 1960: Job No. 5827: New work Order No. E4983
Provision of AWS type of train control on steam locomotives on LMR 1960 programme. 46203 done during p.e. 13 June 1959 probably at the light casual repair 13 April 1959 - 22 May 1959 at a cost of £302-9-0d and charged to Capital.

THE LIVERIES OF 'PRINCESS MARGARET ROSE'

1. FIRST LIVERY — 1st July 1935 (as new)

Basic colour: Crimson Lake with 12 '' high engine numerals in gold leaf shaded black in accordance with the following detailed specification:

ENGINE	Painted Maroon with the exception of the smokebox which is painted black.
Running Angle	Maroon with 1'' black line running along bottom edge and ⅜'' yellow line running adjacent to it.
First Boiler Clothing Lagging Belt (Smokebox end)	Painted black with a ⅜'' yellow line running adjacent to it on the clothing.
Firebox Lagging Belt outside Cab	2'' black line and ⅜'' yellow line adjacent to it.
Cab Side	2¼'' black line running down both sides and bottom edge and ⅜'' yellow line adjacent to it on the inside. The engine numbers are central on the cab side and the horizontal centre line of the numbers is 22'' from the platform plate. Total width of numbers is 44'' and the size of the latter is 12''.
Splashers	Peripheral 1'' black line and adjacent to it ⅜'' yellow line, on the inside.
Buffer Beam	Red
TENDER	Painted maroon. 2¼'' black line all round side and back plates and ½'' yellow line adjacent to it on the inside.
Lightening holes in frame	1'' black line all round and ½'' yellow line adjacent to it on the outside.
Bottom of Frame	1'' black line with ½'' yellow on the inside.
Footsteps	1'' black line on the side and bottom and ½'' yellow line on the inside.
Buffer Beam	Red

14'' letters L M S are painted on the tender tank. The letter 'M' coincides with the centre line of the intermediate wheel. The distances from the centre of the 'M' to the centre of the 'L' and 'S' are 5' 0'' and 4' 9'' respectively. The letters are placed 2' 6'' from the bottom of the tank, i.e. to the bottom of the letters.

1a Detailed Change — 13th January 1939(?)

Numeral size changed to 10 '' high letters in plain block gilt lettering with black shading 'L M S' lettering on tender 14 '' high black shaded. Classification figures and letters 2⅛'' high.

2. SECOND LIVERY — 8th December 1947

ENGINE	Painted glossy black.
Running Angle	2½'' wide maroon band edged with ⅜'' straw line with ⅜'' black line top and bottom of running angle.
First lagging belt (smokebox end) and last lagging belt (front of firebox)	Maroon edged with ⅜'' straw line each side.
Firebox lagging belt (in front of cab)	Maroon edged with ⅜'' straw line each side.
Cab side (sides and bottom)	2½'' wide maroon band around edge with ⅜'' straw line at inside edge. The engine numbers are central on the cab side and the bottom of the numbers is 30'' from the bottom of the cab side. The size of the numbers is 12'' (Gill Sans).
Cylinders casing belts (front and rear)	Maroon edged with ⅜'' straw line each side.
All buffer beam and buffer stocks	Red (vermilion).
All footsteps	Black, no lining.
All tyres	As machined.
TENDER	Painted glossy black.
Tender tank sides	2½'' wide maroon band edged with ⅜'' straw line at inside edge.
Tender frames	Black, no lining.

The tender letters 'L M S' on the tender tank sides are placed with the centre line of the 'M' in line with the centre axle of the intermediate wheel. The distances from the centre of the 'M' to the centre line of the 'L' and 'S' are 5' 3'' and 5' 0'' respectively. The letters are placed 2' 6'' from the bottom of the tank i.e. to the bottom of the letters. The letters are 14'' high (Gill Sans). Both engine numbers and LMS letters are straw coloured lined with maroon edged with straw.

2a. Detail changes of second livery.

For a short period in 1949 the smokebox numberplate was changed to an L.M.S. style 46203. The tender lettering remained L.M.S.

The smokebox number plate was changed again (1949/50) for the style which was to last throughout the B.R. years, although the tender continued with LMS on the tank sides.

3. THIRD LIVERY — 24th May 1951

Basic colour: 'Caledonian' Blue.
Information from drawings Nos D49-18750 (engine) & D49-18749 (tender).

ENGINE	Painted blue with the exception of the smokebox, smokebox saddle and outside steam pipes.
Running Angle	Blue with a ½'' black line along the bottom edge, and a ½'' blue line above that and a ⅛'' white line above the blue (i.e. next to the main blue of the angle). Lining to follow actual edge of running angle throughout.
All firebox clothing bands	Blue.
Handrails	Black.
All parts below platform (running plate)	Black, except motion which is to remain bright.
Cylinder clothing	Black.
Splashers	Blue, lined along the top edge only with ½'' black band, ½'' blue band, ⅛'' white band except where a splasher is extensively screened by external fittings when it should not be lined.
Cab side	Blue with inset lining panel 5'' from bottom and sides and 4'' below cab side windows. Lining as follows: top corners and bottom back corner: from outer edge:- ⅛'' white, ½'' blue, 1'' black with outer corner radius of 4'', plus ½'' blue edged with ⅛'' white on inside with a corner radius of (outer edge of blue) of 2⅝'' struck from a different centre ⅜'' in at an angle of 45 degrees. Bottom front corner adjacent to running angle : From outer edge :- ⅛''white, ½'' blue, 1'' black, with outer corner radius of 7'' (to match 1' radius of edge of cabside plate) plus:- ½'' blue edged with ⅛'' white on inside with a corner radius of 5½'' (struck from a different centre as above.)
Cab side numbers	8'' figures (Gill sans medium) set with tops 10½'' below bottom of cab side windows, and centred in lining panel.
Classification	2'' figure and letter set equidistant between top of cab side numbers and inner edge of lining panel (To be painted in cream lining colour if transfers not available).
Cab Roof	Black

Buffer beam & buffer stocks	Signal red to B.S. colour No 537.
Frame extension	Black
TENDER	Tender tank sides to be blue with inset lining panel 5'' from bottom edge of tender side plate, 1' 5'' from the outer edge of the front beading, 1' 4'' from the back edge and 3'' below the start of the curve at the tank top. At the top corner of the lining panel the front corner follows the inside edge of the beading and is set 9'' away. At the rear top corner a curve of radius 1' 11'' is set 7'' below the horizontal beading at the rear of the tender tank side and runs out to 9'' at the corner radius of the lining panel. The corner radii are 4'' for the outside of the outer ⅛'' white band with a ½'' blue and black band inside. Two further bands of ½'' blue with a 2⅝'' radius (on a different centre) set in by ⅜'' on a 45 degree angle plus a ⅛'' inner white band complete the lining panel.
Tender tank backplate	Blue unlined.
Handrails	Black
Exposed parts on tender top	Black
Buffer Beam & Buffer stocks	Signal red to B.S.colour No.537
B.R. Lion & Wheel crest	One left hand and one right hand required (Lion must face forward). 2' 4'' high transfers to be placed centrally on the panel between the horizontal rows of rivets and between the third and fourth vertical rows of rivets. Bottom of the square block lettered 'BRITISH RAILWAYS' to be 2' 6½'' from bottom of tender tank side plate (10' 8¼'' from leading edge of front beading and 11' 2'' from the back edge of the tender side.

4. FOURTH LIVERY – 17th March 1952 (applied at Derby Locomotive Works.)

Basic colour:- B.R. Brunswick Green applied to boiler, cab sides and front, running angle, tender sides and back.

Cylinder covers	Glossy black lined with two vertical orange lines at both front and rear edges.
Smokebox	Glossy black
Buffer beams	Vermilion
Nameplates	Black background
Lining	Black and orange (next to the green) was applied to the cabside side panel, tender side, and the boiler bands. The running plate angle was lined with a single orange line at both bottom and top edges.

The rest of the framing below running plates and other details, including wheels plain black.

The B.R. Crest on the tender was the Lion & Wheel (handed for each side). In August 1958 the second design of tender transfer replaced the Lion & Wheel. This second design was not handed.

5. FIFTH LIVERY – April 1963

Basic colour: L.M.S. crimson lake per original livery (first) when built, except that the gold numbers and letters carried both black (to the right and below) and red (to the left and below) shading and were of Midland Pattern. The engine numbers were also placed in the post war positions and not central on the cabside panel.

6. SIXTH LIVERY – May 1985

Basic Colour: B.R.Brunswick Green. This repainting was done only to make the locomotive look more respectable after repairs to platework and boiler cladding pending eventual restoration to working order.

7. SEVENTH LIVERY – May 1990

Basic colour: B.R. Crimson Lake applied strictly in accordance with the official painting and lettering drawing No. D60-26081 of 1960. The smokebox numberplate 46203 in L.M.S. style with the second style B.R. emblem on the tender.

ENGINE	Painted maroon with the exception of the smokebox which is painted black.
Running plate	Maroon with 1'' wide black line along bottom edge and ½'' wide yellow line above.
First lagging belt smokebox end	½'' yellow line on inside edge of lagging band (boiler side)
Firebox lagging belt outside cab	½'' yellow line on outside edge of lagging band (boiler side) painted on top of 1½'' wide back band.
Cab side	2½'' black band all round sides and bottom only edged on inside with ½'' yellow band.
Cab roof, wing plate & door, oilboxes & sandboxes	Black
Splasher	1'' wide band all round side plate with ½'' yellow band on inside edge. Splasher tops black.
Cylinder casing bands	Maroon with ⅜'' yellow lines on inside edge.
Footsteps, Backplate only	1⅛'' black band on sides only edged with ⅜'' yellow band on inside edge and continuing across the bottom footstep only ¼'' above the footstep back angle. (No lining on footsteps)
Front buffer beam	Vermilion edged all round with 1'' black and ⅜'' yellow band on inside edge.
Buffer stock (Engine & Tender)	Vermilion with ⅜'' yellow band commencing at front edge of buffer stock footstep.
All motion	Left bright.
TENDER	
Tender side plates	Painted in maroon with 2½'' black band all round (measured from inside edge of beading and tender tank bottom plate) with ½'' yellow band on inside edge.
Tender tank backplate	Painted unlined maroon.
Tender frame lightening holes	1⅛'' black band and ⅜'' yellow band on edge opposite holes.
Tender frame bottom edge	1⅛'' black band and ⅜'' yellow band above (Note lining also runs up at the back angle of the frame as far as the rear buffer beam and up to the brake shaft bush at the front end).
Tender buffer beam	Vermilion edged at the bottom and sides by a 1'' black band edged on the inside by a ⅜'' yellow band.

APPENDIX 4

MILEAGES

Year	*Miles run*	*Year*	*Miles run*	*Year*	*Miles run*	*Year*	*Miles run*
1935	48 585 L	1943	57 016 L	1951	54 428 B	1958	56 192 B
1936	95 467 L	1944	51 086 L	1952	59 619 B	1959	51 431 B
1937	74 941 L	1945	54 674 L	1953	53 119 B	1960	45 469 B
1938	74 017 L	1946	67 434 L	1954	57 967 B	1961	6 012 B
1939	83 612 L	1947	45 690 L	1955	51 678 B	1962	* B
1940	57 999 L	1948	43 695 B	1956	54 457 B	1990	331 P
1941	40 375 L	1949	44 991 B	1957	47 713 B	1991	1 908 P
1942	58 887 L	1950	57 921 B				

L LMS B BR P Preserved

* Not recorded, but over 7600.

LIST OF TENDERS ATTACHED TO 'PRINCESS ROYAL' CLASS 4-6-2 LOCOMOTIVES

Tender No.	Build Date	Attached to Engine	Date Attached	Remarks
9000	1933	6200	27/06/33	Straight-sided. Subsequently rebuilt with curved sides. To engine no. 5073 w/e 08/6/35.
9001	1933	6201	3/11/33	Straight-sided. To engine No. 5074 w/e 15/6/35.
9003	1933	6202	29/06/35	Straight sided subsequently rebuilt with curved sides. Standard but with laminated buffer springs, original type of brake and pick-up gearing and feed water condensate gear for the turbines.
9065	1934	6200	9/05/35	Curved sided.
		6201	20/06/36	To No. 5739 w/e 12/12/36.
9066	1934	6201	28/03/35	Curved sided. To engine No. 5738 w/e 05/12/36.
		6200	20/06/36	
9124	1935	6203	1/07/35	Curved sided. To engine No. 6130 (per Lemon 19/2/37)
9125	1935	6204	19/07/35	Curved sided. To engine No. 5741 (new 31/12/36)
9126	1935	6205	24/07/35	Curved sided. To engine No. 6152
9127	1935	6206	1/08/35	Curved sided. To engine No. 5727 (new 17/10/36)
9128	1935	6207	9/08/35	Curved sided. To engine No. 5742 (new 31/12/36)
9129	1935	6208	16/08/35	Curved sided. To engine No. 6125
9130	1935	6209	23/08/35	Curved sided. To engine No. 5726 (new 10/10/36)
9131	1935	6210	6/09/35	Curved sided. To engine No. 6157
9132	1935	6211	18/09/35	Curved sided. To engine No. 6124
9133	1935	6212	21/10/35	Curved sided. To engine No. 6151

All the tenders in the above three categories were 4000 gallons water capacity and 9 tons coal capacity. They were all built at Crewe.

NOTE: Tender No. 9002 was allocated to Royal Scot No. 6100 for its North American Tour.

Tender No.	Attached to Engine	Date Attached	Intended for Engine	Tender No.	Attached to Engine	Date Attached	Intended for Engine	Tender No.	Attached to Engine	Date Attached	Intended for Engine
9344	6205	29/05/36	5708	9354	6212	28/07/36	5718	9372	6200	23/11/36	5736
	6208	3/07/36			6211	5/12/44			6210	13/08/55	
	6205	11/03/37			6209	4/09/46		9373	6201	28/11/36	5737
9345	6211	29/06/36	5709	9359*	6206	15/10/36	5723	9374	6203	19/01/37	5738
	6212	5/12/44			6207	20/11/46		9375	6204	19/12/36	5739
9353	6205	17/07/36	5717		6206	17/10/47		9376	6207	18/12/36	5740
	6208	11/03/37		9360	6210	25/09/36	5724		6210	20/12/39	
	6210	16/06/39			6208	16/06/39			6200	27/08/55	
	6207	25/12/39		9361	6209	1/10/36	5725				
	6206	20/11/46			6211	4/09/46					
	6207	17/10/47									

All the above were built at Crewe in 1936 and were curved sided with 4000 gallons water capacity and 10 tons coal capacity.

* Fitted with steam-operated coal pusher

9816	46206	18/10/62	Built for 'Princess Coronation' class. Curved sides, increased coal capacity and steam operated coal pusher fitted. (Attached to Engine No. 6253 when new in 1946.)

ALLOCATIONS OF 'PRINCESS MARGARET ROSE'

Date from	Code	Depot	Date from	Code	Depot
4th July 1935		New, first trip Crewe—Euston	14th February 1948	8A	Edge Hill
6th July 1935	1B	Camden	22nd September 1951	66A	Polmadie (on loan)
20th July 1935	27A	Polmadie (on loan)	16th May 1953	8A	Edge Hill
24th August 1935	27A	Polmadie	23rd May 1953	5A	Crewe North
15th February 1936	1B	Camden (on loan)	20th September 1958	8A	Edge Hill
29th February 1936	1B	Camden	20th August 1960	1B	Camden (on loan)
21st October 1939	8A	Edge Hill	10th September 1960	8A	Edge Hill
6th April 1940	14A	Holyhead	5th March 1961	24L	Carnforth (in store out of use)
28th September 1940	5A	Crewe North	9th July 1961		(taken out of store)
2nd November 1940	14A	Holyhead	16th July 1961	5A	Crewe North
9th November 1940	8A	Edge Hill	1st September 1961	24L	Carnforth (in store out of use)
26th December 1942	1B	Camden	24th January 1962		(taken out of store)
3rd April 1943	8A	Edge Hill	27th January 1962	12B	Carlisle Upperby
9th October 1943	5A	Crewe North (on loan)	7th April 1962	12A	Carlisle Kingmoor
27th November 1943	5A	Crewe North	9th September 1962		(stored in serviceable condition)
20th May 1944	8A	Edge Hill	15th October 1962		(taken out of store)
18th October 1947	5A	Crewe North (on loan)	20th October 1962		Withdrawn from service

Following withdrawal 46203 was sold to Messrs Butlins, and was taken to Crewe Works to be restored to L.M.S. Crimson Lake livery. She was then hauled dead on her own wheels from Crewe to Butlins Camp at Pwllheli on 4th May 1963.

Date	Code	Detail	Date	Code	Detail
11th May 1975		Moved by rail from Pwllheli to Derby (stored out of use at Derby Carriage Works and Derby Locomotive Works)	18th August 1991	12B	Carlisle Upperby
			24th August 1991		Carnforth
			7th September 1991	12B	Carlisle Upperby
4th November 1975	18A	Moved to Toton m.p.d.	5th October 1991		Crewe
5th November 1975		Moved to Butterley (Midland Railway Centre)	12th October 1991		Midland Railway Centre
October 1988		Moved into workshops at Butterley Park m.p.d.	24th July 1992		Crewe
15th to 17th May 1990		Test runs with 41E (Barrow Hill) shedplate	6th September 1992		Midland Railway Centre
2nd June 1990		66A Polmadie shedplate carried	12th November 1992	84E	Tyseley
1st June 1991	12B	Carlisle Upperby	(to 9th January 1993)		
22nd June 1991		Carnforth			

'PRINCESS ROYAL' CLASS BOILERS

Note: Where an exact date is shown, this is the date that the boiler was actually fitted.

Engine No.	Original Boiler	2	3	4	5	6	7	8	9	10	11	12	13	Engine Withdrawn
6200	6048 27/06/33	6050 04/35	6048 13/05/37	6048 09/39	6050 04/42	6048 22/10/44	6050 04/08/48	6048 26/07/48	9106 18/01/52	9103 09/56	9107 01/60			17/11/62
6201	6049 03/11/33	6048 11/35	6050 09/37	6049 03/40	6048 10/42	6049 28/07/44	6050 12/11/45	6049 19/07/46	6050 05/11/48	9109 13/02/52	9130 28/07/54	9235 16/09/56	9101 06/60	20/10/62
6202	9100 29/06/35	9236 22/07/36 out of service 21/09/39	9236 07/41 (off 06/43)	9236 09/44	9236 04/47 (withdrawn 03/50)	9236 02/07/52	Engine rebuilt to std. form	*						05/54
6203	9101 01/07/35	9100 15/12/36	9101 18/12/38	9106 20/12/41	9102 26/07/44	9106 24/10/47	9108 23/04/51	9101 14/09/55	9100 14/08/58					20/10/62
6204	9102 19/07/35	9105 01/38	9109 10/40	9103 06/44	9108 20/08/46	9236 25/08/50	6048 30/05/52	6049 06/06/55						07/10/61
6205	9103 24/07/35	9108 12/40	9104 10/42	9109 26/01/45	9235 27/09/48	9105 06/08/52	9107 04/01/56	9109 10/58						25/11/61
6206	9104 01/08/35	9235 06/37	9100 07/39	9108 01/43	9235 09/43	9104 19/07/45	9102 23/01/48	9101 02/10/50	9100 23/02/55	9105 03/58				03/11/62
6207	9105 09/08/35	9104 08/37	9102 02/40	9101 01/42	9108 10/43	9100 20/05/46	9105 29/03/49	9102 21/11/51	9109 09/11/55	9106 05/58				25/11/61
6208	9106 16/08/35	9109 04/38	9104 03/40	9107 08/42	9235 18/09/45	9104 31/03/48	6049 25/08/50	6050 06/10/52	9104 01/57	9236 01/60				20/10/62
6209	9107 23/08/35	9101 02/37	9106 09/38	9103 07/41	9105 09/43	9107 26/11/45	9109 24/11/48	9104 24/08/51	9108 11/01/56	9102 12/58				29/09/62
6210	9108 06/09/35	9105 12/40	9236 09/43	9106 08/44	9101 24/07/47	9103 04/04/50	9107 10/01/53	6048 21/11/55	6050 03/58					07/10/61
6211	9109 18/09/35	9102 02/38	9107 10/39	9102 07/42	9101 04/44	9103 10/01/47	9100 10/05/49	9235 10/11/52	9102 23/01/56	6048 09/58				07/10/61
6212	9235 21/10/35	9107 10/37	9235 08/39	9100 07/43	9105 20/12/45	9107 08/03/49	6049 13/10/52	9236 15/01/54	9101 post 8/58	9108 01/60				07/10/61

* Engine damaged in accident 8/10/52 & taken out of service.

DYNAMOMETER CAR TESTS

Report No. 59, 1935

DYNAMOMETER CAR No.1 TESTS.

Engines Nos.6203. 3 rows of Superheater Elements.
6209. 4 rows of Superheater Elements.
Royal Scot Trains. Euston - Glasgow.

Dynamometer Car Tests were made with the above engines working the regular Royal Scot trains between Euston and Glasgow. The trains ran to normal timings and the actual loads hauled by each engine respectively are given below :-

Engine No.6209. 4 Rows of Superheater Elements.

Date	Route.		Load.		
Nov.18th.	Euston - Glasgow	(540	tons to	Crewe
		(476	" "	Symington
		(337	" "	Glasgow.
Nov.28th.	Euston - Glasgow.	(540	tons to	Crewe.
		(443	" "	Symington.
		(304	" "	Glasgow.
Nov.30th.	Glasgow - Euston.	(279	tons to	Symington.
		(470	" "	Euston.
Dec.3rd.	Euston - Glasgow.	(536	tons to	Crewe.
		(474	" "	Symington.
		(355	" "	Glasgow.

Engine No.6203. 3 Rows of Superheater Elements.

Date	Route.		Load.		
Nov.25th.	Euston - Glasgow	(544	tons to	Crewe.
		(480	" "	Symington.
		(343	" "	Glasgow.
Nov.27th.	Glasgow - Euston.	(314	tons to	Symington.
		(481	" "	Euston.

Tests were also made on November 20th when the results obtained were not comparable owing to the light loads hauled, and on December 17th and 19th when general weather conditions and fog influenced the timekeeping of the trains to such an extent as to seriously affect the results obtained.

STEAM CHEST TEMPERATURES.

In order to compare the steam chest temperatures of the two engines, a mercury bulb pyrometer was fitted to the R.H. outside steam chest of each engine.

Records were taken throughout each day's test of the temperatures registered, and a summary of these will be found in Tables Nos.2 and 3.

COAL.

Grimethorpe coal was used throughout the tests and an allowance of 16 cwts was made for lighting up from cold and 11.1/4 cwts when the engine was warm.

In addition allowances for standing, light running and shunting were assessed at 4 cwts for the down trip, and 3 cwts for the up trip respectively.

WATER.

The water consumption was measured in the Dynamometer Car by the usual air pressure indicator. Steam was used for carriage warming purposes throughout the tests.

WEATHER.

The general weather conditions experienced on each day of the tests were similar.

OPERATION OF ENGINES.

The engines were worked by Camden and also Carlisle men between Euston and Carlisle, and by Polmadie men between Carlisle and Glasgow, the general cut off employed on the level and easier gradients being 17% - 20%. Where practicable full regulator opening was used, and in tables 2 and 3 will be found a summary of boiler steam pressures, engine operation, and steam chest temperatures recorded when working over the more severe gradients of the route.

STEAMING.

ENGINE No.6209. (4 Rows of Standard Superheater Elements)

Nov.18th. 10.0 a.m. Euston - Glasgow.

Full boiler pressure not maintained between Euston - Carlisle, minimum pressure recorded 203 lbs per sq.inch at Shilton and between Tebay and Shap Summit. Average boiler pressure maintained between Beattock and Beattock Summit 242 lbs per sq.inch at a cut off of 43%.

Nov.28th. 10.0 a.m. Euston - Glasgow.

Full boiler pressure not maintained to Rugby, minimum pressure 170 lbs per sq.inch. From Rugby to Lancaster minimum pressure 210 lbs per sq.inch. From Lancaster to Carlisle minimum pressure 195 lbs per sq.inch (between Tebay and Shap Summit). Average boiler pressure maintained up Beattock bank 235 lbs per sq.inch, cut off 48%.

Nov.30th. 10.0 am Glasgow - Euston.

Steaming completely satisfactory throughout.

Dec.3rd. 10.0 a.m. Euston - Glasgow.

Steaming completely satisfactory throughout.

ENGINE No.6203. (3 Rows of Standard Superheater Elements

Nov.25th. 10.0 a.m. Euston - Glasgow.

Steaming satisfactory throughout.

Nov.27th. 10.0 a.m. Glasgow to Euston.

Steaming completely satisfactory to Crewe, after which very poor, minimum boiler pressure 160 lbs per sq.inch at Roade. The engine was examined at Camden Shed, but no defects were found to account for this serious loss of pressure.

From the above it would appear that the unsatisfactory steaming of the engines was largely due to mismanagement, as the recovery effected in the steaming of each engine by the Scotch crews was most marked.

The back damper door only was used on each engine, and this was regulated from 1/4 to 3/4 open as required.

TIMEKEEPING.

Sectional timekeeping was in general well maintained by each engine, but owing to the large number of speed restrictions and signal checks experienced during these tests, the overall running time was frequently exceeded.

Table No.1 gives the booked and actual running times of each engine over the heavier gradients.

RESULTS OBTAINED.

Table No.5 gives the full particulars of the results during the tests with both engines on all the trains worked, **under satisfactory test conditions.**

Table No.4 shows the average results of each engine on :-

1. Euston to Glasgow Route.
2. Glasgow to Euston Route.
3. Combined average results of each engine over both routes.

In the case of Engine No.6209 when working between Euston and Glasgow the figures given are the average of three trips over that route.

From Table No.4 a clear reduction in coal and water consumption is shown by the 4 row element Engine No.6209 when compared with the 3 Row Element Engine No.6203.

On the combined average results the reduction amounted to 4.9% in coal and 5.7% in water per drawbar horse-power hour.

From the average steam chest temperatures recorded an increase of 7% is effected by the 4 Row Engine No.6209.

TABLE No.1. Sectional Timekeeping.

Engine No.6209 (4 Rows of Elements). Euston - Glasgow.

SECTION	Booked Time. Mins.	ACTUAL TIME. Nov.18	Nov.28	Dec.3rd	
		Mins Secs	Mins Secs	Mins Secs	
Euston - Tring	38	39. 5	37. 30	⚹ 43. 25	
Bletchley - Roade	13	13. 0	12. 40	13. 25	
Stafford - Whitmore	17	16.10	15. 30	16. 0	
Carnforth - Oxenholme	15	14.30	14. 5	14. 40	
Oxenholme - Tebay	17	18. 0	16. 25	17. 15	
Tebay - Shap Summit	10	11. 0	10. 0	10. 25	
Beattock - Beattock S	20	21.20	20. 30	+ 23. 55	

⚹ Signal check Camden
+ Severe slipping due to frosty rail.

Glasgow - Euston

SECTION	Booked Time. Mins.	ACTUAL TIME Nov.30	
		Mins Secs	
Symington -Beattock S	22	21. 45	
Carlisle - Plumpton	21	22. 5	
Penrith -Shap Summit	21	19. 5	
Crewe - Whitmore	13	⚹ 15. 30	⚹ Signal stop
Rugby - Roade	23	21. 55	Crewe North
Bletchley - Tring	17	14. 35	Jcn

ENGINE No.6203 (3 Rows of Elements). Euston - Glasgow.

SECTION.	Booked Time Mins.	ACTUAL TIME Nov.25	
		Mins. Secs	
Euston - Tring	38	⚹ 45. 35	⚹P.W.S Willesden
Bletchley - Roade	13	+ 17. 35	+ P.W.S Wolverton
Stafford - Whitmore	17	14. 40	
Carnforth-Oxenholme	15	13. 20	
Oxenholme-Tebay	17	18. 5	
Tebay - Shap Summit	10	10. 35	
Beattock -Beattock S	20	21. 15	

Glasgow - Euston

SECTION.	Booked Time Mins.	ACTUAL TIME Nov.27	
		Mins. Secs.	
Symington-Beattock S	22	23. 10	
Carlisle -Plumpton	21	21. 45	
Penrith -Shap Summit	21	21. 25	
Crewe - Whitmore	13	14. 50	
Rugby - Roade	23	24. 55	
Bletchley - Tring	17	13. 40	

TABLE No.2.

SECTION	Engine No.	BOILER PRESSURE lbs per sq.in. Average.	Minimum	CUT OFF % Average Maintained.	Maximum.	Steam Chest Temperature. F° Average.	Maximum.
EUSTON - TRING		240	233	23	42	494	540
BLETCHLEY - ROADE		238	230	22	27	537	545
STAFFORD - WHITMORE	6203 3 Rows of Super- heater Elements.	243	240	24	24	547	550
CARNFORTH - GRAYRIGG		233	228	26	32	529	534
TEBAY - SHAP SUMMIT		228	218	34	41	527	540
BEATTOCK - BEATTOCK SUMMIT		233	218	40	45	535	540

SECTION.	Engine No.	BOILER PRESSURE. lbs per sq.in. Average.	Minimum.	CUT OFF % Average Maintained	Maximum.	Steam Chest Temperature. Average	Maximum.
UDDINGSTON - CLEGHORN.		238	228	25	26	520	525
SYMINGTON - BEATTOCK S.		235	228	26	29	520	540
CARLISLE - PLUMPTON.	6203 3 Rows of Super- heater Elements.	239	233	26	31	497	530
PENRITH - SHAP SUMMIT		243	236	25	30	523	527
CREWE - WHITMORE.		220	218	26	26	522	525
RUGBY - KILSBY TUNNEL.		190	178	29	29	519	530
BLETCHLEY - TRING.		173	160	29	30	505	510

T A B L E   3.

SECTION.	ENGINE No.	Boiler Pressure. lbs per sq.in. Average	Minimum	CUT OFF. % Average Maintained.	Maximum.	STEAM CHEST TEMPERATURE. F° Average	Maximum
EUSTON - TRING		222	205	24	30	467	585
BLETCHLEY - ROADE		218	215	19	26	565	570
STAFFORD - WHITMORE	6209 4 Rows of Super- heater Elements.	231	224	22	25	569	580
CARNFORTH - GRAYRIGG		229	222	26	33	573	582
TEBAY - SHAP SUMMIT		217	210	37	45	574	580
BEATTOCK - BEATTOCK SUMMIT.		236	227	35	47	581	590

SECTION	ENGINE No.	Boiler Pressure. lbs per sq.in. Average	Minimum.	CUT OFF. % Average Maintained	Maximum.	STEAM CHEST TEMPERATURE. Average	Maximum
UDDINGSTON - GLEGHORN		242	240	23	24	570	580
SYMINGTON - BEATTOCK S		242	240	27	30	545	595
CARLISLE - PLUMPTON	6209 4 Rows of Super- heater Elements.	237	235	27	32	542	585
PENRITH - SHAP SUMMIT		232	225	27	32	580	585
CREWE - WHITMORE		235	230	25	25	565	580
RUGBY - KILSBY TUNNEL		237	235	25	25	567	578
BLETCHLEY - TRING		230	225	21	22	572	575

TABLE No.4.

ROUTE	EUSTON- GLASGOW		GLASGOW- EUSTON		COMBINED RESULTS.		
ENGINE	6203 3 Row Elements	6209 ✱ 4 Row Elements	6203 3 Row Elements	6209 4 Row Elements	6203 3 Row Elements	6209 4 Row Elements	Increase or Decrease % 4 Row Elements
COAL Total Weight (during test)	19208	18807	18368	16975	18788	17891	- 4.8%
lbs per mile.	47.6	46.6	45.5	42.0	46.4	44.3	- 4.7%
lbs per D.B.H.P.hr	3.23	3.10	3.23	3.04	3.23	3.07	- 4.9%
lbs per sq.ft grate area per hour.	53.9	52.9	52.9	50.7	53.5	51.8	- 3.2%
WATER. Total Gallons (during test)	15945	15070	14830	13945	15387	14507	- 5.7%
lbs per Mile.	39.5	37.3	36.7	34.1	38.1	35.7	- 6.3%
lbs per D.B.H.P.hr	26.8	24.8	26.1	25.0	26.4	24.9	- 5.7%
EVAPORATION. lbs water per lb coal	8.30	8.01	8.10	8.22	8.20	8.11	- 1.1%

✱ Mean value 3 trips.   AVERAGE RESULTS.

T A B L E No. 5.

ROUTE	EUSTON - GLASGOW				GLASGOW - EUSTON	
ENGINE (STANDARD ELEMENTS)	6203 3-Row		6209 4-Row		6203 3-Row	6209 4-Row
DATE	25/11/35	18/11/35	28/11/35	3/12/35	27/11/35	30/11/35
Weight of train behind drawbar (tons)						
DOWN TRAINS } To CREWE	544	540	540	538		
CARLISLE	480	476	443	474		
SYMINGTON	480	476	443	474		
GLASGOW	343	337	304	335		
UP TRAINS } To SYMINGTON					514	279
EUSTON					481	470
TRAIN MILES	404.4	404.3	404.5	404.5	404.5	404.6
TON MILES excluding engine	199421	197659	189699	196962	188605	183343
" " including engine	260146	258385	250425	257688	249331	244069
AVERAGE RUNNING SPEED. M.P.H.	51.0	51.2	53.0	51.2	52.6	54.4
MAXIMUM RUNNING SPEED.	82.0	78.0	78.0	80.0	81.0	78.0
WORK DONE. H.P.Mins.	356787	373338	389362	332335	341801	334993
H.P.hours.	5946.45	6222.3	6489.37	5538.75	5696.68	5583.22
H.P.Mins per ton mile excluding engine	1.79	1.89	2.06	1.69	1.81	1.83
COAL (GRIMETHORPE)						
Total weight lbs.	19208	18592	20189	17640	18368	16975
lbs per mile	47.6	46.0	49.9	43.6	45.5	42.0
lbs per ton mile excluding engine	.096	.094	.106	.090	.097	.093
" " " including engine	.074	.072	.081	.069	.074	.069
lbs per D.B.H.P.hour	3.23	2.98	3.11	3.18	3.83	3.04
lbs per sq.ft of grate per hour	53.9	52.3	58.9	49.7	52.9	50.7
WATER.						
Total gallons	15945	14845	16105	14260	14830	13945
Gallons per mile	39.5	36.75	39.8	35.3	36.7	34.1
lbs per ton mile including engine	.612	.574	.644	.554	.596	.572
lbs per D.B.H.P.hr.	26.85	23.9	24.9	25.8	26.1	25.0
EVAPORATION.						
lbs per lb of coal.	8.3	8.0	8.05	8.09	8.1	8.22

Tests were run on November 20th, December 17th and 19th, but not been included owing to the test conditions being unsatisfactory from fog and general weather conditions.

GRADIENT PROFILES EUSTON–GLASGOW

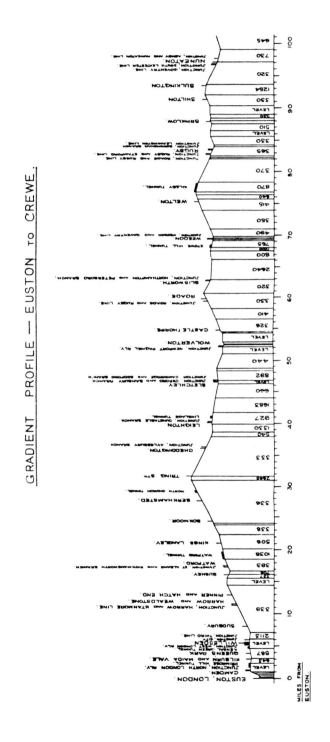

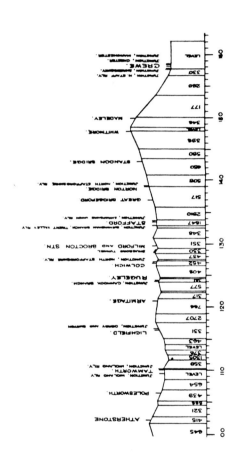

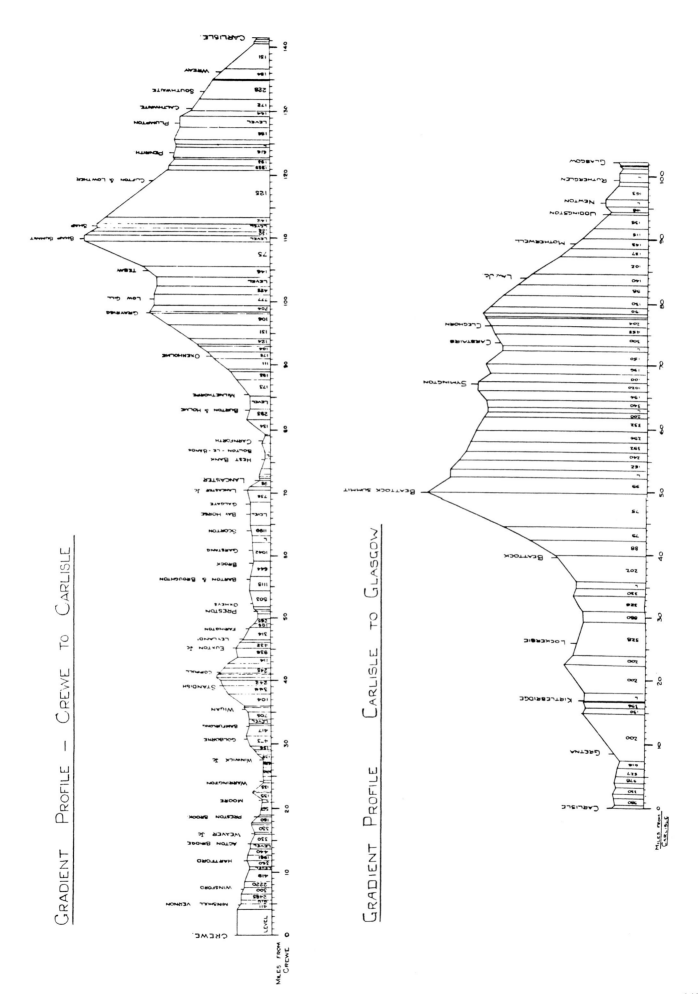

GRADIENT PROFILE — CREWE TO CARLISLE

GRADIENT PROFILE — CARLISLE TO GLASGOW

SPECIAL NOTICE FOR MOVEMENT TO DERBY

B R I T I S H   R A I L W A Y S

LONDON MIDLAND REGION

S P E C I A L   N O T I C E   O.G. 379

EXCEPTIONAL LOAD — PENYCHAIN TO DERBY LOCOMOTIVE WORKS VIA INTO AND OUT OF CRICCIETH, PORTMADOC, HARLECH, FAIRBOURNE, DOVEY JUNCTION, MACHYNLLETH, WELSHPOOL, ENGLISH BRIDGE JN., INTO AND OUT OF ABBEY FOREGATE JN., SHREWSBURY, WHITCHURCH, CREWE GRESTY LANE NO. 1 , BASFORD HALL SS NORTH & MIDDLE, INTO AND OUT OF BASFORD HALL SS SOUTH, UP AND DOWN STOKE GOODS LINE, CREWE N. STAFFS 1945 , KIDSGROVE, LONGPORT, STOKE, CRESSWELL, UTTOXETER, STENSON JN., AND L. & N.W. JN.

DESCRIPTION AND DIMENSIONS

Privately owned ex L.M.S Class 8P 4-6-2 Steam Tender Locomotive No. 46203 "Princess Margaret Rose" DEAD ON OWN WHEELS.

Length over buffers:- 74ft. 4¼ins. Weight : 124 tonnes.
Width over leading footsteps:- 7ft. 9ins. at 1ft. 3ins. and 2ft. 9ins. ARL.
Width over cylinders: 8ft. 11½ins. at 5ft. 0ins. ARL.
Width over side windscreens : 9ft. 7⅞ins. between 8ft. 6.1/16ins. and 10ft. 0¼ins. ARL.
Extreme height (over cab roof): 13ft. 3ins.
Gross Trailing Weight:- 190 tonnes.

MARSHALLING OF TRAIN

Hauling Locomotive.
Freight brakevan.
Tube Wagon.
Dead Locomotive No. 46203.
Tube Wagon.
Freight Brakevan.

SITE ARRANGEMENTS
SATURDAY/SUNDAY, 10/11 MAY 1975

Site working to be arranged by Divisional Manager, Stoke in conjunction with Area Manager, Shrewsbury.

SERVICE

SPECIAL TRAIN 9X98 SUNDAY 11 MAY, 1975 as under:-
(Times shown in brackets are passing times)

Penychain	dep	08PR00	Crewe GL No. 1			(19 55)
Criccieth	arr	08PR20	Crewe Basford Hall	arr	20D00	
	dep	08 40		dep	22PR35	
Porthmadog		(09 00)	Basford Hall SS South	arr	22PR40	
Harlech		(09 40)		dep	22 50	
Barmouth	arr	10E30	North Stafford Sdgs.		(23 00)	
	dep	10E40	Signal KC 30	arr	23*21	
Tywyn		(11 30)		dep	23*26	
Dovey Jn.		(12 20)	Kidsgrove		(23*28)	
Machynlleth	arr	12E38	Etruria		(23 41)	
	dep	13L00	Stoke		(23 45)	
Cemmes Road		(13 22)	Stoke Jn.		(23 47)	
Talerddig		(13 58)	Caverswall	arr	23E58	
Caersws	arr	14E32			MON. 12 MAY	
	dep	14E42		dep	00E13	
Newtown		(15 04)	Cresswell		(00 21)	
Welshpool	arr	16E02	Uttoxeter		(00 45)	
	dep	16E12	Tutbury		(01 05)	
Westbury		(16 48)	Egginton Jn.		(01 13)	
Sutton Bridge Jn.		(17 32)	North Stafford Jn.		(01 22)	
via Loop			Stenson Jn.		(01 24)	
Abbey Foregate	arr	17E40	L. & N. W. Jn.		(01X36)	
	dep	18RR00			GL	
Shrewsbury		(18 05)	London Road Jn.		(01 39)	
Harlescott Crossing		(18 10)	Derby E.S. No. 1		(01 42)	
Whitchurch	arr	19E00	Derby Loco Works	arr	01 45	
	dep	19E10				
Willaston	arr	19 45				

Continued.

POWER AND TRAINCREW ARRANGEMENTS

CREWE DD 316 (CLASS 24) to be worked to Pwllheli on Saturday, 10 May (DM STOKE to arrange) and work as Crewe DD 310 (Sun), with LD to Penychain and 9X98 to Crewe, return LD/AC to Shrewsbury (for 07 15 Mon.) and as programmed.
TOTON DD 164 (CLASS 25) at Derby work LD to Crewe and 9X98 Crewe to Derby and as programmed
MACHYNLLETH TC (AM SHREWSBURY to arrange) by road transport to Pwllheli and work LD C4 CO from Pwllheli to Penychain and work at site until 08 00 hours return by road transport (See 1st relief from Machynlleth).
MACHYNLLETH TC (AM SHREWSBURY to arrange) by road transport to Penychain for departure 9X98 08 00 to Machynlleth.
SHREWSBURY TC (AM SHREWSBURY to arrange) by road transport to Machynlleth and work 9X98 13 00 Machynlleth to Abbey Foregate.
SHREWSBURY TC work 9X98 18 00 to Crewe B. Hall return LD.
DERBY TC work LD to Crewe and 9X98 22 35 to Derby Loco Works.

RESTRICTIONS APPLICABLE TO THE LOAD THROUGHOUT THE JOURNEY

1. The dead Locomotive must be empty of coal and water.

2. Windscreens to be folded back.

3. An empty runner wagon or wagons (which may include a freight brakevan) having a total length of not less than 40ft. over buffers must be marshalled between the hauling locomotive and dead locomotive No. 46203.

RESTRICTIONS TO BE OBSERVED DURING THE JOURNEY BETWEEN PENYCHAIN AND SHREWSBURY

1. Propelling of the load between Penychain and Criccieth is specially authorised subject to the requirements of Sectional Appendix Table F1 being strictly observed.

2. FABRIC   Must not exceed speed of:-

  (a) FIVE m.p.h. when passing over Old Chaple Viaduct, through Barmouth Tunnel and over Barmouth Viaduct situated between Barmouth and Morfa Mawddach ($100\frac{1}{2}$ – $99\frac{1}{4}$ m.p.s.)

  (b) FIVE m.p.h. passing through Aberdovey No. 4 Tunnel situated between Aberdovey and Penhelig ($84\frac{1}{2}$ – 84 m.p.s.)

  (c) FIVE m.p.h. passing through Aberdovey No. 3 Tunnel situated between Penhelig and Abertafol (84 – $83\frac{3}{4}$ m.p.s.)

  (d) FIVE m.p.h. passing through Aberdovey Nos. 2 and 1 Tunnels situated between Abertafol and Gogarth ($82\frac{1}{4}$ – 82 m.p.s. and $81\frac{1}{4}$ – 81 m.p.s.)

  (e) 15 m.p.h. maximum elsewhere between Penychain and Shrewsbury.

3. Must NOT travel via the No. 3 Platform Line at Shrewsbury Station.

4. LACER   Not to use crossovers between platforms.

5. To be confined to running lines throughout.

6. NOTRAMO   Not to travel more than 25 miles without stopping for examination.

7. GOBI   The routing as shown in the heading must be observed.

RESTRICTIONS TO BE OBSERVED DURING THE JOURNEY BETWEEN SHREWSBURY AND DERBY

1. Passage of the load under LIVE AC Electrified Lines is STRICTLY PROHIBITED.

2. AT WILLASTON The train must be brought to a stand and not be allowed to proceed until the signalman has received confirmation that isolation of AC Electrified Lines into Basford Hall has taken place.

3. AT KIDSGROVE OUTER HOME SIGNAL NO. KG30 the train must be brought to a stand and not be allowed to proceed until the Signalman has received confirmation that isolation of AC Electrified Lines between Kidsgrove and Stoke Junction has taken place.

4. FABRIC   Must not exceed speed of 10 m.p.h. through Kidsgrove Station.

RESTRICTIONS TO BE OBSERVED DURING THE JOURNEY BETWEEN SHREWSBURY AND DERBY (Continued...)

5.   SULTAN   Must travel over the Up Main Line through Stoke Station.

6.   TO STOP and proceed with extreme caution through Meir Tunnel (Bridge No. 20) between Longton and Caverswall (3 - 3½ m.p.s.)

7.   SULTAN   Must travel over the Goods Lines at Derby.

8.   FABRIC   Must not exceed a MAXIMUM speed of 25 m.p.h. between Shrewsbury and Derby.

9.   LACER   Not to use crossovers between platforms.

10.   To be confined to running lines throughout (Except may stable in Crewe Basford Hall)

11. NOTRAMO   Not to travel more than 25 miles without stopping for examination.

12.   GOBI   The routing as shown in the heading must be observed.

SIGNALLING OF TRAIN

Block Signalling as per Telegraph Code "OCLO" will apply.

ISOLATION OF AC ELECTRIFIED LINES

Divisional Maintenance Engineer, Stoke to arrange as necessary.

OPENING OF SIGNALBOXES

Signalboxes to be opened specially or remain open as necessary.

ACCOMPANIMENT

Private owners Caretaker to travel on the dead locomotive throughout.
Members of the Midland Railway Company to ride in the brakevan.

MISCELLANEOUS INSTRUCTIONS

Area Managers must arrange to advise all concerned in connection with the passage of this load, including Signalmen and P. Way Staff.

ACKNOWLEDGEMENT

The following to acknowledge receipt by wire IMMEDIATELY to GENMAN (04/7) CREWE using the code:-

                        "ARNO O.G. 379"

DIVISIONAL MANAGERS	—	Stoke, Nottingham.
CONTROL	—	Chester, Stoke, Nottingham.
D.C.E.	—	Crewe
A.M./A.A.M./STAFF & ADMIN.	—	Shrewsbury, Crewe, Stoke, Machynlleth, Burton-on-Trent, Derby.
B.o P.	—	Crewe

CREWE
DATE : 5.5.75
EXTN : 2975/2243
REF : 04/7/86

                                    K. DIXON
                                MOVEMENTS MANAGER

PERFORMANCE LOGS

LOADED TEST RUN — 17th May 1990

Locomotive: Ex L.M.S. Pacific No. 46203 'Princess Margaret Rose'

Stock: Support Coach 35476 plus 10 Mk. 1 & 2 Mk. 2 coaches Nos. 4962, 4965, 4944, 4978, 4886, 4958, 4915, 4928, 4937, 17052, 17054, 18706.

Total load (tare): 463 tons.

Driver: Driver Reg. White (Derby No.4 Shed).
Fireman: Driver Lindsay Shelton (Derby No.4 Shed).
Traction Inspector: Chief Inspector Harry Leyland (Derby).
Mechanical Inspector: Inspector Colin Wood (DM & EE Derby).
Conductor: Senior Conductor Arthur Seale (Derby).

The locomotive carried the headboard 'THE RED ROSE'.

Miles	Location	Elapsed Time	Speed	Notes
0.00	DERBY (dep. 13.24.40)	00.00		
1.46	m.p.127	03.58		
	Spondon Jn.			
2.46	m.p.126	05.31	39	
3.46	m.p.125			
	Borrowash			
4.46	m.p.124	07.17	63	
5.46	m.p.123	08.10	68	
6.46	m.p.122	09.00	72	p.w.s.
7.46	m.p.121	10.15	48	
8.11	Long Eaton Station			slow for platform
8.19	m.p.120¼	13.04		
8.69	m.p.119¾	14.50	34	
9.40	m.p.120 Trent Jn.	16.31		
10.15	Long Eaton Jn.	16.47		
10.40	m.p.121			
11.40	Toton m.p.122			
11.65	m.p.122¼	19.53		
12.01	Stapleford & Sandiacre	20.03	60	
12.40	m.p.123	20.38		
13.15	m.p.123¾			p.w.s.
13.20	Stanton Gate			
13.40	m.p.124	22.40	30	
14.40	m.p.125	24.22	35	
15.40	m.p.126	25.35	49	
16.40	m.p.127	26.40	55	
16.90	m.p.127½	27.09		
17.40	m.p.128	27.39	60	
	Shipley Gate			
18.40	m.p.129	28.37		
18.90	Langley Mill m.p.129½	29.07	60	
19.40	m.p.130	29.36		
19.90	m.p.130½	30.06	60	
20.40	m.p.131	30.34	64	
20.90	m.p.131½	31.02	64	
21.40	m.p.132	31.31	62	
21.90	Codnor Park Jn.			
23.15	m.p.133¾	33.14	61	
	Pye Bridge			
23.90	Coates Park North			
24.40	m.p.135	34.30	59	
25.50	Alfreton Tunnel			
25.40	m.p.136			
	Alfreton & Mansfield Parkway	35.42		
26.40	m.p.137	36.54	50	
	Westhouses & Blackwell	37.02		
				p.w.s. 45
27.90	m.p.138½	38.51		
28.40	m.p.139	39.74	32	
29.40	m.p.140	41.13	42	
30.40	m.p.141	42.52	36	sigs.
30.90	m.p.141½	44.22	20	
		45.56		sig. stop
		48.28		
		50.00		
31.40	m.p.142			
31.54	Clay Cross South Jn.			
32.40	m.p.143	51.31	40	
33.40	m.p.144	52.41	51	
34.40	m.p.145	53.42	59	
35.40	m.p.146	56.13	16	sigs.
35.65	CHESTERFIELD			
	Tapton Jn.			
36.40	m.p.147	60.00	22	
37.65	m.p.148¼	62.08	35	
	Whittington			
37.90	m.p.148½	62.35	33	
38.40	m.p.149	63.19	41	
39.05	Barrow Hill			
39.40	m.p.150	64.28	52	
40.21	Foxlow Jn.	65.32		
40.40	m.p.151	65.57	37	
41.40	m.p.152	67.17	45	
41.90	Eckington & Renishaw			p.w.s. 30
42.40	m.p.153	69.02	34	
42.90	m.p.153½	69.55	34	sigs.
43.65	m.p.154¼	71.03	40	
44.40	m.p.155	72.20	35	
45.00	Beighton Jn. m.p.155½	73.51		
46.15	m.p.156¾	74.53	72	
46.30	m.p.47	76.04		
46.80	Woodhouse Station m.p.46½	76.52	41	
47.30	m.p.46	77.38	39	
47.80	m.p.45½	78.21	42	
48.30	m.p.45	79.01	45	
49.05	m.p.44¾	79.21	45	
49.30	m.p.44	80.19	40	
49.80	Darnall Station	81.11		
	m.p.43¾	81.52		
	m.p.43½	82.15	39	
	m.p.43	83.03	38	p.w.s.
	m.p.159¼	83.59		
51.74	Nunnery Main Line Jn.	85.02		slow
52.20	SHEFFIELD arr.	88.10		
0.00	SHEFFIELD (dep. 15.32.30)	00.00		
0.51	m.p.158			
1.01	Heeley m.p.157½	03.27		
1.51	m.p.157	04.30		
2.01	m.p.156½	05.26	29	
2.51	m.p.156	06.16	36	
3.51	m.p.155	07.51	38	
4.01	Dore & Totley m.p.154½	08.35		
4.51	m.p.154	09.19	41	
	Bradway Tunnel			
6.51	m.p.152	12.00	45	
6.96	Dronfield	12.28		
7.51	m.p.151	13.00	60	
8.01	Unstone m.p.150½	13.27	67	
8.51	m.p.150	13.51	75	
9.26	m.p.149¼	15.11		
10.51	Broomhouse m.p.148	15.24	77	
11.01	m.p.147½	15.48	75	
11.51	m.p.147	16.13		
12.01	Tapton Jn. m.p.146½	16.39	69	
12.26	CHESTERFIELD	16.53	69	
12.51	m.p.146	17.05	69	
13.01	m.p.145½	17.31	69	
13.51	m.p.145	17.58	67	
14.01	m.p.144½	18.23	72	
14.51	m.p.144	18.49	69	
15.01	m.p.143½	19.14	72	
15.51	m.p.143	19.39	72	
16.01	Clay Cross m.p. 142½	20.06	67	
16.51	m.p.142	20.29		
16.75	m.p.147½	20.40		
	Clay Cross Tunnel			
18.25	m.p.146	21.56	71	
18.75	m.p.145½	22.21	72	
18.85	Stretton			
19.25	m.p.145	22.46	72	
19.75	m.p.144½	23.10	75	
20.25	m.p.144	23.33	79	
20.75	m.p.144½	23.56	79	
21.25	m.p.143	24.18	82	
21.75	m.p.142½	24.41	78	
22.25	m.p.142	25.03		
22.50	Wingfield	25.13	84	
23.25	m.p.141	25.46		
24.25	m.p.140	26.32	78	
	Wingfield Tunnel			p.w.s.
25.25	m.p.139	27.26	67	
25.56	Crich Jn.	27.48		
	Ambergate North Jn.			
25.75	m.p.138½	27.59	78	
	Toadmoor Tunnel (out)	28.29		
26.25	m.p.138			
26.50	m.p.137¾ Ambergate South Jn.	28.50		
27.25	m.p.137	29.34		
27.75	m.p.136½	30.00	69	
28.25	m.p.136	30.27	68	
28.55	Belper Station	30.44		
29.25	m.p.135	31.16		
29.75	m.p.134½	31.40	75	
	Milford Tunnel			
30.75	m.p.133½	33.27		
31.25	m.p.133	32.50	78	
31.75	m.p.132½	33.12	82	
32.25	m.p.132			
32.75	Little Eaton Jn. m.p.131½	33.55	84	
34.25	m.p.130	34.17	82	
34.75	m.p.129½	35.01		
	Derby Nottingham Road	35.25		
35.25	m.p.129	35.57		sigs.
	Derby North Jn.			
35.75	m.p.128½			sigs.
36.25	m.p.128	40.11		
36.40	DERBY arr.	41 12		

From m.p.152 (South of Bradway Tunnel) to coming to a stand at m.p.129 (just over ½ mile north of Derby), a distance of 28.74 miles, the average speed was 73.16 mph.

Timed by J.B. Radford.

THE RICHARD LEVICK MEMORIAL SPECIALS

Derby — Sheffield — Derby (twice)

Date: Saturday 2nd June 1990
Locomotive: Ex L.M.S. Pacific No. 46203 'Princess Margaret Rose'
Stock: Support Coach 35476, Open firsts 122 (3106), 123 (3109), 124 (3110), Miniature buffet car 132 (1861), Corridor brake composite 129 (21272), open first 357 (3112).
Pullman parlour seconds 347, 349, 350, 351, RBR 1657, Pullman parlour seconds 352, 353.
Total Load: 523 Tons(tare) 555 tons(gross).
Driver: Driver Tom Blakeman (Derby 4 shed.
No. 1 Fireman: Driver Alan Porter (Derby 4 shed).
No. 2 Fireman: Driver Alec McPherson (Derby 4 Shed).
Traction Inspectors: Inspector Ron Dye (Run 1), Inspector John Sumner (Run 2).

			RUN 1				RUN 2		
Miles	Location		Booked Time mins.	Actual Time m. s.	Speed mph	Notes	Booked Time mins.	Actual Time m. s.	Speed mph	Notes
0.00	DERBY	dep		0.00				0.00		
1.46	m.p.127			3.50	33			3.32	41	
	Signal 405	arr		6.22		signal stop				
		dep		7.39						
2.46	m.p.126			8.42						
2.63	Spondon Station			9.02				4.56	43	
3.46	m.p.125			10.45	29			5.56		
	Borrowash			11.15						
4.46	m.p.124			12.04	46			6.59	57	
5.46	m.p.123							7.59	60	
6.46	m.p.122			14.13	56			8.53	67	
7.46	m.p.121			15.15	58	brakes		10.00	54	
8.11	Long Eaton Station					20 restriction		11.29		
	Sheet Stores Jn.				16					
8.46	m.p.120 (towards Derby)			18.44	15			12.39	33	
	Trent South Jn.							14.54		
	Long Eaton Jn.			20.38	20					
9.40	m.p.120 (Trent)			20.52				15.29	33	
10.11	Old Long Eaton Station			22.16	36					
10.40	m.p.121			22.38	34			17.02	39	
	Toton			24.09				17.42		
11.40	m.p.122							18.20	46	
11.65	m.p.122¼			24.25				18.52		
12.01	Stapleford & Sandiacre									
12.40	m.p.123			25.20	49			19.32	51	
12.90	m.p.123½			26.17						
13.20	Stanton Gate			27.21	15	p.w.s.				
13.40	m.p.124			28.15				21.23		
14.40	m.p.125			30.33	33			23.42	38	
15.40	m.p 126			32.08	38			25.06		
16.05	Ilkeston Jn.									
16.40	m.p.127			33.32	43			26.21	49	
17.40	m.p.128			34.51	45.5			27.33		
	Shipley Gate									
18.40	m.p.129			36.11	45			28.49	47	
19.30	Langley Mill Station			37.21				29.50		
19.40	m.p.130			37.31	45			30.04	48	
20.40	m.p.131			38.45	48.60			31.18		
21.40	m.p.132			40.01	47.40			32.23	50	
21.90	Codnor Park Jn.			40.39				33.11		
22.40	m.p.133									
22.90	m.p.133½			41.57						
23.40	m.p.134			42.36	45.5			35.08	46	
23.90	Coates Park North			43.16						
24.40	m.p.135			43.59	43.40			36.30	42	
24.55	Alfreton Tunnel South			44.12				36.42		
25.40	m.p.136			45.26	41.40			37.54		
25.50	ALFRETON & MANSFIELD PARKWAY		35			booked stop not taken				
26.40	m.p.137							39.07		
	Westhouses & Blackwell									
	Doe Hill				45	p.w.s.				
27.40	m.p.138			47.52				40.26	51/40	
28.40	m.p.139			49.11	45.60			42.42	40	
28.90	Morton Sidings			49.54						
29.40	m.p.140			50.33	44			43.21		
30.40	m.p.141			52.25	50/39	p.w.s.		44.26	58	
31.40	m.p.142			54.06						
31.54	Clay Cross South Jn.			54.17	48.6					
32.40	m.p.143			55.20				46.27	62	
33.40	m.p.144			56.29	52			47.27	60	
34.40	m.p.145			57.41	50	approach control		48.54	41	approach control
35.40	m.p.146			59.32				51.17		
35.65	CHESTERFIELD		61	60.32	15		56	52.10		
35.80	Tapton Jn.			61.15	18	20 restriction		53.04	19	20 restriction
36.40	m.p.147			62.25				54.21		
37.40	m.p.148			64.03	41			56.08	35	
38.25	Whittington			65.18				56.59		
38.40	m.p.149			65.33	40			57.42	37	
39.05	Barrow Hill Jn.			66.09						
39.40	m.p.150			66.42	52			58.59	47	
40.21	Foxlow Jn.			67.14				59.51		
40.40	m.p.151			67.45	57			60.06	54	
41.40	m.p.152			68.43	62			61.08	58	
					20	p.w.s.				
41.90	Eckington & Renishaw			69.15				61.45		
42.40	m.p.153			70.07	43			62.44	38	
43.40	m.p.154			72.07				64.40	31	
43.71	Killamarsh			72.10						
44.40	m.p.155			73.53	34			66.35	31	

Dist	Location		No.	Time	Speed	Notes	No.	Time	Speed	Notes
44.90	Beighton Jn.		73	76.45			68	68.25	18	
	Beighton Station							69.46		
46.30	m.p.47			77.35				70.42		
46.41	Woodhouse Jn.			78.17				71.15		
46.80	Woodhouse Station			79.00	34			72.05		
47.30	m.p.46			79.24	33			72.31		
48.30	m.p.45			81.06	35			74.19	33	
49.30	m.p.44				29			76.17	30	
49.80	Darnall Station			83.57	38			77.27	38	
50.10	m.p.43					p.w.s. 20				p.w.s. 20
	m.p. 159¼							81.14		
	signal at Nunnery M.L. Jn.	arr						81.45		signal stop
		dep						83.33		
51.65	Nunnery Main Line Jn.		84	87.30	slow		73	84.42		slow
52.15	SHEFFIELD	arr	86	90.12			81	87.59		
0.00	SHEFFIELD	dep		0.00				00.00		
0.51	m.p.158									
1.01	Heeley m.p.157½			4.12	25			3.17	35	
1.51	m.p.157			4.28	26			4.39		sigs.
	Up passenger loop	arr						7.12		put inside loop
		dep						10.50		to allow HST to pass
2.51	m.p.156			6.39	27			13.11		
3.51	m.p.155			8.52	26			16.07	22	
4.26	DORE & TOTLEY		14	10.35			14			
4.51	m.p.154			11.05	54			18.34		
4.75	Bradway Tunnel North End							19.09	25	
6.51	m.p.152			15.15	55.4					
6.96	DRONFIELD							23.29	50	
7.51	m.p.151			16.23	53			24.04		
8.01	Unstone m.p.150½									
8.51	m.p.150			17.19	64			26.41		
9.51	m.p.149			18.14	72				73/74	
10.51	Broomhouse m.p.148			18.58	75				74	
11.51	m.p.147			19.50	69			27.42	71	
12.01	Tapton Jn.									
12.26	CHESTERFIELD		24	20.31	65		24	28.08	69	
12.51	m.p.146							28.20		
13.51	m.p.145			21.41	65			29.14	67	
14.51	m.p.144			22.39	62			30.09	66	
15.51	m.p.143			23.39	60			31.06		
	Clay Cross South Jn.			24.30	57					
16.51	m.p.142			24.41				32.05		
17.25	m.p.148									
16.98	Clay Cross Tunnel North							32.34		
17.99	Clay Cross Tunnel South							33.36		
18.25	m.p.146			26.33	53			33.54	57	
18.85	Stretton									
19.25	m.p.145			27.36	57			34.54	60	
20.25	m.p.144			28.41	60			35.52	62	
21.25	m.p.143			29.33	62			36.46	67	
22.25	m.p.142							37.39	68	
22.50	South Wingfield			30.40	66			37.60	70	
23.25	m.p.141			31.21	67			38.31	69	
24.25	m.p.140			32.19	68			39.23	68	
24.51	Wingfield Tunnel North			32.28				40.10		
25.25	m.p.139			33.06	69			40.30	54	
25.56	Crich Jn.			33.21				sigs		
25.88	Ambergate North							slow		
26.09	Toadmoor Tunnel North			33.55				42.03		
26.25	m.p.138			34.06	60			42.50		
26.50	Ambergate South Jn.			34.21	57					
	Broadholme Loop									slow through loop to pass failed train
27.25	m.p.137			35.06	60					
28.25	m.p.136			36.06	60			49.40		
28.55	BELPER			36.22	64			50.02		
29.25	m.p.135			36.58	69			50.56		
29.94	Milford Tunnel (North)			37.36				51.48		
31.15	DUFFIELD									
31.25	m.p.133			38.45	67			53.14	52	
32.25	m.p.132			39.45				54.00		
33.18	Little Eaton Jn.							55.13		
34.25	m.p.130			41.36	56			56.16	60	
34/75	m.p.129½							56.46		
						braking				braking
35.25	m.p.129			42.43	49			57.25	42	
	Derby North Jn.									
36.40	DERBY	arr	57	46.09			57	60.40		

Summary of speeds:

	Derby — Sheffield	Sheffield — Derby
Booked average speed	36.40 m.p.h.	38.30 m.p.h.
Actual Run 1	34.72 m.p.h. (Max speed 62 m.p.h.)	47.30 m.p.h. (Max speed 75 m.p.h.)
Actual Run 2	35.60 m.p.h. (Max speed 67 m.p.h.)	36.36 m.p.h. (Max speed 74 m.p.h.)

Timed by J.B.Radford

APPLEBY – GARSDALE 1991.

Miles	Location	22nd June 448.5/475 tons		6th July 448/465 tons		24th August 448/465 tons		4th October 454/480 tons	
		m. s.	speed	m.s.	speed	m.s.	speed	m.s.	speed
0.00	Appleby S.B.							0.00	-
0.12	APPLEBY STATION	0.00	-			0.00	-	0.58	
0.37	MP 277			0.00	-			1.38	
0.87	MP 276.5	2.43	28			2.55	25	2.35	34
1.37	MP 276	3.30	41	2.31	36.5	3.48	38	3.15	49
1.87	MP 275.5							3.49	56
2.37	MP 275	4.41	54.5	3.43	53	5.00	53	4.19	61.5
2.87	MP 274.5							4.50	58.5
3.37	MP 274	5.52	48	4.55	48	6.10	51	5.21	55.25
3.87	MP 273.5							5.56	52
4.37	MP 273	7.13	42.5	6.14	44	7.26	46	6.30	49
4.87	MP 272.5							7.09	
5.37	Griseburn	8.40	36.5	7.42	40	8.49	42.5	7.46	47
6.37	MP 271	10.22	39	9.11	42	10.09	45.5	9.04	47
6.87	MP 270.5							9.40	49.5
7.37	MP 270	11.49	42	10.32	45	11.25	49	10.16	51
7.54	Crosby Garrett.							10.29	
7.87	MP 269.5							10.52	53
8.62	MP 268.75	13.27	49	12.05	51	12.52	54	11.40	56
8.87	MP 268.5							11.56	
9.37	MP 268	14.24	46	12.58	49	13.42	53	12.27	54.5
9.87	MP 267.5							13.02	50.75
10.37	MP 267	15.49	40	14.18	43	14.52	49	13.36	50.75
10.87	KIRKBY STEPHEN	16.26	37.5	14.52	41	15.22	47	14.12	49
11.37	MP 266	17.23	38.5	15.43	43	16.06	48.5	14.49	50.25
11.87	MP 265.5							15.26	47.75
12.37	MP 265	18.59	37	17.11	40.5	17.24	44.5	16.05	46.5
13.37	MP 264	20.38	36	18.43	37.5	18.46	43	17.24	44.5
13.87	MP 263.5							18.05	44.5
14.37	MP 263	22.09	43	20.13	44	20.06	48	18.42	47.75
14.87	MP 262.5							19.19	47.5
15.37	MP 262	23.32	44	21.31	45	21.20	47	19.59	45.25
15.87	MP 261.5							20.39	43.75
16.37	MP 261	24.59	41	22.53	43	22.38	46.5	21.22	42.5
16.87	MP 260.5	25.43	41	23.34	43	23.17	45	22.05	41.5
17.37	MP 260							22.49	41
17.62	MP 259.75	26.46	42	24.37	42	24.17	44	23.10	accelerating
18.37	MP 259							24.09	48
19.37	MP 258	28.50	56	26.39	59	26.18	58	25.17	53.25
20.70	GARSDALE	31.10		29.46		28.35		27.45	

Logs 1,2,3 by Alastair Wood, 4 by Stephen Leyland.

Drivers: 1. Willie Alexander, 2, 4 Kenny Stubbs, 3 Jackie Eden.
Fireman: Paul Kane (all).
Inspectors 1, 2, 3 Jimmy McLellan, 4 Jimmy Boyle

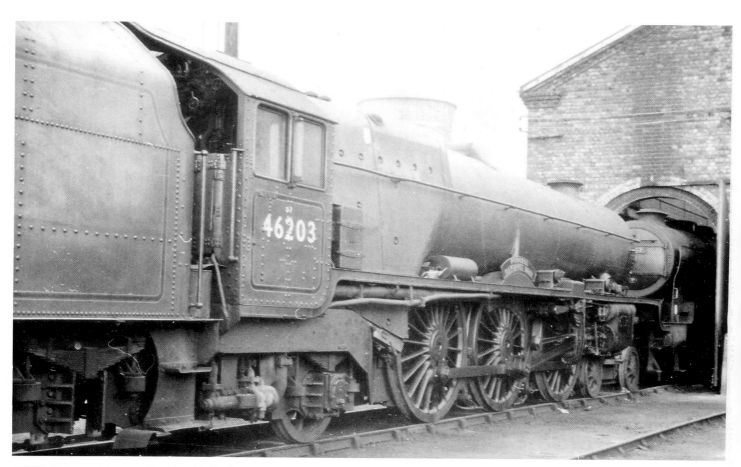

46203 'Princess Margaret Rose' at Willesden m.p.d on 20th August 1961

Peter Fox

DIARY OF EVENTS FOR 6203

Date		Working/Location	Reference
1935			
Jul	P	Crewe Works	Official LMS
4th Jul	R	Crewe – Euston	
6th Jul	R	Allocated to Camden m.p.d. (1B)	
6th Jul	O	Euston – Carlisle on 'Royal Scot'	O.S. Nock
17th Jul	P	Brent Signal box 10.00 a.m. Glasgow – Euston	K. Nunn coll.
20th Jul	R	Allocated Polmadie m.p.d. (27A) - on loan	
1st Aug	P	On Euston – Glasgow arr. Glasgow	J.F. Clay
2nd Aug	P	On Glasgow – Euston dep. Glasgow	J.F. Clay
11th Aug	P	Kirkby on Express	A.G. Ellis coll.
24th Aug	R	Allocated to Polmadie m.p.d. (27A)	
26th Aug	P	Camden m.p.d.	H.N. James
Aug	P	Lichfield	P.E. Haynes
Sep	P	Bushey on down 'Royal Scot'	H. Gordon Tidey
Oct	P	Bushey on down express	J.B. Molesworth
25th Nov	R	Dynamometer Car Test Run Euston – Glasgow	
27th Nov	R	ditto	
?	P	Symington	Real Photos
?	P	Oxenholme	r.a. Stephenson
?	P	Stonehaven	r.a. Stephenson
1936			
29th Feb	R	Allocated Camden m.p.d. (1B)	
19th Mar	R	Entered Crewe Works for Light Repairs	
6th Apr	R	Re-entered traffic	
8th Apr	R	Entered Crewe Workd for Light Repairs	
15th Apr	R	Re-entered traffic	
3rd May	R	Test train Euston – Crewe reached 102.5 m.p.h.	L.M.S. Magazine
7th May	O	Euston – Glasgow down 'Mid-Day Scot' timed by Cecil J. Allen	
14th May	P	Gretna on up express	H.C. Casserley
15th Jun	R	Entered Crewe Works for Light Repairs	
19th Jun	R	Re-entered traffic	
6th Aug	R	Entered Crewe Works for Heavy Repairs	
17th Aug	R	Re-entered traffic	
?	P	Dillicar Troughs on up express	M.W. Earley
?	P	On shed at Camden	P. Ransome Wallis
?	P	Near Winsford on down 'Mid-Day Scot'	Rev. E. Treacy
?	P	Lune Valley on down 'Royal Scot'	Railway Magazine
?	P	Bushey on down 'Royal Scot'	Railway Magazine
?	P	Crewe North	J.L. Stevenson
30th Nov	R	Entered Crewe Works for Heavy General Repair.	
15th Dec	R	Boiler No. 9100 fitted in works.	
31th Dec	P	Official photos taken representing all class with new tender No. 9374 fitted.	
1937			
19th Jan	R	Re-entered traffic	
5th Aug	R	Entered Crewe Works for Heavy Service Repair Order No. 3098	
10th Sep	R	Re-entered traffic	
29th Nov	R	Entered Crewe Works for Light Overhaul	
13th Dec	R	Re-entered traffic	
1938			
5th Jun	P	Berkhampstead on up express	H.C. Casserley
Sep	P	Camden on empty stock	Photomatic
?	P	Queens Park	Rev. E. Treacy
?	P	Location unknown hauling express	P. Ransome Wallis
28th Oct	R	Entered Crewe Works for Heavy General Overhaul and boiler No. 9101 fitted.	
1939			
12th Jan	R	Re-entered traffic	
31st May	P	Northchurch Tunnel on down express	H.C. Casserley
?	P	Passing Bushey on down 'Royal Scot'	C.R.L. Coles
?	P	Being turned on Camden turntable	Real Photos.
?	P	Kings Langley on express	A.G. Ellis coll.
?	P	Passing Kilburn down 'Mid-Day Scot'	Rev. E. Treacy
?	P	Passing Wavertree Junction up express	Rev. E. Treacy
?	P	Passing Edge Hill up express	Rev. E. Treacy
21st Oct	R	Transferred to Edge Hill m.p.d. (8A)	
28th Dec	R	Entered Crewe Works for Light Service repair	
1940			
13th Jan	R	Re-entered traffic	
6th Apr	R	Transferred to Holyhead m.p.d. (7C)	
28th Sep	R	Transferred to Crewe North m.p.d. (5A)	
24th Sep	R	Entered Crewe Works for Light Overhaul	
12th Oct	R	Re-entered traffic	
2nd Nov	R	Transferred to Holyhead m.p.d. (7C)	
9th Nov	R	Transferred to Edge Hill m.p.d. (8A)	
1941			
25th Jan	R	Entered Crewe Works for Heavy Repair	
22nd Feb	R	Re-entered traffic	
15th Nov	R	Entered Crewe Works for Heavy General Overhaul Boiler No. 9106 fitted	
20th Dec	R	Re-entered traffic	
1942			
28th Mar	R	Entered Crewe Works for Light Overhaul	
16th Apr	R	Re-entered traffic	
13th Nov	R	Entered Crewe Works for Heavy Service Repair	
15th Dec	R	Re-entered traffic	
26th Dec	R	Allocated to Camden m.p.d. (1B)	
1943			
?	P	Passing Camden on down express	Rev. E. Treacy
3rd Apr	R	Transferred to Edge Hill m.p.d. (8A)	
27th Jul	R	Entered Crewe Works for Heavy Service Repair	
18th Aug	R	Re-entered traffic	
21st Sep	R	Entered Crewe Works for Light Overhaul	
30th Sep	R	Re-entered traffic	
9th Oct	R	Transferred to Crewe North m.p.d. (5A) - on loan.	
27th Nov	R	Transferred to Crewe North m.p.d. (5A)	
1944			
20th May	R	Transferred to Edge Hill m.p.d. (8A)	
11th Jun	R	Entered Crewe Works for Heavy General Repair and boiler No. 9102 fitted	
22nd Jul	P	Piloting Loco. No. 6125 on up express at Euston	H.C. Casserley
26th Jul	R	Re-entered traffic	
1945			
21st May	R	Entered Crewe Works for Heavy Service Repair	
30th Jun	R	Re-entered traffic	
26th Oct	R	Entered Crewe Works for Light Overhaul	
16th Nov	R	Re-entered traffic	
24th Dec	R	Entered Crewe Works for Heavy Overhaul	
1946			
9th Feb	R	Re-entered traffic	
29th Jul	R	Entered Crewe Works for Light Service Repair	
Jul	P	Tring 2.40 p.m. Euston – Liverpool express	L.M.S. Official
7th Sep	R	Re-entered traffic	
28th Sep	P	Tring on express	R.F. Deardon (c/o NRM)
1947			
18th Jan	R	Entered Crewe Works for Light Overhaul	
19th Feb	R	Re-entered traffic	
26th Apr	P	Kenton on down express	Ian Allan Library
17th Jun	P	Northchurch Tunnel Euston – Liverpool express	Ian Allan Library
18th Oct	R	Transferred to Crewe North m.p.d. (5A) on loan	
18th Sep	R	Entered Crewe Works for Heavy General Repair, boiler No. 9106 fitted (24/10/48) and re-liveried in L.N.W.R. black.	
8th Dec	R	Re-entered traffic	
31st Dec	O	Worked Carlisle – Glasgow sleeper	S.R.P.S.
1948			
14th Feb	R	Transferred to Edge Hill m.p.d. - Shed code 8A	
10th Apr	R	Crewe works for Heavy Overhaul on tender	
5th May	R	Re-entered traffic	
26th Jun	P	Ashton near Liverpool on down express	L. Hanson
3rd Jul	P	Brinklow, Rugby on down express	G. Coltas
14th Nov	R	Entered Crewe Works for Light Service Repair	
23rd Dec	R	Re-entered traffic	
1949			
18th Feb	R	Entered Crewe Works for Heavy Casual Repair	
13th May	R	Entered Crewe Works for Light Casual Repair	
5th Aug	R	Entered Crewe Works for Light Casual Repair	
1st Sep	R	Re-entered traffic	
16th Oct	R	Entered Crewe for Unclassified Repair - Boiler diaphragm bolts loose.	
28th Oct	R	Re-entered traffic	
?	P	Passing Crewe Station on up express	P. Ransome Wallis
1950			
25th Mar	P	Nr. Bourne End 8.15 a.m. Liverpool – Euston express	E.D. Bruton
2nd Jun	R	Entered Crewe Works for Light Intermediate Repair	
3rd Jul	R	Re-entered traffic	
Jul	P	Down express location unknown	Rev. E. Treacy
?	P	Bushey on down express	C.R.L. Coles
1951			
17th Apr	R	Entered Crewe Works for Heavy General Repair boiler No. 9108 fitted. Re-liveried in Caledonian Blue	
24th May	R	Re-entered traffic	
26th May	P	Crewe North m.p.d.	J.E. Wilkinson
3rd Jun	P	Crewe North m.p.d.	F. Ashley
13th Jun	P	Willesden Junction down 'Merseyside Express'	H.C. Casserley
16th Jun	P	Berkhamstead on down express	H.C. Casserley
29th Jun	P	Berkhamstead on down express	H.C. Casserley
30th Jun	P	Wembley on down express	C.R.L. Coles

30th Jun	P	Watford on down express	N.E. Stead
Summer	P	Leaving Euston with down express	Rev. E. Treacy
22nd Sep	R	Transferred to Polmadie m.p.d. (66A)	
4th Nov	P	Polmadie m.p.d.	J.L. Stevenson
13th Nov	R	Sent to Derby Works for Heavy Intermediate Repair and new front end frames.	

1952

	P	Derby Works No. 8 Erecting Shop	D. Merrifield
26th Feb	P	Derby Works No. 8 Erecting Shop	J.B. Radford
	R	Re-liveried in Brunswick Green	
	P	Derby No. 4 Shed	J.B. Radford
4th Mar	R	Re-entered traffic	
19th Mar	P	Derby No. 4 Shed	R.J. Buckley
4th Apr	R	Crewe Works for Unclassified Repair	
8th Apr	R	Entered Crewe Works for Unclassified Repair – Motion plate repair.	
10th Apr	R	Re-entered traffic	
20th Apr	P	11.15am Glasgow – Manchester express at Polmadie	H.C. Casserley
13th May	P	Tebay on 11.15 a.m. Birmingham – Glasgow express	J.E. Wilkinson
23rd May	P	Tebay on 9.25 a.m. Crewe – Perth express	J.E. Wilkinson
26th May	P	Scout Green on down express	E.D. Bruton
2nd Jun	P	Dillicar Troughs on 11.15 a.m. Birmingham – Glasgow express	E.D. Bruton
6th Jun	P	Shap Wells on down 11.15 a.m. Birmingham – Glasgow express	E.D. Bruton
16 Aug	O	11.15 a.m. Glasgow – Birmingham	
22nd Aug	O	'Up postal' Glasgow – Euston	
30th Aug	P	Shap 11.15 a.m. Birmingham – Glasgow express (W87)	J.E. Wilkinson
?	P	Climbing Beattock with down express	Rev. E. Treacy

1953

28th Feb	P	Beattock Station 9.25 a.m. Crewe – Perth express	J.L. Stevenson
22nd Mar	P	Tebay up 'Mid-Day Scot'	J.E. Wilkinson
29th Apr	R	Entered Crewe Works for Light Casual Repair	
15th May	R	Re-entered traffic	
16th May	R	Transferred to Edge Hill m.p.d. (8A)	
23rd May	R	Transferred to Crewe North m.p.d. (5A)	
27th Jun	P	Shap Wells 11.25 a.m. Birmingham – Glasgow express	J.E. Wilkinson
9th Aug	R	9.45 a.m. Perth-Euston express to Crewe – Bad coal report	
Summer	P	Camden Bank on down express	Rev. E. Treacy
20th Aug	R	Entered Crewe Works for Heavy Casual repair	
24th Sep	R	Re-entered traffic	
17th Oct	P	Scotty Bridge, Greenholme 11.25 a.m. Birmingham – Glasgow express	J.E. Wilkinson
29th Oct	R	Entered Crewe Works for Heavy Intermediate Repair Cast steel inside cylinders fitted. Tell-tale device fitted to inside big ends.	
4th Dec	R	Re-entered traffic	

1954

22nd Feb	R	Entered Crewe Works for Heavy Casual Repair	
19th Mar	R	Re-entered traffic	
5th Apr	P	Dutton Viaduct on Birmingham – Glasgow express	N.E. Preedy coll.
15th May	P	Shap on up 'Mid-Day Scot'	J.E. Wilkinson
5th Jun	P	Kensal Green on down 'Mid-Day Scot'	S. Creer
Jun	P	Backing out of Euston No. 1 Platform	G. Rixon
3rd Jul	P	Low Moor on 11.15 a.m. Birmingham – Glasgow express W211	J.E. Wilkinson
31st Jul	P	Tebay on down express (42424 banker)	J.E. Wilkinson
Summer	P	Greskine Box on down express	Rev. E. Treacy
8th Sep	R	Entered Crewe Works for Heavy Casual Repair	
15th Oct	R	Re-entered traffic	

1955

19th May	P	Shap on up 'Mid-Day Scot' passing Low Moor.	J.E. Wilkinson
21st May	P	Shap on 11.25 a.m. Birmingham – Glasgow express	J.E. Wilkinson
Jun	P	Hest Bank 11.25 a.m. Birmingham – Glasgow express	A.S. Darnborough
23rd Jul	P	Carlisle Station on Birmingham – Glasgow W67	D. Buttefield
24th Jul	P	Polmadie m.p.d. with W67 code on.	D. Anderson
30th Jul	P	Strawfank Junction up express W69	W.S. Sellar
19th Aug	R	Entered Crewe Works for Heavy General Repair and boiler No. 9101 fitted	
19th Oct	R	Re-entered traffic	
29th Oct	R	Entered Crewe Works. Domed regulator fitted, new brake hangar pins and hot box on tender repaired.	
10th Nov	R	Re-entered traffic	
28th Dec	P	Crewe on 5.15 p.m. Inverness-Euston parcels	

1956

8th Feb	R	Entered Crewe Works for Light Casual Repair	
13th Mar	R	Re-entered traffic	
21st Apr	P	Wreay on up 'Mid-Day Scot'	M. Dunnett
22nd Apr	P	Polmadie m.p.d. before working up 'Mid-Day Scot'	D. Anderson
28th Apr	P	Heaton Norris on Euston – Manchester express	N.E. Preedy coll.
21st Jul	P	Greenholme Cutting on Euston – Perth express	J.E. Wilkinson
18th Oct	P	Shap on Birmingham – Glasgow express	G.A. Barlow
28th Oct	R	Entered Crewe Works for Heavy Intermediate Repair	

| 21st Dec | R | Re-entered traffic | |
| 29th Dec | R | (Period ending) fitting of strengthened axlebox guides | |

1957

6th Jan	R	Crewe Works for Casual Repair	
11th Jan	R	Re-entered traffic	
26th Jan	P	Scout Green on 11.15 a.m. Birmingham – Glasgow express	J.E. Wilkinson
13th Mar	P	Rugby on Crewe – Euston express	M. Mitchell
3rd Apr	P	Backing out of Euston after working express from Crewe	A.R. Butcher
1st Jun	R	Entered Crewe Works for Light Casual Repair	
3rd Aug	R	Re-entered traffic	
24th Aug	O	10.30 a.m. Euston-Carlisle express banked out of Euston by 42487	
7th Sep	S	Speed indicator fitted	
23rd Sep	R	Entered Crewe Works for Unclassified Repair	
26th Sep	R	Re-entered traffic	
Sep	P	Crewe on down 'Mid-Day Scot'	E. Oldham
18th Oct	R	Entered Crewe Works for Light Casual Repair	
7th Dec	R	Re-entered traffic	
?	P	Leaving Carlisle with up express	Rev. E. Treacy

1958

3rd May	P	Carstairs on down express	D. Anderson
9th Jun	P	Acton Grange on up express	N.E. Preedy coll.
13th Jun	R	Entered Crewe Works for Heavy General Repair boiler No. 9100 fitted and second B.R. Transfer applied to tender.	
14th Aug	R	Re-entered traffic	
Summer	P	Near A74 on express	Rev. E. Treacy
6th Sep	R	Steam operated cylinder drains fitted.	
20th Sep	R	Transferred to Edge Hill m.p.d. (8A)	

1959

13th Apr	R	Entered Crewe Works for Light Casual repair	
22nd May	R	Re-entered traffic	
13th Jun	R	(Period ending) AWS fitted	
Jun	P	Location not known	A.G. Ellis
Jun	P	Up 'Merseyside Express' at Headstone Lane	D. Cross
22nd Jul	O	Liverpool – Euston on 'Red Rose' timed by Watford on up 'Merseyside Express' (17 vehicles)	O.S. Nock
25th Jul	P		
15th Aug	P	On 'Manxman' Express	Photographer not known
Aug	P	Up 'Manxman' at Winsford	P. Hughes
Summer	P	Tring on up express (W48)	Photographer not known
5th Sep	P	Preston on down 'Royal Scot'	W. Ashcroft
9th Sep	R	Entered Crewe Works for Heavy Intermediate Repair	
6th Nov	R	Re-entered traffic	
?	P	Edge Hill m.p.d.	J.R. Carter

1960

29th Jan	O	Liverpool Lime Street	M. Graham
16th Mar	O	Liverpool Lime Street	M. Graham
14th May	O	Lichfield Trent Valley	M. Graham
17th May	O	Lime Street	M. Graham
14th Jun	R	Entered Crewe Works for Heavy Casual Repair	
Jun	P	Lichfield on Euston-Liverpool express	J.B. Radford
12th Aug	R	Re-entered traffic	
20th Aug	R	Transferred to Camden (1B) on loan	
29th Aug	P	Carpenders Park on down express	B. Fleming
10th Sep	R	Transferred to Edge Hill m.p.d. (8A)	
11th Sep	O	Lime Street Station	M. Graham
29th Nov	R	Entered Crewe Works for Heavy Intermediate Repair. New Tyres fitted to locomotive and tender.	

1961

7th Feb	P	Outside Crewe Works Paintshop	S. Taylor
9th Feb	R	Re-entered traffic	
15th Feb	P	Near Valley on up express	A. Chandler
24th Feb	P	Coppull on Crewe – Carlisle parcels	A.C. Gilbert
5th Mar	R	Put in store at Carnforth (10A)	
18th Apr	P	In store at Carnforth	W. Ashcroft
9th Jul	R	Removed from Store	
15th Jul	R	Transferred to Crewe North m.p.d. (5A)	
27th Jul	O	06.35 a.m. Euston – Crewe express	
5th Aug	P	Dillicar Water Troughs on 1S53	A.J. Macbeath
5th Aug	P	Tebay Station 1S53	B. Barlow
			K. Linford
7th Aug	P	Chester General on Bangor – Euston express	S.D. Wainwright
20th Aug	P	Willesden m.p.d.	P. Fox
25th Aug	O	On 10.05 a.m. Glasgow – Birmingham express	A.J. Macbeath
30th Aug	P	Preston m.p.d.	R.C. Cutler
1st Sep	R	Into store at Carnforth	
Oct	P	Carnforth in store	M. Collier
8th Oct	R	Taken out of store	

1962

27th Jan	R	Transferred to Carlisle Upperby m.p.d. (12B)	
28th Jan	O	12.20 p.m. Crewe – Carlisle parcels 3L09	R. Herbert
31st Jan	O	3.30 p.m. Carlisle – Crewe Freight	R. Herbert
8th Feb	P	Aston (near Loade) on up Windermere express	K. Fairey
8th Feb	O	8.40 a.m. Carlisle – Euston 1A33	R. Herbert
15th Feb	O	1.05 p.m. Euston – Perth 1S81	R. Herbert
20th Feb	O	10.23 p.m. Monument Lane – Carlisle parcels 3L06	R. Herbert
22nd Feb	O	6.50 p.m. Crewe – Glasgow parcels 3S07	R. Herbert
24th Feb	O	4.28 a.m. Carlisle – Crewe fish 3K13	R. Herbert

24th Feb	P	Coppull 12.46 p.m. Crewe–Carlisle parcels	A.C. Gilbert
28th Feb	O	3.30 p.m. Carlisle-Crewe freight	R. Herbert
4th Mar	P	Perth m.p.d.	N.E. Preedy coll.
5th Mar	O	Glasgow (St Enoch)–London (St Pancras) express to Carlisle	
21nd Mar	O	11.45 p.m. Glasgow–Willesden parcels 3M10	R. Herbert
21st Mar	O	1.05 p.m. Euston–Perth 1S81	R. Herbert
31st Mar	O	12.20 p.m. Crewe–Carlisle parcels 3L09	R. Herbert
4th Apr	O	8.40 a.m. Carlisle to Euston 1A33	R. Herbert
5th Apr	O	10.25 p.m. Willesden to Carlisle milk empties 1L98	R. Herbert
7th Apr	R	Transferred to Carlisle Kingmoor m.p.d. (12A)	
21st Apr	O	Perth m.p.d.	M. Graham
26th Apr	P	Departing Carlisle on Euston–Perth express	S.C. Crook
26th Apr	O	Arriving Perth on Euston–Perth express	M. Graham
3rd May	O	12.20 Crewe–Carlisle parcels 3L09	R. Herbert
30th May	P	Rockcliffe on 1.30 p.m. Euston–Perth express	R.H. Leslie
21st Jun	O	Carlisle on 10.00 a.m. Euston–Aberdeen express	A.J. Macbeath
25th Jun	O	Carlisle on 10.00 a.m. Euston–Aberdeen express	A.J. Macbeath
Jul	P	Backing down to Carlisle station	N. Thexton
28th Jul	P	Rockcliffe on Euston–Perth express	R.H. Leslie
?	P	Passing Kingmoor on down express	Rev. E. Treacy
18th Aug	P	Carlisle waiting to take 4.27 p.m. Perth express	G.W. Dawson
18th Aug	P	Quintishill on 10.15 a.m. Euston–Perth express	R.H. Leslie
18th Aug	P	Beattock on 4.27 p.m. ex-Carlisle–Perth express	S.C. Crook
26th Aug	P	Beattock on down express	D. Cross
27th Aug	O	Carlisle on 10.00 a.m. Euston–Aberdeen express	A.J. Macbeath
27th Aug		Passing Rockcliffe on Euston–Perth express	S.C. Crook
27th Aug	P	Passing Carstairs on Euston–Aberdeen express	D. Cross
28th Aug	P	Abingdon on express	D. Cross
29th Aug	P	Carlisle Station on 10.00 a.m. Euston -?	P. Fitton
29th Aug	P	Passing Kingmoor Shed Carlisle on down express	Rev. E. Treacy
29th Aug	P	Coatbridge Central on 10.00 a.m. Eust–Aberdeen	W.A.C. Smith
30th Aug	O	Carlisle on 10.00 a.m. Euston–Aberdeen express	A.J. Macbeath
30th Aug	P	Lamington on 10.00 a.m. Euston–Aberdeen express	Photographer unknown
30th Aug	P	Beattock Station 10.00 a.m. Euston–Aberdeen express	D. Cross
31st Aug	O	Carlisle on 1.20 p.m. Euston–Perth express	A.J. Macbeath
6th Sep	P	Carlisle Station on 3.49 p.m. to Glasgow express	M. Collier
6th Sep	P	Carstairs Station on 3.49 p.m. Carlisle–Glasgow express	M. Collier
8th Sep	P	Carlisle Kingmoor m.p.d.	G. Rixon
8th Sep	P	Leaving Carlisle on Euston–Perth express	G. Rixon
8th Sep	P	Beattock on Euston–Perth express	Peter J. Robinson
?	P	Leaving Beattock with down Perth express	D. Cross
9th Sep	R	Put in store at Carlisle Kingmoor	
15th Oct	R	Taken out of store	
20th Oct	R	Withdrawn from service	

1963

Mar	P	Crewe Works	G. Matthews
Apr		Sold to Messrs Butlins	
3rd May	P	Crewe North m.p.d.	D. Russell
4th May	P	En-route Crewe–Pwllheli	N. Kneale

From 5th May 1963 until 10th May 1975 6203 remained at Pwllheli Holiday Camp.

1975

10/11th May   Moved dead on own wheels to Derby via Crewe.

4th Nov	Moved from Derby to Toton m.p.d.
5th Nov	Moved from Toton to Butterley, Midland Railway Centre.

From 5th November 1975, 6203 remained located at Butterley and was housed in the carriage shed until October 1987 when she was moved into the new museum building on Swanwick site.

1988

Oct	Sold to Brell Ewart and restoration to working order commenced.

1990

8th May	Fire lit in locomotive for first time since 1962
11th May	Locomotive steamed for first time at Midland Railway Centre
12th May	Locomotive running in Swanwick to Ironville (MRC)
13th May	Light engine running in Swanwick to Ironville (MRC)
14th May	Light Engine running in Swanwick to Ironville (MRC)
15th May	Light test run for B.R. Butterley–Derby–Sheffield–Derby
16th May	Weighed at B.R. Technical Centre, Derby
17th May	Loaded Test Run Derby–Sheffield–Derby
2nd Jun	'Richard Levick Memorial' train. Derby–Sheffield–Derby x 2
3rd Jun	On display at Coalville Open Day in steam
15th Sep	'White Rose' Derby–Sheffield–Derby
10th Nov	'Red Rose' Nottingham–Didcot–Nottingham

1991

30th Mar	In steam Swanwick (MRC) Light engine Swanwick–Ironville
24th May	Steam test for B.R. light engine Swanwick–Ironville
25th May	Hauled three main line diesels via Leicester to Coalville
26th May	On display in steam at Coalville open day
31st May	Butterley–Sheffield–Leeds–Carnforth L.E + Support Coach
1st Jun	Carnforth–Blackburn L.E.
	Blackburn–Hellifield–Appleby 'Cumbrian Mountain Express'
22nd Jun	Appleby–Blackburn 'Cumbrian Mountain Express'
4th Jul	Blackburn–Appleby 'The Midlander'
5th Jul	Appleby–Farringdon Jnction 'Cumbrian Mountain Express'
6th Jul	In steam at Carnforth Steamtown on Crag Bank shuttle
17th Aug	Carnforth–Workington 'Cumbrian Coast Express'
24th Aug	Appleby–Farringdon Jnction 'Cumbrian Mountain Express'
7th Sep	Farringdon Jnction–Appleby 'Cumbrian Mountain Express'
4th Oct	Carlisle–Crewe 'The Westmorelander'
12th Oct	Crewe–Holyhead–Crewe 'Ynys-Mon Express'
	Crewe–Butterley L.E. + Coach
13th Nov	Swanwick–Ironville filming for Railscene
15th Nov	B.R. Steam Test Butterley
17th Nov	Service Train MRT 5 trains

1992

26th Jun	In steam Swanwick Junction
27th Jun	Service Train MRT 5 trains
28th Jun	Service Train MRT 4 trains
30th Jun	B.R. Steam Test Butterley
24th Jul	Swanwick–Crewe L.E. + Coach
4th Aug	Crewe–Blackburn L.E. + Coach
5th Aug	Faringdon Junction–Carlisle 'Cumbrian Mountain Express'
12th Aug	Carlisle–Crewe L.E. + Coach
23rd Aug	Crewe–Holyhead & return 'Cymru Coaster'
6th Sep	Crewe–Holyhead & return 'Ynys Mon Express'
7th Sep	Crewe–Swanwick L.E. + Coach

P = photo : R = Official Records : O = Observation
r.a Stephenson = Rail archive Stephenson

46203 'Princess Margaret Rose' makes a fine sight as she sweeps through Darwen station with 'The Westmorelander' special from Carlisle to Crewe on 4th October 1991.

N.R. Knight

BIBLIOGRAPHY

Various official records, publications and timetables of the London Midland & Scottish Railway.

Speeding North with the Royal Scot. Laurie Earl (in collaboration with Horace Greenleaf),Oxford University Press, 1939.
William Stanier. O.S. Nock, Ian Allan, 1964
Stanier Pacifics at Work. A.J. Powell, Ian Allan, 1986
The L.M.S. Pacifics. J.W.P. Rowledge, David & Charles, 1987
The Stanier Pacifics of the L.M.S. Cecil J. Allen, Ian Allan, 1948
Locomotive Panaroma Volume 1. E.S. Cox, Ian Allan, 1965
60 Years of West Coast Express Running. O.S. Nock, Ian Allan, 1976
The West Coast Pacifics. John F. Clay and J. Cliffe, Ian Allan, 1976
L.M.S. Locomotive Design and Construction. A.F. Cook, R.C.T.S., 1990
Great Locomotives of the L.M.S. O.S. Nock, Patrick Stevens Ltd., 1989
Locomotive Liveries of the L.M.S. D. Jenkinson and R.J. Essery, Roundhouse Books, Ian Allan, 1967

ACKNOWLEDGEMENTS

We would like to express our sincere thanks to all those who provided information and photographs for this book enabling us to produce what we believe is the most exhaustive account of the history of a single locomotive yet published.

Our special thanks to Dr. John Coiley and the staff at the National Railway Museum, York for considerable assistance in providing us with material from official records and photographs of 46203 and permission to reproduce the official record cards of the locomotive.

Thanks are also due to J.W.P. Rowledge for checking the text, to Alan Wilson for giving exhaustive details of the basis for shopping of locomotives, to Neville Stead for the detective work in tracking down photographers whose records of 'Princess Margaret Rose' at work form an essential part of this book, and to all those who gave permission to reproduce them without fee — a splendid gesture.

There is a long list of those many people, of both professional railwaymen and enthusiasts alike who have helped make this book possible and we thank them all.

Brian Radford and Brell Ewart
November 1992

An historic moment as the two preserved 'Princess Royal' class locomotives meet on the Settle–Carlisle line at Appleby station, the change over point for the locomotives working separate legs of the 'Cumbrian Mountain Express' on 22nd June 1991.

Howard Routledge